With great skill, Dr. Sittser has tackled one of the knottiest problems that face Christ's people. These pages are aware of the host of differences that baffle us; they are alert to the biblical resources that can help us cope; they are alive with suggestions and illustrations with which we can all identify. No one who cares about obeying Christ's call to love can afford to ignore Sittser's work.

DAVID ALLAN HUBBARD
president emeritus, Fuller Theological Seminary

Jerry Sittser must have often prayed Saint Francis's prayer, "Lord, make me an instrument of thy peace" in order to have written *Loving Across Our Differences*. With moving personal candor and striking biblical integrity, Sittser challenges our pluralistic church to claim our essential unity in Jesus Christ. Though Sittser and I would come to different conclusions on some of the issues he addresses, he invites me to imagine a church with space enough for us both and for all who acknowledge the claim of Christ on our lives and on the world. This book lets us catch a glimpse of what the new creation just might turn out to be.

JOANNA M. ADAMS
pastor, Trinity Presbyterian Church, Atlanta

Jesus' best-known command, "love one another," is also the least obeyed. It's the most difficult thing Jesus asked us to do. Jerry Sittser doesn't make it any easier, but he shows how it is possible. He does it by embedding the love command in a network of New Testament "mutuality commands" that support and nourish Jesus' command to love. This is accurate exegesis embraced by passionate concern and worked out in contexts in which any of us can recognize ourselves; the result is a book that will develop spiritual maturity in its readers and deepen the life of love in the church.

EUGENE H. PETERSON
James M. Houston Professor of Spiritual Theology, Regent College

Gerald L. Sittser

*With Questions
for Study & Discussion*

INTERVARSITY PRESS
DOWNERS GROVE, ILLINOIS 60515

InterVarsity Press® is the book-publishing division of InterVarsity Christian Fellowship®, a student movement active on campus at hundreds of universities, colleges and schools of nursing in the United States of America, and a member movement of the International Fellowship of Evangelical Students. For information about local and regional activities, write Public Relations Dept., InterVarsity Christian Fellowship, 6400 Schroeder Rd., P.O. Box 7895, Madison, WI 53707-7895.

Scripture quotations, unless otherwise noted, are from the New Revised Standard Version of the Bible, copyright 1989 by the Division of Christian Education of the National Council of the Churches of Christ in the U.S.A., and are used by permission.

Cover photograph: SuperStock, Inc.

ISBN 0-8308-1668-2

Printed in the United States of America ∞

Library of Congress Cataloging-in-Publication Data

Sittser, Jerry L., 1950-
    Loving across our differences/Gerald L. Sittser.
      p.   cm.
    Includes bibliographical references.
    ISBN 0-8308-1668-2
    1. Church membership. 2. Love—Religious aspects—Christianity.
3. Religious pluralism—Christianity. 4. Multiculturalism—
Religious aspects—Christianity. 5. Christian life—Presbyterian
authors. I. Title.
BV4525.S58   1994
250—dc20   94-414
                                                                          CIP

15   14   13   12   11   10   9   8   7   6   5   4   3   2   1
04   03   02   01   00   99   98   97   96   95   94

In memory of my wife,
Lynda Dethmers Sittser,
whose life so wonderfully reflected
Jesus' commandment that
we love one another as he has loved us all.

1 The New Commandment _____ 9

PART ONE: FOUNDATIONAL COMMANDS
2 Greet One Another_____ 27
3 Be Subject to One Another_____ 45
4 Forbear One Another_____ 62

PART TWO: SUSTAINING COMMANDS
5 Forgive One Another_____ 85
6 Confess Sin to and Pray for One
Another_____ 103
7 Serve One Another _____ 119
8 Encourage One Another _____ 140

PART THREE: CRISIS COMMANDS
9 Comfort One Another _____ 157
10 Bear One Another's Burdens _____ 177

PART FOUR: CONFRONTATIONAL COMMANDS
11 Stir Up One Another _____ 199
12 Admonish One Another _____ 218
Epilogue _____ 245
Notes_____ 249
Questions for Study and Discussion_____ 251

Acknowledgments

As in all human endeavors, the authorship of this book cannot be traced to the hand of one person, though only one person's name appears on the front cover. I wrote it, but many people have contributed along the way. The credit should go to many, not just to one.

I want to thank several groups of people in particular. First, to the people of the churches I have belonged to over the years—Emmanuel Reformed Church of Paramount, California; First Reformed Church of Orange City, Iowa; First Reformed Church of South Holland, Illinois; First Presbyterian Church of Spokane, Washington. Thank you, dear friends, for your obedience to Jesus' new commandment.

Second, to the people who told me their stories and gave me permission to use them as case studies in the book, with the understanding that I would change the names and the extraneous details. Thank you for your vulnerability, example and integrity.

Third, to the friends and colleagues who read parts or all of this manuscript—Forrest Baird, Doug Dye, Robin Garvin, Linda Hunt, Monica Martens, Steve and Richelle Mills, Roger Mohrlang, Lorrie Nelson, Dave Peterson, Ron Pyle, Dale Soden, Andy Sonneland, Kathy Storm, Jack and Diane Veltkamp. Thank you for your time, insights and suggestions.

Finally, to my friends at InterVarsity Press, especially my editor, Rodney Clapp. Thank you for your willingness to take this second risk and for your standard of excellence.

1

THE NEW
COMMANDMENT

*J*ust as I have loved you, you also should love one another," Jesus said. "By this everyone will know that you are my disciples, if you have love for one another" (Jn 13:34-35). This "new commandment" is, as Jesus stated, the secret to the church's witness in the world. The unbelieving world will identify Christians as true disciples of Christ when they see them love one another.

As simple as this mandate sounds, we know through personal experience that it is not so simple after all. We may be able to obey this command with our friends and allies in the church, although even then it is often a matter of hit-or-miss. It is another matter altogether with strangers and enemies. What does this command require in a church—local, denominational, ethnic, national, international—that is characterized by diversity, disagreement, distrust and division? What does love require in a pluralistic church?

I am writing this book to explore how Christians can fulfill this mandate. I decided to write it for two reasons. The first comes out of my awareness of what appears to be the impossibility of doing what Jesus commands in the church today. Pluralism poses a real problem for the prospects of obeying these words. The second comes out of my own unusual experience of the church at work. How the church responded to my catastrophic need shows that the church has the potential to be the community that Jesus intends it to be.

The Challenge of Pluralism

My first reason for writing this book is obvious enough to most Christians. Pluralism in the church makes the new commandment appear completely out of reach. I had no trouble finding good examples of this. One friend told me about a controversy that surfaced in his church during the Persian Gulf War. Several leaders of the church thought it would be an appropriate gesture if they put an American flag in the sanctuary, which would remind the members of the congregation to pray for American soldiers and to perform their patriotic duties. My friend raised questions about their suggestion. In his mind it was a case of confusing patriotism and Christian faith. He argued that the Christian's first loyalty is to the kingdom of God and the church, which transcends national borders and flies a flag under which all people can be united. "Christians in America have more in common with Iraqi Christians than with pagans in their own country," he said. The controversy soon ended (the flag was put in the narthex of the church). Still, a larger question remains. How should Christians handle differences of opinion in the church?

What happens in congregations also happens in denominations. I am active in a local congregation of the Presbyterian Church, U.S.A. In 1991 the Presbyterian national assembly met to discuss, among other topics, the report of a special task force that had been appointed two years earlier to study sexuality from a Christian perspective. The general reaction to the report was extremely negative. Conservative groups accused the task force of approving of extramarital affairs, advocating homosexuality and compromising biblical morality. Supporters of the committee accused their conservative critics of defending the injustice of heterosexism, holding to narrowmindedness and being hopelessly out of date. Rancor flowed in both directions. The controversy reinforced the division between conservatives and liberals in the denomination. It was one of several factors that caused some churches to leave the denomination altogether. While I am sure that this controversy will eventually fade, a question remains. How should Christians address theological and ethical controversy in the church?

These are only two of dozens of examples I have collected over the past two years. I could have used many others—a practicing homosexual who wants to join a conservative church and is turned away, a temperamental church music director who appears to aim higher than his choir can reach and is resented for it, a popular church elder who divorces his wife and starts to date someone else from the same church, a division in a mainline congregation between prolife and prochoice parties, a preacher who has alienated an influential segment of the congregation because he is accused of being more interested in social action than in biblical preaching.

What does it mean to love one another as Jesus has loved us? How can Christians get along with each other? How can we address our differences with civility and reach unity in spite of our differences? How should we respond when neither side is willing to compromise? How can we put up with the nagging irritations of church membership? What does love require in a pluralistic church?

The Options

Three answers to these questions appear possible. First, we could try to accept diversity in the church without reservation and to embrace tolerance as an absolute good. This answer—the most popular in our society but troublesome from a biblical point of view—smacks of relativism. Are all differences in the church good? Is there nothing that sets Christians apart, except for their diversity? Are there no standards—of belief, conduct, character—to which all Christians should, or at least try to, measure up? "Political correctness" has perhaps reached creedal status in American culture. That does not mean that it should become the standard for life in the church.

Second, we could eliminate diversity, erase the differences among us and strive for sameness. This answer—the most culturally unrealistic but the most prevalent through much of church history—demands judgment, discipline and conformity. Who is to decide what that "sameness" should be? How will the decision be made? Can any individual Christian assume that his or her interpretation of the Bible is the correct one? Does might, in the end, make right? This option has only succeeded in dividing the church, suppressing open debate, destroying healthy diversity and shedding innocent blood.

Third, we could strive for unity in our diversity. This answer—the most difficult and demanding of the three—requires sacrifice, servanthood, compromise, struggle. It is the way of love, which is neither relativistic nor judgmental but truthful and wise.

This book will address the third option. I believe that the New Testament shows us very clearly what such love requires in a pluralistic church. It reveals the requirements of love in the many mutuality commands that appear in the New Testament. These "one another" passages give love shape, texture and color. They show Christians how to translate love into concrete and specific actions, how to pursue the high calling of love in a church filled with difficult people, how to make diversity a healthy instead of a destructive force. The intent of this book is to discern what it means to love fellow Christians so that we neither exalt diversity as if it were an absolute good nor eliminate it as if it were an absolute evil, but rather discern how we can nurture unity in our diversity so that the church can be everything God wants it to be, Jesus' body and bride here on earth. This third alternative requires that we learn to live in a fine balance between forgiveness and confession, forbearance and admonition, friendliness and exhortation. It pushes us to take the New Testament's mutuality commands seriously.

Diversity of Belief

Though there are many kinds of diversity in the church, I have two kinds in mind. The first is diversity of belief. It surfaces daily in differences of theological, ethical and political opinion. Most Christians in America today experience such diversity with feelings of pain and confusion. They are combatants or casualties in the fight over abortion, homosexuality, inerrancy, eschatology, secular humanism, tongues speaking, aid to the contras, South Africa or the rights of Palestinians. And the list could go on.

Many denominations in America are strained to the breaking point because their members disagree so sharply over these and other issues. Catholics are quarreling over papal authority, birth control, women in church office and academic freedom. Protestants are divided between liberal and conservative in almost every major denomination. In *The Struggle for America's Soul* Robert Wuthnow argues that the split between conservative and liberal is the dominant conflict in the Protestant church today. However destructive these disagreements are, there is little indication that resolution is anywhere in sight. If anything, the conflict is just heating up, with both sides poised to fight over any number of issues. And neither, it seems, is ready to compromise. Thus fundamentalists and moderates in the Southern Baptist Convention have disputed for at least ten years now over theological issues like inerrancy. Presbyterians are struggling over the biblical understanding of human sexuality. Episcopalians are divided over the ordination of women. Methodists are polarized over their understanding and practice of evangelism in the church. Rare is the Christian today who has not been involved in some kind of theological or ethical controversy.

Diversity of belief usually threatens us at a distance, since most of us surround ourselves with people who think and believe like we do. After enlisting in an army of Christians who line up on the right side of the issues—on our side, of course—we then receive training to defend our point of view, dig our trenches so that we are invulnerable to attack, and fight the enemy "out there" somewhere (in that small group, that church, that region of the country, that seminary, that denomination or that special interest group) whom we strongly disagree with and dislike but don't really know personally. It is enough to know what they believe;

it confuses the issue to know who they are. Personality has nothing to do with it. They are wrong and we are right. That is all that matters.

Several years ago my late wife, Lynda, fell into a long conversation with an acquaintance whom she had not seen for several years. For some reason the subject of abortion came up. Lynda was surprised to learn that this friend supported abortion on demand; he was equally surprised that Lynda opposed abortion on demand. Early on in the conversation he said, with a hint of sarcasm in his voice and a puckish grin on his face, that any Christian who was not, like himself, prochoice was simply wrong. Lynda responded by asserting that any Christian who was not prolife was wrong. The long discussion that followed these bold statements demonstrated that both of them had spent very little time actually talking with a fellow Christian who did not believe as they did. They had arrived at their positions on abortion without listening firsthand to an intelligent person from the other side. Their conversation was one of those rare occasions when both sides crawled out of their trenches, white flag in hand, to negotiate with the enemy face to face.

The easiest way to deal with diversity of belief is to caricature, slander and condemn. I work in an academic setting, and I am appalled at how often academics, who are expected to be objective, careful and rational, use name-calling and other cheap methods to expose their opponents and to score points. Thus any persons who have questions about the morality of homosexuality are labeled "homophobic," which is a convenient way to dismiss them altogether rather than to deal honestly with their questions. Likewise, anyone who challenges affirmative action is "racist," and anyone who appeals to the authority of Scripture is a "fundamentalist." Conversely, anyone who sympathizes with a prochoice position is "liberal" and a willing participant in the "new holocaust." Anyone who questions the exclusive nature of Christianity is a "universalist" who has betrayed the faith and capitulated to culture. Never mind the reasons why any of these people believe what they do.

Even their use of terms is telling. Opponents of abortion call the other side pro-abortionists, not prochoicers. Supporters of abortion call the other side anti-abortionists or antichoicers, not prolifers. Both sides, in other words, select terms that shed the worst possible light on the other. Neither is willing to yield linguistic ground in this life-and-death "struggle for America's soul."

The problem with diversity of belief is exacerbated by the motivation that we have to fight in the first place. I have often pondered the reasons for this lack of generosity toward other Christians and the zeal with which we cling to our own beliefs. Why do some Christians infuriate and threaten us so much? Sometimes it is because our own petty egos can't stand it when people think and behave differently. Pride seems to play some role in these controversies. At other times, however, it may actually reflect a healthy commitment to protect the faith from all enemies. The Christian faith is, among other things, a religion of definite beliefs and morals. Because we believe it is true, we feel a compulsion to defend it against all opposition. Insiders can imperil the faith more than outsiders, just as traitors operating behind the battle lines are more dangerous than obvious foes we face on a field of battle. People who claim to be Christian but in word and deed violate what we consider true Christianity are greater threats to the faith because they have greater power to do the kind of damage that is hard to detect and to defend against. Traitorous Christians can undermine the faith in a way secular opponents never could. They are like spiritual termites, eating away at the foundation while going undetected. When the survival of Christianity is at stake, the defense of it against such inside menaces can become anything but civil and irenic.

Diversity of Style

The second kind of diversity has more to do with style than with substance, although the two are sometimes difficult to separate. Diversity of style deals with the little issues that irritate and frustrate us, not the big ones that alarm us and make us fighting mad. In most cases it involves people whom we know well and see often but feel uneasy around, usually for a specific reason. We may dislike a fellow soprano in the choir who shows up late for rehearsals and then sings poorly during worship on Sundays. Or we may distrust an elder who exercises leadership too dominantly and insensitively, though she thinks of herself as genuinely spiritual and kindhearted. Or we may feel crowded by a friend who demands too much time and energy from us but never seems to give anything in return. Or we may take offense at a member of a small group who talks too much without having much to say. Or we may feel uncomfortable around friends who prefer a contemporary sound in choir music and congregational singing. The church is full of such different—and often difficult—people. Their presence is more like healthy food with a peculiar taste than like rotten food that we spit out of our mouths. They are there. We feel their presence. We think about them often. We consider them a problem. Yet we are not quite sure what to do about our feelings because nothing really significant seems to be wrong.

When Love Faces Human Need
This challenge of pluralism provided the initial impetus for writing this book. That theme will still predominate in the chapters that follow. It is what set this project in motion, so it will be the book's primary focus But I felt compelled to finish the book, once I had started it, for another reason. My own experience of the church as it obeyed these mutuality commands made the topic of this book even more timely and relevant to me. I was the grateful beneficiary of the church functioning at its best. My own experience helped me to see what the church is capable of doing, if only it could be less selective and exclusive and more compassionate and inclusive. What happened to me as a result of the church's obedience showed promise for what could happen for many other people in need.

In the fall of 1991 my family was involved in a terrible tragedy. My wife, Lynda, home-schooled our children and had just completed a social studies unit on Native American culture. She decided to conclude the unit with a field trip. So on a Friday afternoon Lynda, our four children and I piled into our minivan to attend a pow-wow at a nearby Indian reservation. My mother, Grace, who was visiting us for the weekend, came along as well. We had dinner with members of the tribe and then attended the pow-wow. My two daughters even danced in the ceremony. We left at 8:30 p.m. to drive home. Ten minutes later we were struck head-on by a drunken driver who was going eighty miles an hour and missed a curve. My mother, my wife and my daughter Diana Jane were killed in the accident. I tried to save them, but their injuries were too severe. So I watched helplessly as each of them died.

The accident devastated my children and me. It plunged me into a terrible darkness, bewildered me with unanswerable questions and left me with overwhelming responsibilities. The weight of grief was more than I—more than anyone—could bear.

Christians friends responded immediately. The church took action. My children and I were enveloped by the love of the body of Christ. In the months that followed I found myself saying often, "What would we do, where would we be, without the church?" Close friends rushed to my side and stayed there. They cared for my children, especially my youngest, John, who broke his femur in the accident. Kathy Bruner, the wife of a colleague of mine at the college, stayed with John daily for three weeks at my home while he was in traction and later in a body cast. Ron and Julie Pyle, close friends since we arrived at Whitworth, came forward to provide child care for John after he recovered from his injuries. Julie has become John's surrogate mother. The college and our home church worked together to provide meals two or three times a week for as long as it was required (friends signed up for a whole year, although we only took advantage of their service for a few months). Thousands of people prayed for us faithfully and sent cards and letters. Counselors offered to meet with me and the children. Students volunteered to do yard work. The outpouring of support was unimaginable. Fellow believers comforted us, served us, bore our burdens, encouraged us. They fulfilled many of the mutuality commands that this book will explore. They did not take the grief away—no one could do that. They did, however, make the grief more bearable.

The tragedy and the events that followed showed me what the church is capable of doing. Sadly, the church does not seem to rise to the occasion very often. Our case was clear-cut, obvious and convenient. Our family was well known in the community, Lynda as a musician, I as a leader and speaker. We had developed deep friendships with many people in our community and around the country. We had opened our home to the needy and used our gifts to build the church. Who wouldn't respond to our needs, considering the loss we had suffered? That bothered me. I began to think about the people whose needs are not as obvious as ours were (and still are) but are still serious—the divorced, the unemployed, the terminally ill, the severely depressed. I thought, too, about people whose suffering is taken as a personal victory by their opponents, who see the pain as a sign of God's judgment.

Over time I realized that the love poured out to me and my children was too selective, directed, as it was, toward the "deserving." I concluded that there is enough resource of concern and compassion in the church. Energy, money, time and commitment are there. Quantity and even quality of love are not the issue. Rather, the issue is our exclusivity and selectivity. We think we have the right and duty to decide whom to love and how to love them. But the Bible does not give that right to us. It commands us to "love one another." It does not attach conditions to this command.

The Weight of Evidence
The Bible not only commands us to "love one another"; it commands us over and over again. The weight of evidence is overwhelming. "This is my commandment, that you love one another as I have loved you. No one has greater love than this, to lay down one's life for one's friends" (Jn 15:12-13). "I ask not only on behalf of these, but also on behalf of those who will believe in me through their word, that they may all be one. As you, Father, are in me and I am in you, may they also be in us, so that the world may believe that you have sent me" (Jn 17:20-21; see also 1 Jn 4:11-12, 20-21). The apostle Paul emphasized the same idea. "Let love be genuine; hate what is evil, hold fast to what is good; love

one another with mutual affection; outdo one another in showing honor" (Rom 12:9-10; see also Gal 6:9-10 and Col 3:14).

Jesus underscored the importance of this command on more than one occasion. He said that the disciples' greatest impact on the world would come from mutual love. "By this everyone will know that you are my disciples, if you have love for one another" (Jn 13:35). Love for one another would distinguish the disciples from other social groups and movements. It would prove that they were true believers in Jesus, establish the authenticity of their witness and serve as the primary strategy for their evangelistic outreach. Jesus also said that love for one another would confirm the divine origin of his ministry. Their "oneness" in love would cause the world to believe that the Father had sent his Son (Jn 17:20-23). The fruit of Jesus' ministry—love among believers—would bear witness to the truth of it—God's love for us in Christ. Love for one another, in other words, would verify that Jesus really did come from God and was, in fact, God become human.

The apostle Paul reasoned similarly. He argued that the cross of Christ breaks down the "dividing wall" of hostility that separates Jews and Gentiles, men and women, slaves and free, sophisticates and Philistines, liberals and conservatives (Eph 2:11-22). The cross makes us "one" by exposing our condition as helpless sinners and by giving us all grace. It thus abolishes all those distinctives—religious heritage, education, gender, race, wealth, power, prestige, ethnicity and so forth—that make one group feel superior to another, and it clears out a piece of level ground at the foot of the cross on which all of us can stand as equals, as both sinners and saints. Thus Paul appealed in the name of Christ that Christians simply affirm the unity that was effected in the cross. "I appeal to you, brothers and sisters, by the name of our Lord Jesus Christ, that all of you be in agreement and that there be no divisions among you, but that you be united in the same mind and the same purpose" (1 Cor 1:10). He pleaded that believers make "every effort to maintain the unity of the Spirit in the bond of peace," since, in his mind, there was only one body, one Spirit, one hope, one Lord, one faith, one baptism, one God and Father of us all (Eph 4:3-6). He urged that leaders build up the body of Christ until "all of us come to the unity of the faith and of the knowledge of the Son of God" (Eph 4:13).

Yet Paul was a realist. He recognized and encouraged diversity in the church too. There are different types of personalities and different gifts of the Spirit. These differences sometimes threaten to divide the church. Paul used the metaphors of "joints" and "ligaments" to show how the church could experience unity in its diversity (see Eph 4:16 and Col 2:18-19). Different parts of the human body, each having a unique function, are connected together by joints and ligaments so that they can work together toward one goal. Likewise, different parts of the body of Christ are supposed to be linked together in love so that diversity in the body of Christ serves rather than hurts the ultimate mission of the church. These spiritual joints and ligaments, which we could define as the commitment to strive for "the common good," to have "the same affection and sympathy," to "love one another" in Christ, enable the different personalities, interests, perspectives, gifts, abilities, convictions and callings of Christians to function together as a single organism. Thus diversity strengthens the church only if mutual love first unites it. Without such love, diversity will divide and destroy the church every time conflict erupts.

This unity in love will protect us from becoming prisoners to ourselves—to our pet doctrines, rituals, causes, programs, movements or methods. It will also keep us from using the faults, errors and excesses of other believers to excuse our own. It will therefore break the cycle of polarization that begins when a party within the church appoints itself as the one group that is capable of compensating for the weakness of another. Such compensation, of course, usually leads to overcompensation, which arouses the other side to do the same. Thus the more "conservative" one party becomes, the more "liberal" the other becomes. The more "mission-minded" one becomes, the more "social-activist" the other becomes. The more "progressive" one becomes, the more "traditional" the other becomes. The more "inclusive" one becomes, the more "exclusive" the other becomes. This cycle often continues until the body of Christ is torn apart by suspicion, overreaction and imbalance. It does not help the body of Christ when, as the apostle Paul intimated, the eye exaggerates its importance because it feels that the nose is gaining too much power.

The Direction

Mutual love has many implications, as I have already intimated. We shall be exploring these by investigating how the New Testament teaches us to love. Through its many mutuality commands—"greet one another," "forbear one another," "admonish one another"—the New Testament shows us what love requires in the concrete circumstances of life. We will be studying these commands in the chapters that follow, making sure to give proper attention to how these commands fit together into a larger whole. Some of them, as we shall see, establish the foundation on which relationships can grow (for example, "greet"); others equip us to maintain those relationships over a long period of time ("encourage"); still others enable us to help people in crisis ("comfort"); and the last group directs us to confront fellow Christians who have compromised the essentials of Christian faith and morality ("admonish"). Our discussion will not be abstract, superficial or sentimental. We will take a close look at very concrete and difficult cases. We will ask, for example, what it means to love those who not only *have* a burden but seem, at least to us, to *be* a burden, or what it means to love fellow Christians with whom we have major theological and ethical disagreements.

These commands, as I have already said, are "mutual." Mutuality does not imply that we should treat others exactly as they treat us, as if it were a spiritual version of "you scratch my back and I'll scratch yours." Our obedience cannot be based on how others respond to us first. It cannot be reduced to keeping accurate records, so that the liabilities of serving do not outstrip the assets of being served. Mutuality does not imply that all things must be equal.

It does imply, however, that all things should be shared. We are commanded to show love to others; we are reminded that we need love from others. We must always be committed to the former and aware of the latter, for we are neither helpless infants who are always in a state of need nor divine beings who stand above need altogether. On some occasions we may face circumstances that will require us to give much and receive little in return. Parents surely face these circumstances at times with their children. So do church leaders with faltering church members. So do husbands with wives, and wives with husbands. At such times the relationship will seem very one-sided, and one person will have to carry the relationship alone, like a good Samaritan, because the other is incapable or unwilling. On other occasions, however, we may face circumstances in which our own pressing needs will force us to receive much from others and give little in return. Physical pain, mental agony, spiritual depression, bitterness of soul, unconquerable sin or apathy will make us so needy that we will feel that we have nothing at all to give to others except our problems.

It is therefore unrealistic and impractical to expect to receive from others exactly what we have given to them, or vice versa. It is also unbiblical. Our responsibility is twofold. We must invest ourselves in our fellow believers without reservation, and we must embrace their gifts of love to us. Whom we invest in and whom we receive from will not always be the same person. Mutuality requires that love be given liberally and received gratefully, that love be distributed impartially and cherished as a rare treasure. It cannot be confined to two people or groups alone, both of whom watch and weigh to make sure that each is giving only to the degree that each has received, for in that situation no love will be shared at all. Mutual love is unconditional concern and undeniable need meeting at the crossroad of our relationships in the body of Christ.

As you read this book I ask you to keep two groups of people in mind. I have already discussed them at the beginning of this chapter. The first group comprises people you know personally and see frequently—spouses, children, parents, relatives, colleagues, associates, friends at church—but sometimes have trouble understanding and loving. These are the people who differ from you more in style than in substance, although, as I said before, the two are sometimes hard to distinguish. The second group includes Christians you see less frequently, or not at all, and know only through reading and study, informal reports, media coverage, hearsay or rumor. This latter group comprises people whose convictions and conduct offend you, whether they be fundamentalists, liberals, charismatics, bureaucrats, ecumenists, prolifers or radical feminists. These people differ from you in belief, although, once again, belief and style often go hand in hand. Keeping these people in mind, I invite you to join me in obeying Jesus' commandment that we love one another, especially as we consider the tremendous diversity in the church today.

PART 1
FOUNDATIONAL COMMANDS

2

GREET
ONE ANOTHER

*L*ook at yourself in a mirror sometime. You don't really see yourself in a mirror as you really are, however carefully you study that image staring back at you. What you see in the mirror depends almost entirely on what you think others see in you and, like a mirror, reflect back to you in their approving or condemning faces. People are better mirrors than real mirrors are. They give us eyes to interpret the image of ourselves that we see every morning and evening on the bathroom wall. So what do you see? A selfish snob, a caring friend, an engaging countenance, an arrogant beast, a crazy clown, a boring personality, a raving beauty, a near lunatic, a brilliant mind, a lazy bum, an ugly face, a creative artist? What you see of yourself in the faces of others determines what you see in the mirror; and the same holds true, obviously, for your friends. You are a mirror for them, as they are for you.

We hold in our hands the power to transform or to destroy our fellow human beings. A mirror on the wall can only reflect the face of the one gazing into it; it cannot interpret that image. That is left up to the one looking at it. What we see in the mirror depends on what we see of ourselves in the faces of each other.

In the late nineteenth century Frederick Treves, a London physician, spotted the picture of a hideously deformed creature on the marquee of a "freak" exhibition and decided out of scientific curiosity to take a closer look at this most unfortunate of creatures called "the Elephant Man." Winding through a dark, dusty passageway, he finally entered a large room. A showman barked at the freak to stand up and uncover himself for the visitor. Treves recorded what followed:

The most striking feature about him was his enormous and misshapened head. From the brow there projected a huge bony mass like a loaf, while from the back of the head there hung a bag of spongy, fungous-looking skin, the surface of which was comparable to brown cauliflower. On the top of the skull were a few long hairs. The osseous growth of the forehead almost occluded one eye. The circumference of the head was no less than that of the man's waist. From the upper jaw there projected another mass of bone. It protruded from the mouth like a pink stump, turning the upper lip inside out and making of the mouth a mere slobbering aperture. . . . The nose was merely a lump of flesh, only recognizable as a nose from its position. The face was no more capable of expression than a block of gnarled wood.

The rest of his body had similar deformities. Folds of spongy skin hung from both front and back. The right arm was overgrown, his legs deformed. Yet there were signs here and there of normal appearance, like his left arm and shoulder, which made the rest of his body seem all the more hideous.

Treves was so fascinated by the creature that he brought him to the hospital and quartered him there. He wanted to study his deformities and use him as a scientific exhibit before the London academy of physicians. Quite sure that the man was an imbecile, Treves was shocked one day to discover that his specimen was a real human being, intelligent, sensitive and kind. He also had a name, John Merrick. Merrick had learned to read and write before his mother abandoned him at the age of five. From that point on his life had been a succession of experiences as horrible as the appearance of his body. Though treated like an animal, he had nevertheless preserved vestiges of humanity deep within himself. Treves wrote:

> His troubles had ennobled him. He showed himself to be a gentle, affectionate and lovable creature, as amiable as a happy woman, free from any trace of cynicism or resentment, without a grievance and without an unkind word for anyone. I have never heard him complain. I have never heard him deplore his ruined life or resent the treatment he had received at the hands of callous keepers. His journey through life had been uphill all the way, and now, when the night was blackest and the way most steep, he had found himself, as it were, in a friendly inn, bright with light and warm with welcome. His gratitude to those about him was pathetic in its sincerity and eloquent in the childlike simplicity with which it was expressed.

Treves and Merrick soon became good friends, and Merrick began to recover his health and enjoy the security of living in the environment of the hospital. Still, Treves noticed that something seemed to hold Merrick back from becoming a whole human being, some terrible secret perhaps, some hidden fear or some painful memory. Treves considered what he could do to shake Merrick loose from his bondage. He finally decided to invite Merrick to visit a widow friend of his as the first step toward introducing him to a wider circle of friends. The idea was risky, for most people, especially women, recoiled in horror and disgust upon meeting Merrick. They could not see past his deformities. But when Treves introduced Merrick to his friend, she graciously wished him a good morning, smiled at him warmly and then took his hand in hers. As Merrick let go of her hand, he rested his huge head on his knees and began to sob. Treves discovered the reason later:

> He told me afterwards that this was the first woman who had ever smiled at him, and the first woman, in the whole of his life, who had shaken hands with him. From this day the transformation of Merrick commenced and he began to change, little by little, from a hunted thing into a man.

Looking back on the incident, Treves believed that the kind touch of a woman changed Merrick's entire life.

I don't know many people like John Merrick, real freaks who have had to endure deformity, pain and rejection for a lifetime. Still, I know many people who *feel* like John Merrick, at least some of the time. Like Merrick, they are longing and waiting for the same acceptance that one dear widow extended to Merrick. That, in essence, is what it means to "greet one another."

Initiative and Generosity

Like all words used in the New Testament, the word we translate as "greet" has its own unique background. It was used widely in the Greek world, as "dear" and "friend" are in our culture. It was employed in several ways. For example, when people wanted to *welcome* guests into their home they would use the term. When people wanted to communicate special attention and affection to loved ones they would add a kiss to their greetings; *cherish* would be a good synonym in this case. When people wanted to greet superiors they would accord them special *honor* through such gestures as a bow. Finally, people writing letters to friends or associates would begin their communications with a *salutation,* which served a similar purpose to our "Dear so-and-so." In the Greek culture of the New Testament period, then, the term "greet" denoted the embracing of another human being in loving affection. It conveyed a sense of warm acceptance and genuine interest. It went far beyond our superficial "hello." It was a way of saying, "I'm glad you're alive; I'm glad I know you; I'm glad we're friends."

The Gospels give the term their own distinctive stamp. Jesus poured special meaning into it, conforming the idea to his own unique ministry. He presented two negative examples to make his point. He used the Pharisees as the first example of what not to do.

> But woe to you Pharisees! For you tithe mint and rue and herbs of all kinds, and neglect justice and the love of God; it is these you ought to have practiced, without neglecting the others. Woe to you Phari-

sees! For you love to have the seat of honor in the synagogues and to be greeted with respect in the marketplaces. Woe to you! For you are like unmarked graves, and people walk over them without realizing it. (Lk 11:42-44)

The Pharisees followed the practice of dressing up in their religious garb and strolling through the marketplaces, where they expected to be treated with respect and greeted by the common people. Jesus warned his disciples not to behave so pretentiously and arrogantly. They were not to expect a greeting from others, as if they were superiors waiting to be acknowledged by inferiors; they were to give a greeting first. To put it in a popular idiom, they were to be "there you are" people rather than "here I am" people. They were to behave like Jesus, who paid special attention to the ones everybody else overlooked and who did not use his popularity, prestige and greatness to separate himself from the common folk. He was an initiator in relationships. He acted immediately to welcome, affirm and encourage whoever crossed his path.

Jesus cited the Gentiles as the second negative example.

You have heard that it was said, "You shall love your neighbor and hate your enemy." But I say to you, Love your enemies and pray for those who persecute you, so that you may be children of your Father in heaven; for he makes his sun rise on the evil and on the good, and sends rain on the righteous and on the unrighteous. For if you love those who love you, what reward do you have? Do not even the tax collectors do the same? And if you greet only your brothers and sisters, what more are you doing than others? Do not even the Gentiles do the same? Be perfect, therefore, as your heavenly Father is perfect. (Mt 5:43-48)

Jesus acknowledged that the Gentiles were friendly, but only to their own kind. Their self-interest led them to be nice to the people who were nice in return. Such strict reciprocity did not require true faith or demonstrate genuine love. There was no risk in it at all. Jesus said that his disciples had to do better by greeting those who were not part of their natural circle of friends. That included the foreigner, the newcomer, the oddball—even the enemy. Jesus required that his disciples treat people as if they really counted for something, which of course they do, at least in the eyes of God.

Jesus commanded his disciples, therefore, to be generous with their greetings. They were not to let differences in color, personality, interest, background, social status, economic level and religious conviction tempt them to show favorites in the family of God, nor to let an expectation of repayment lead them to welcome into their lives only those who would return the favor. Jesus warned against such base motives and actions. "When you give a luncheon or a dinner, do not invite your friends or your brothers or your relatives or rich neighbors, in case they may invite you in return, and you would be repaid. But when you give a banquet, invite the poor, the crippled, the lame, and the blind, And you will be blessed, because they cannot repay you" (Lk 14:12-14). As James exhorted, believers should avoid any display (or even suggestion) of partiality. We are to treat the poor no differently than we treat the rich, women no differently than men, children no differently than adults, the marginal no differently than the powerful. Jesus himself set a worthy example. He went out of his way to include women, lepers, children, the poor and common folk in his circle of friends. He was generous with his greetings. We are to do the same.

Thus the passage about the Pharisees (Lk 11) teaches us that we must take the initiative in greeting others and not wait for them to act first. The passage about the Gentiles (Mt 5) implies that we should be generous with our greetings, extending them not only to friends and family, who usually respond to us in kind, but also to outsiders and enemies, who may not be willing or capable of greeting us in return. To greet one another, therefore, is to demonstrate in word, deed, gesture and attitude that people are important to God and therefore to us, no matter who they are, where they come from, what they believe or how they live.

While this command should affect all of our relationships, it is especially applicable in our relationships in the body of Christ, where we are prone to draw sharp doctrinal and moral boundaries in our concern for and commitment to the faith. To give greetings in the church is a way of affirming people, embracing them in love and showing them that we will not erect any barriers—cultural, religious, economic, political—that may create distance, suspicion and misunderstanding in the relationship. Such a greeting is particularly important in our initial encounters with Christians, when openness, trust and immediate acceptance create a climate for future growth in the relationship.

This reciprocal command played a dominant role in the apostle Paul's life. He encouraged others to obey it, and he practiced it himself. Thus in his letter to the Romans he wrote: "Welcome one another, therefore, just as Christ has welcomed you, for the glory of God" (Rom 15:7). In his mind, no Christian had the right to impose artificial standards on the body of Christ that made one group appear to be superior to another. Whether circumcised or uncircumcised, slave or free, male or female, educated or uneducated, strong or weak, Christians were to do what pleased others. That meant that they were to embrace each other in love, regardless of their differences. Moreover, in virtually every one of his letters Paul extended his greetings to his Christian brethren or relayed the greetings of others. "The churches of Asia send greetings. Aquila and Prisca, together with the church in their house, greet you warmly in the Lord" (1 Cor 16:19). Through his many years of ministry Paul established an extensive network of relationships and enlarged that network through the greetings he extended. The popular view of Paul is of a stern and judgmental man. Reading the final chapter of many of his letters reveals another side—and probably the more accurate side—of the apostle. He was a man who knew how to welcome, include and affirm.

Nowhere is this more evident than in the final chapter of Romans. Paul's example shows us how powerful and positive the act of greeting can be. He provides a model for our greeting of others. We will look more closely at the ways he extended greetings—by acknowledging people, by commending accomplishments, by expressing affection and by conferring a blessing.

Acknowledging People

Most people these days know how it feels to be a stranger, largely because our society has become so mobile. Take a typical American family: Ethel, a single parent, and her three children. Recently divorced, Ethel decided to move to a bigger city where she landed a good job at a large corporation. She was welcomed as a newcomer to her place of employment and, in spite of feeling isolated and lonely for a while, eventually began to make friends.

The same cannot be said, however, of her life outside of work. She bought a house in a new suburban subdivision and hoped that both she and the children would develop friendships there. But her neighbors did not seem to be interested. They were either too busy or too private to be neighborly.

Fortunately, Ethel also had the church to turn to. Her past experience in the church had been positive; she had always considered herself a church insider up to this point in her life. Still, this was the first time she had to go church shopping, and she was nervous about it. Over the next year she learned what it was like to hunt for a parking place and a nursery, what it was like to be seated in the sanctuary under the gaze of many who were sizing her up as the visitor, what it was like to practice new ways of worshiping, what it was like to meet a crowd of people afterward who didn't know what to say once they had learned her name, asked where her husband was and inquired about the reasons for her move. Sometimes she learned what it was like to be completely ignored, as she often was in large churches, the members of which probably weren't acquainted well enough with each other to know who was a visitor and who wasn't. In church after church she met many people but made no friends, and sometimes she didn't meet anyone at all.

Ethel finally found a church home, but not before she went through the agony of being an outsider. Through this experience she learned what many Christians already know, that churches often make it difficult for newcomers to feel welcomed, wanted and needed.

Genuine acknowledgment and acceptance of people is a rare gift that few of us have and all of us need. Most of us forget names once we hear them and overlook people once we meet them. We usually pay attention to the people we already know, or to the ones we want to know. The few powerful, popular, witty, rich and successful people attract the biggest following, even at church. The quiet, elderly, odd, ordinary and undesirable are often left alone, like the lepers of Jesus' day were.

I am impressed by the masterful way Paul extended greetings to the Romans (see Rom 16). He referred to many people by name, some of whom he had never met in person but knew only through mutual friends. There were no invisible people to Paul; there were only individuals with names, backgrounds, interests, needs. Paul also remembered something special about them. He remembered that Epaenetus was "the first convert in Asia," that Andronicus and Junias were "in Christ" before Paul was and were highly respected by the other apostles, that Prisca and Aquila had "risked their necks" for Paul. He remembered the interesting details about people that set them apart and made them unique. Finally, he made his brethren in Rome feel like they belonged. Scholars have discovered that half of the list of names in Romans 16 are those of slaves and women, two groups that had very little social power and respect in those days. Paul made outsiders feel welcomed. He did not base his greetings on what would enhance his prestige and advance his own interests. Unlike many of us, Paul did not calculate who were the right people to know. He practiced what he preached: "From now on, therefore, we regard no one from a human point of view. . . . If anyone is in Christ, there is a new creation: everything old has passed away; see, everything has become new!" (2 Cor 5:16-17).

Christian groups can become exclusive over time, however sincere is their desire to welcome newcomers and outsiders. Thus churches can become ingrown; colleges can become closed to new influences and fresh perspectives; bureaucracies and committees can become stifled by "old boy" networks, making it almost impossible for new blood to get involved. It is easy for us to keep "our people" in power and, consequently, to alienate new people who have not had the time or interest to join our party or take up our cause. Moreover, it is natural to concentrate on the friendships we already have—over coffee on Sunday mornings, at the office during the week or in a weekly Bible study—usually at the expense of developing new ones. We often exclude people without knowing it, especially if they don't speak our language, occupy our social and economic level, share our interests or hold our religious convictions. It takes work to include newcomers. Many of us don't have the time, energy or interest to do it. We feel most comfortable seeing, talking to and working with the people we have known for years. We thus recoil from the responsibility of spotting new faces in a crowd, learning new names, building new friendships, welcoming new people.

The size of a group doesn't seem to matter either. The proverbial "small and friendly" church is probably a myth. One reason, among many, why it remains small is because it may, quite unintentionally, be closed to new people. I have visited small churches that made me feel as if I had offended them by coming, and I have visited large churches that made me feel as if I were the only visitor they had seen in a year.

A few years ago Lynda and I visited a large church in the Minneapolis area. We attended one of the Sunday morning services because we had read about the church's beautiful architecture and wanted to see the building in action. We arrived early enough to study the building, and we planned to leave immediately after the worship service. Our plans were thwarted, however, by the friendliness of the people; they would not let us go! After worship we were greeted by dozens of people who, much to our surprise, were somehow able to identify us as visitors, though there must have been fifteen hundred people at the church. They learned our names, engaged us in conversation, discovered our interests and introduced us to people who had similar interests. Three times we were invited to someone's home for dinner. One couple invited us to a Messiah sing-along at their home. We chatted with people in the church narthex for an entire hour before we could break away. And we were by no means the last people to leave. Is it any wonder that we wanted to return? We only regretted not living closer to Minneapolis.

However, we might not be able to leave inclusion of outsiders to spontaneity. Many churches require their members to serve as greeters before Sunday morning worship. In all the churches I have visited, no greeter has ever bothered to learn my name or to introduce me to other members. There were too many people to greet and too little time available to do it well. Most churches also follow the custom of having the pastor shake hands with parishioners after worship. Again, I have rarely had a meaningful encounter with the pastor in that setting. A line of people, often extending down to the very front of the sanctuary, usually keeps pastors from concentrating their energies on just one person for any length of time. Perhaps churches need to designate certain people to be responsible to meet newcomers after worship. Their mission would be to identify visitors, welcome them to the church and introduce them to others. They could even invite them for dinner or coffee. Obviously they would have to be long-standing members who know most people at the church and who feel comfortable engaging strangers in conversation. Likewise, Christian colleges could appoint veteran faculty and staff members to help their new colleagues to adjust to life at an unfamiliar institution. We would hope, of course, that such formal strategies would be superfluous, assuming that the work of greeting outsiders was already being carried on spontaneously. Still, they might be necessary, since many Christians do not have the time, interest, maturity or capability to welcome newcomers. It is better to organize it than to leave it up to chance.

Commending Accomplishments

Still, acknowledging people is not the only way to extend greetings to our brothers and sisters in Christ. Another way is by commending their accomplishments and by announcing to others the useful service that they have rendered to God. Again, Paul was a master at this. He began his litany of greetings at the end of his letter to the Romans by singling out Phoebe, the carrier of the letter, for special praise. "I commend to you our sister Phoebe, a deacon of the church at Cenchreae, so that you may welcome her in the Lord as is fitting for the saints, and help her in whatever she may require from you, for she has been a benefactor of many and of myself as well" (Rom 16:1-2). The terms Paul used to describe her worthiness carry special authority: sister, deacon, benefactor. After honoring Phoebe, he charged the believers in Rome to receive and assist her, so that she would be able to execute her responsibilities speedily.

Paul accomplished two purposes in this short introduction of Phoebe. First, he made her feel important and useful, which is reason enough to commend others for their godly character and their productive labor. Paul merely practiced then what behavioral science has now proven. People respond best when they are praised, not when they are criticized. Second, he created a sense of mutual respect and obligation between Phoebe and the Roman Christians. Both had high expectations of and admiration for each other before they ever met because Paul had prepared the way.

Paul thus reminds us of something we already know through personal, and often painful, experience. We wield the power to enhance or to destroy the reputation of people simply by how we talk about them. The Bible is brutally direct in warning us about how we use the tongue (Lk 12:1-3; Mt 12:36; Jas 3:2-12; Eph 4:29). Who will not bear witness, perhaps with shame, to the influence that an evil report can have on how we think about others? It's easy to make up our mind about people before meeting them because we listen to—and sometimes seek out—the "informed" opinions of others. We often do not give people a chance to show us who they are and what they want to be, especially if that departs radically from the reputation they have developed thus far. Sadly, this practice is standard fare in the body of Christ. We spread our poison in such insidious ways. "Ed is an obnoxious and difficult student," a second-grade teacher at a Christian school says to his colleagues in the teacher's lounge, thus giving Ed a reputation that may stalk him during the rest of his years in elementary school. "She's competent, all right, but her ambition and thirst for power are just too much for me," a supervisor in a Christian organization says to his boss about Jane, though that supervisor has never addressed the issue in her evaluation. "He's rigid, narrow and uptight," a veteran pastor says about a new minister just appointed to a denominational committee.

Each person has at least two sides, and the difference between the two is often a matter of what we want to see and to communicate to others. For example, what is the difference between spiritual discipline and fanatical devotion? Between assertiveness and aggressiveness? Between flexibility and irresponsibility? Between attention to detail and fastidiousness? The difference between the two often comes down to the side we choose to see. We extend godly greetings in the body of Christ when we decide to look at and put forward the best side of our brothers and sisters in Christ without, of course, overlooking their weaknesses. Surely Phoebe wasn't a perfect woman. Neither was Paul stupid and naive. He simply decided to share a good report about her, though he could have done otherwise. He considered it his responsibility to accent the positive, especially when talking about her in public. He reserved the right to address the negative in face-to-face encounters.

This manner of greeting will demand a special effort from us when dealing with our Christian opponents. We will inevitably face the temptation of recruiting newcomers or, as newcomers, of being recruited to the "right" side in the battle against some enemy out there. Frequently cast in the role of both leader and newcomer, pastors, professors and similar types are often encouraged to join a side or to take up a cause, especially when they first arrive at a church, college or other Christian institution. "You could really enhance the evangelical witness at a time when we really need to counteract the influence of _____." Or: "Your commitment to social justice will provide a useful corrective to people like _____, who are too narrow and privatistic in their faith." They are not allowed, in other words, to make up their own mind about people. That is too risky, and the stakes are too high! Instead, they have to be given the right angle on things. They have to be informed about the real issues dogging the institution. They have to be recruited to join a party of people whose minds are already made up.

The apostle Paul did not always share good reports about people. He could be—and on occasion was—direct and clear in his denunciation of those whom he considered threats to the faith. "By rejecting conscience, certain persons have suffered shipwreck in the faith; among them are Hymenaeus and Alexander, whom I have turned over to Satan, so that they may learn not to blaspheme" (1 Tim 1:19-20). Paul appeared to follow this rule: fellow Christians deserve rebuke when they depart radically from Christian belief and Christian morality. We will explore this issue further in the chapter on admonition.

Expressing Affection

The first Christians attached a physical greeting to their verbal one: "Greet one another with a holy kiss" (Rom 16:16). This "holy kiss" was practiced regularly in the apostolic church, and by the second century was included in the communion liturgy. Even today many churches "pass the peace"—usually a handshake or a hug—as a way of turning the attention of believers to one another, even during formal worship.

Modern culture has perverted our understanding of sexuality. We don't know how to use our bodies to show filial love to one another. This uncomfortableness with the body is ironic since the body has become something of an icon and idol in Western culture. We may be conscious of our bodies, but we don't feel comfortable using them in relationships unless it is for erotic purposes. We are thus forever treating people as if they had nothing but a body, to enjoy for purposes of pleasure, or as if they didn't have a body at all. The difference between the way many men gaze at sex goddesses and the way they ignore old women proves the point. The Christian "holy kiss" reminds us that our greetings should convey affection and that our bodies should be used to show love instead of lust.

Again, Paul expressed such affection in word as well as in action. Many of his letters communicate a certain and unmistakable tone of real love. For example, to the Philippians he wrote:

It is right for me to think this way about all of you, because I hold you in my heart, for all of you share in God's grace with me, both in my imprisonment and in the defense and confirmation of the gospel. For God is my witness, how I long for all of you with the compassion of Christ Jesus. (Phil 1:7-8 mg)

And the conclusion to his letter to the Romans contains phrase after phrase that communicates real emotion. He calls Ampliatus and many others his "beloved in the Lord." He calls Andronicus and Junias his "relatives" and Urbanus his "co-worker in Christ." Paul said verbally what he no doubt demonstrated physically. He greeted his fellow Christians with true affection.

We live in a different culture today. The concept of the holy kiss must be translated into expressions that are more suitable to our time and place. Style may vary but intent should remain the same. A Presbyterian handshake has just as much power to communicate affection as a Pentecostal hug or a Middle Eastern kiss. The point is not so much what we do but what we want to convey. A handshake can be kind and gracious or cold and lifeless; a hug can be warm and hearty or calculating and suggestive. We must always sound the depths of our hearts. Do we really want to embrace one another in love? Are we willing to use our total selves to show such love? Are we impartial in the affectionate greetings we give?

In the body of Christ some people stand in special need of holy affection. These are the "untouchables" of our culture. Jesus embraced the untouchables of his day—lepers, children, women, tax collectors. We have our own to love—the elderly, the poor, the sick and the ugly. I know widows who long for the tender touches that their spouses once gave. I know homely people who want to be known and treated as something other than a displeasing face or figure. I know terminally ill people who crave to have someone break through the barrier of their illness. I met a young woman years ago who told me that she had never, since entering junior high, been touched by a man. She was starved for love and affection. We may rightly fear giving other people "the wrong impression"; we may recoil from "leading people on." These concerns, however, should not keep us from showing love to others. We must respect limits but not withhold love. Untouchables have a special need for demonstrations of genuine caring.

We have much to learn from churches whose members are more expressive and free. A good friend of mine, raised in white, middle-class culture, spent an entire year working as an intern in an inner-city church. In his religious background the greeting during worship lasted about twenty seconds and consisted of a few friendly handshakes and subdued "hellos." The greeting in his new setting meant something very different. During his first Sunday there he arose, as he had always done before, to smile politely and shake a few hands. He quickly learned that that was not the custom they followed there. He was hugged by one person after another, all of whom welcomed him to their church. He sat down five minutes later to catch his breath, only to discover that he was the only one sitting down. The greeting took another ten minutes before formal worship resumed. Such was his introduction to the holy kiss in an African-American church. Over the next several months he loosened up and learned to greet his brothers and sisters in Christ with his whole self.

Conferring a Blessing

Still, not even word, gesture and holy affection are enough. Our greeting must include something else, and that is the divine blessing. It should confer a spiritual benediction upon both the people we already know and the people we meet for the first time. Paul usually included a benediction of grace and peace in his letters. "The God of peace be with all of you. Amen" (Rom 15:33). "The grace of the Lord Jesus be with you. My love be with all of you in Christ Jesus. Amen" (1 Cor 16:23-24). "The grace of our Lord Jesus Christ be with your spirit, brothers and sisters. Amen" (Gal 6:18). Here our greetings convey both human love and divine favor, the former actually being a conduit for the latter. Paul was not merely talking about a blessing; he was literally imparting it.

In doing so, Paul was drawing on a rich Old Testament custom. The "blessing" was standard practice among the people of God from the very beginning. Fathers pronounced a blessing on their children, a leader on the people. The blessing was given through prophetic utterance or conferred by the giving or changing of a name. The blessing communicated God's favor on a person. The loss of blessing was considered a terrible curse, as we learn from the example of Esau, who wept bitterly when his father decided to let the blessing on Jacob stay, though he had received it under false pretenses.

Esau's cry—"O Father, bless me!"—has echoed down through the ages in the hearts of those who have never felt or received the kind of greeting that carries with it the blessing of God. Children, parents, spouses, lovers, colleagues and friends want to know that our love for them reflects the love of God, that our love for them channels the love of God. People want to know that God's favor rests on them. They depend on us, at least in part, to receive that blessing.

Every night before my wife retired to bed she slipped into the rooms of our four children and prayed for them, laying her hands gently on their heads. She was bestowing upon them God's blessing. I have carried on that custom since her death. Our children need it desperately. But then who doesn't? We have the responsibility to channel God's favor to one another as we give hearty and joyful greetings and impart to each other, in unspoken prayer, God's grace and peace.

Our Christian enemies need that blessing too. I do not want to pretend that tensions do not exist in the church today. I am not proposing that we ignore or dismiss them, but I am suggesting that we mitigate them by praying the favor of God on our Christian opponents whenever we meet them, whether it is in cordial or adversarial situations. They belong to God, as we do; they believe in God, as we do; they stand in need of God, as we do. The substance of our disagreements and controversies might not change, but the spirit of the relationship and the manner of communication often will, if in our greetings we bestow God's blessing on them. They need to be reminded that though we may differ with them in matters of theology or practice, we still regard them as

Christian brethren. We cannot assume in the heat of battle that they will believe it, unless we take pains to communicate it. The burden of proof is on us, not them. We must remember, as Jesus taught, that greetings should be initiated and given generously, even when they are not returned.

The good news of the gospel is that God has already greeted us in Christ Jesus. Jesus told us so in the parable of the prodigal son, which is really a story about a longing and loving father. Recognizing that he had to let his ungrateful and selfish son go, the father waited anxiously for some sign of his son's return. When he finally spotted him at a distance, the father rushed out to greet him, welcomed him home with a hug, clothed him with a robe, put a ring on his finger and gave him shoes to wear. Then he killed a fatted calf and threw a great big party for him. Jesus said that that father is like God, who embraces us in love, however prodigal we have been, and gladly makes us a part of his family, however undeserving we are. He charges us to do the same for our Christian brothers and sisters.

3

BE SUBJECT TO ONE ANOTHER

*L*ynda and I used to watch old movies on public television. It gave us a chance to enjoy classic entertainment and to watch the performances of great actors and actresses, many of whom have long since died. Over the years we saw several movies of one of the screen's greatest, Fred Astaire, who appeared in dozens of films over a span of four decades. We never seemed to tire of his movies, in spite of the predictable plots and mediocre acting. Astaire's dancing astonished us. He was a master on the dance floor—the quintessential example of grace, effortlessness and sophistication. He looked at home in tails and a top hat.

After his death Ginger Rogers, his most famous dancing partner, was interviewed on *Nightline*. She lauded his abilities. He was so good, she said, that he never seemed to be leading and she following. The film clips that were shown that night supported her claim. Astaire and Rogers were elegance in action. There was between them a fluidity, a seamlessness. They were so good that it was impossible, as she said, to tell who was leading and who was following. They were two people dancing as one.

Astaire and Rogers manifested in dance what God wants all of us to experience in life. He intends life to be whole; he wants relationships to be harmonious so that, regardless of the social status we have, the social role we play and the social order we live in, there will be little or no difference between leader and follower, powerful and powerless. Like Astaire and Rogers, our relationships will have a seamlessness.

Of course what God intends and how we live are very different. Astaire and Rogers only show how far we fall short of God's ideal. Their oneness exposes our disunity; their wholeness our brokenness. Their fluidity on the dance floor unmasks our competitiveness and hostility. In human society today—and that of course includes the church—we spend most of our time not dancing gracefully but tripping over each other's feet. Mutual subjection is God's way of nurturing and preserving harmony in a fragmented world, unity in broken relationships, healing in a sick and unjust society, love in a divided church. If greeting one another enables us to create a positive atmosphere in human relationships, as if we had an opportunity of showing what heaven is like on earth, then subjection allows us to function in relationships that are very much rooted in the realities—sometimes painful realities—of earthly existence. Life on earth does not always mean intimacy and harmony. Few of us experience the kind of natural oneness in relationships that Rogers and Astaire demonstrated on the dance floor. For most of us, social relationships often lead to conflict, disappointment and frustration. Sometimes the problem is interpersonal, between, say, two close friends, with one or both clearly at fault. At other times the problem is not anyone's fault in particular but comes as the result of the social role assigned to us and the social order in which we must live. In the chapter on admonition we will address the former problem—interpersonal conflict. In this chapter we will address the latter problem—the social order itself.

Subjection is the one command that speaks to those who have to deal with the problem of living within a social order that is not always to their or someone else's liking. This command, in other words, speaks to those who live in the real world of institutions, job descriptions, chains of command, power struggles and social roles. It speaks not simply to people as they are in God's eyes but to people as they live in society, who function as husband or wife, parent or child, boss or subordinate, teacher or student, official or citizen, chair or member, pastor or people.

Of all the mutuality commands, this one is perhaps the most difficult to understand and to obey. Americans these days are absolutely obsessed with securing their personal rights, advancing their own interests and gaining as much power as they possibly can. The idea of subjection is foreign and offensive. It runs counter to everything we believe. It appears to buttress the power of those who, like husbands, teachers, owners and leaders, already seem to have too much; it even seems to give them a convenient excuse to wield it selfishly and greedily. It also appears to keep the powerless in their place and to prevent them from improving their station in life, as if their only option in life were to be subservient to others. Marxists argue that the biblical notion of subjection is a classic illustration of how Christianity supports unjust social order and prevents the powerless from recognizing their servile status, developing a sense of class-consciousness and challenging the powers that be. They conclude that Christianity is inherently conservative, oppressive and destructive. It is part of the old social order that we must do away with. Only then will society become truly just.

This rejection of subjection is partly the fault of the church itself, which has often distorted the biblical meaning of this command. Throughout its two millennia of existence the church has applied it almost exclusively to those who occupy traditionally subordinate roles in society—wives, children, laborers, slaves, followers and ordinary church members—and has resisted applying it to those who hold positions of power in society—husbands, parents, masters, rulers and church leaders. The church has thus made the former group feel inferior and servile, as if they naturally belonged in subordinate positions and were required to accept it as the way God designed life to be lived. It has made the latter group feel invincible and arrogant, as if they had an absolute right to power and the absolute freedom to use it any way they wanted.

Most Christians, then, are not going to embrace this command without a struggle first. Wives will struggle because it seems to require them to assume a subordinate position, thus forcing them to yield every time to the wishes, demands and even abuse of their husbands. Children will struggle because it seems to give absolute authority to parents, thus setting back their quest for early and absolute independence. Employees will struggle because it seems to deprive them of the right to challenge the authority of their employers, thus preventing them from sharing the benefits of ownership, wealth and power. And ordinary church members will struggle because it seems to require them to accept the church as it is and to follow church leaders who do not always uphold biblical principles of leadership.

As we shall see, however, the biblical idea of subjection is not reminiscent of an earlier, backward age. It is revolutionary, progressive and liberating. It has as much to say to the dominant as to the subordinate, to the powerful as to the powerless. It is intended, I believe, to create equality in society without undermining the need for stability and order. Rightly understood, it will make all of us uncomfortable, even as, ironically, it will set all of us free.

The Problem

Though this command addresses Christian life in secular society (for example, the apostle Paul commands us to be subject to governing authorities), I will limit discussion in this chapter to relationships in the church. There is a reason for this. As I see it, secular society usually dictates how most relationships are ordered, even in the church. Christians, in other words, often pattern their relationships after models that they inherit from secular society. Sometimes the church even lends its theology to legitimate that secular social order. My purpose is to explore the proper Christian response to the social order as it affects the way that Christians relate to each other.

To be subject to one another assumes that we live in a social order, under authority and within certain social roles. Behind the command, then, is the assumption of the reality of order. In Greek culture the word translated "to be subject" was used with reference to the ordering of society, which was considered the expression of certain natural laws. In Hebrew culture that order was attributed to God's creation. He made the world and created it to function a certain way. He pronounced the created world good; its order was good, too, since it embodied harmony and wholeness.

Still, the belief that God created social order as a good thing does not imply that the order we now have is a good thing. The Bible teaches that the good order of creation has gone bad. It is now distorted and destructive. That is true for Christian institutions as well as for secular institutions. We are no longer living in the Garden; life is not now what God designed it to be. That is the clear message of the Bible.

Evidence of this distortion is everywhere. Many of us have witnessed or participated in the disordering of God's ordered creation, in the church as well as in secular society. We have been victims of or been involved in church splits, abuse of church office, clergy sexual miscon-duct, lawsuits between Christians or Christian organizations. We have sat on committees that did business instead of ministry. We have participated in church feuds that sapped the spiritual vitality of congre-gations. We have watched helplessly as fellow church members struggled over a theological and moral issue until all perspective was lost, all civility exhausted, all affection and generosity withheld—for the sake of the "cause." We have experienced the gradual erosion of church life because the church operated better as an institution than as an organism. We have worked with denominational hierarchies that pushed a prevailing ideology—whether on the left or on the right—with more passion and conviction than they strived to preach the gospel.

This distortion of church life is so common that it has become the rule rather than the exception. It is simply the way church life is in our experience. The Bible at this point is bluntly realistic about life in the world. It does not whitewash problems in the church (or it would never contain a book like 1 Corinthians). Neither does it accept these problems as inevitables. It is not naively optimistic and utopian; it is not pessimistic and cynical. It affirms that God's world is good but that it has gone bad, that God's intended order for the world is good but that it has been distorted, that power used for the right reasons is good but that it is now being used selfishly.

Possible Solutions

This tension introduces us to a complex problem for Christians. It is impossible to separate the good order that God has created from the perversion of that order that we experience every day. Social order is willed by God; it is also perverted by sin. It is a created good; it has become evil. We can't live with it and we can't live without it. This is the fundamental problem that Christians must address in the church today.

Many Christians have identified this problem over the years and have offered solutions. The first is some form of radicalism. Utopianism, for example, assumes that it is possible to recover the perfection of an earlier time, as if, under the right circumstances, the Garden of Eden could be rediscovered and colonized once again. Utopian communities have proved to be horrible failures, however, because they do not take into account human sinfulness and the impact of that sinfulness on society. Leaders of these communities think that they can withdraw from evil society, but they always end up bringing the evil with them.

Another example of radicalism is egalitarianism, which assumes that there is no divine order for society at all. Every expression of order—church polity, church office, church committee—is the product of human invention or convention. The institutional church is humanly constructed and can be changed with no fear of violating the will of God. If anything, it should be done away with so that equality can prevail among all Christians. The error of this approach is in thinking that because the present order is evil then order itself must be bad. Ironically, those who oppose the idea that order in the church is a divinely created good usually end up creating one that is more corrupt and unjust than the one they helped to destroy.

The second solution is conservatism. Conservatives often assume that since order is good, either the present order or some past expression of it must be good. They argue that the way things presently are or were in the past is the way they ought to be, thus equating the order God created with the order that we have today or had yesterday. Conservatives who defend the "traditional" church base their defense on exactly this argument. They are right insofar as they recognize that social order is inevitable and can be good; they are wrong in identifying a particular social order of the present or past as the order God created. This confusion too often justifies traditionalism, inertia and even injustice.

Again, the problem for Christians is that order was created as a good thing by God but has became an evil thing in the hands of fallen human beings. Subjection is the mutuality command that enables us to acknowledge that order is necessary and good without assuming that this present order is what God ultimately intends. Subjection is the posture that we assume to live in the real world, which God created and human beings have distorted.

The Meaning

Though the command applies to Christians in secular society, as I mentioned before I will limit our discussion to the church. Subjection creates harmony in the church by affirming the need for order, on the one hand, and by transforming that order through love, on the other. It assumes that an institution like the church is good but not necessarily as presently constructed; that structures intended to govern the church are good but not necessarily as presently designed; that roles within this institution are good but not necessarily as presently prescribed. The command is given to all Christians, regardless of age, gender, race, wealth, power or position. We are to "be subject to one another out of reverence for Christ," as Paul writes (Eph 5:21).

The principle of subjection applies to the real, ambiguous and difficult circumstances in which Christians must live. It enables believers to live for Christ in a wide variety of settings, whatever these settings may happen to be and however far they may happen to depart from our ideal.

Subjection helps believers to adapt to the church as it is without becoming fatalistic; it also gives believers the freedom to change the church without becoming rebellious and unruly. Thus subjection is both radical and conservative. It requires Christians to honor the principle of order—that is the conservative side of the command, which keeps believers from being rebellious. It also empowers Christians to correct its distortions and make it better—that is the radical side, which protects believers from fatalism. Subjection helps Christians to live in the church as it is; it also enables Christians to change it.

The principle of subjection addresses the institutional church where it is most vulnerable, at just those points where it is most easily distorted and corrupted. On the one hand, it speaks to those in power by redefining what leadership means and power requires. People who occupy dominant positions in the church—bureaucrats, pastors, elders and so forth—tend to use power to advance their own interests at the expense of their subordinates, who often lack power in the institution. For the powerful, subjection mandates service and sacrifice, as Jesus instructed those who are "first" and "great" (Mk 10:35-45). As the apostle Peter charged:

> Now as an elder myself and a witness of the sufferings of Christ, as well as one who shares in the glory to be revealed, I exhort the elders among you to tend the flock of God that is in your charge, exercising the oversight, not under compulsion but willingly, as God would have you do it—not for sordid gain but eagerly. Do not lord it over those in your charge, but be examples to the flock. And when the chief shepherd appears, you will win the crown of glory that never fades away. (1 Pet 5:1-4)

Leaders of the church must also meet the highest moral and spiritual standards. "Now a bishop must be above reproach, married only once, temperate, sensible, respectable, hospitable, an apt teacher, not a drunkard, not violent but gentle, not quarrelsome, and not a lover of money" (1 Tim 3:2-3).

On the other hand, subjection challenges those without power by

52

calling them to trust Christ's lordship even as they occupy subordinate positions in the church. These people tend to respond to their powerlessness either by resisting authority or by giving in to it. Resentment, manipulation and rebellion result from resistance; fatalism, hopelessness and compromise are some of the consequences of resignation. In the former case, subjection requires that we show honor, give respect, go beyond the call of duty. In the latter case it means that, when the occasion merits, we resist human authorities in the church, but always in the spirit of Christ's humility and lowliness.

The Bible enjoins every believer to be subject, whatever their role is in the church. Subjection must begin with the self first. It demands a personal decision, based not on ideal circumstances but on the power and grace of God. Subjection is not conditioned on the behavior of other people. It is not based on their worthiness or fairness. It does not require perfection of someone else before we strive for perfection ourselves, nor is it dependent on securing our own personal rights first. The apostle Paul did not tell leaders to serve those under their spiritual charge only if they were deserving, nor did he command Christians to respect church authorities only if they exercised ideal leadership. The Bible does not make this command conditional. All Christians are to be subject in the particular settings and roles in which they find themselves. It is as simple as that.

Simple, perhaps, but not easy. That is why the apostle Paul adds this phrase, "as to the Lord," to the command. Nearly every reference to subjection in the Bible contains a qualifier like this one. "Wives, be subject to your husbands as you are to the Lord. . . . Husbands, love your wives, just as Christ loved the church" (Eph 5:22, 25). Subjection assumes the lordship of Christ and requires Christians to live by faith. No one can be subject to another human being if he or she is not first subject to Christ.

We take risks when we obey this command. What if church leaders head in the wrong direction once we stop pressuring them? What if friends at church settle into bad habits once we no longer nag them to measure up to our standards? What if it appears that subjection indulges weakness, accepts the social status quo and reinforces the worst habits in fellow Christians who desperately need changing? It appears that we stand to lose a great deal if we take this command to heart. Only faith will enable us to carry it out in spite of the risks.

Subjection involves attitude as well as action. It requires that we give up being manipulative in relationships in order to get our own way. It may appear possible to be subject without a real change of heart, but sooner or later such token obedience will be exposed as a sham. Leaders may draw attention to their sacrificial labors and devotion to the job as a way of obligating followers to show unquestioning loyalty to them. That is not subjection, it is manipulation. Followers may do what leaders ask but complain constantly behind their backs about their incompetence and unfairness. That, too, is manipulation. Each person can do the right action but make the beneficiary pay a psychological price. It is, in effect, taking back with one hand what is given with the other. An attitude of manipulation and calculation violates the principle of subjection.

Though subjection requires that we yield to Christ, who is Lord of life, it does not mean that we must always yield to others. Forsaking power in the name of subjection does not mean that we should hand it over to another person who doesn't deserve it and shouldn't have it. It is possible to be subject to another person without always yielding to their wishes or obeying their commands. Subjection does not imply that Christians submit to abuse, tolerate evil and cover for people who live irresponsibly. It does not create "codependents."

Paul enjoined Christians to be subject to their rulers, who were appointed by God "as his instruments of wrath." Yet Peter and John refused to stop preaching the gospel, though the Jewish authorities ordered them to be silent. "We must obey God rather than any human authority," they said. That could be construed as outright rebellion. Yet they were willing to suffer the consequences of their disobedience and went willingly and joyfully to jail for it. Thus they upheld the principle of order—they were subject—without capitulating to the evil of that order. Martin Luther King Jr. behaved similarly during the civil rights movement. Like Peter and John, he honored the principle of subjection but refused to accept an unjust social order. He lived in this tension by willingly and graciously accepting the consequences for his disobedience. He, too, went to jail, continued to love his enemies and did not harbor hatred in his heart. Likewise, members representing a minority point of view at a church or in a denomination might become even more marginalized because of their vocal opposition. They would remain subject if they accepted their declining influence graciously and reasonably, but without giving up or giving in.

Subjection is not, therefore, the same as resignation. It does not lead to fatalism, tolerate injustice, encourage passivity or yield to evil. If anything, it overcomes evil by doing good. It changes the social order through the power of love.

Subjection in the Life of One Church

However simple this command is in principle, its application to the complexities of church life is far from simple. The story of one congregation I have observed at a distance comes to mind when I consider the complexities of subjection. I had a long conversation with Seth Mullins, the pastor of North Community Church, about how his church survived the unhappy departure of a major splinter group. And I know two couples who left the church some years ago with that splinter group, one of whom later returned to the church after having wrestled with the principle of subjection.

The contrast between the stories of these two couples underscores both the importance of subjection and the difficulty of obeying it. Both couples began to separate from North Community after they joined a fellowship within the church that became more important to them than the church itself. Their experience in that group only exacerbated the disappointment they felt in North Community, which seemed to fall far short of what they thought the church could and should be. Doug, the leader of this fellowship, had serious disputes with other leaders at the church, and he voiced the sentiment of the whole group by accusing Seth, the pastor of the church, of being a pawn of the other side. The issues themselves were trivial (such as dress codes at their Christian academy), as were the accusations leveled against the pastor. The personalities involved, however, made the difference. They turned insignificant issues into a major dispute. Doug finally left the church and took fifty people with him.

Both couples went with this group, although for different reasons. For Bob and Terri it was a matter of spiritual disappointment because the church wasn't delivering what they wanted. Bob said that he continued to love and respect their former pastor, Seth. He admitted that for him it was a simple matter of "wanting more" and being disappointed that he wasn't getting that "more" at North Community. Terri explained that she simply took up Doug's cause. When Doug and his wife began to complain about Seth, she joined in. When they decided to leave, she naturally followed them. The other couple, Todd and Andrea, had more definite and volatile reasons. Todd believed that Seth was unsuitable to be a minister. Moreover, Todd accused Seth of claiming something about the church that the church could not deliver. "This is the only true church," Todd heard the pastor say repeatedly. "If you don't come here, you're going to miss out." Todd did not like that kind of pressure and did not believe it was true. So he and his wife also joined the group that left.

Bob and Terri didn't stay with the splinter group for long. They moved to Seattle, where they became involved in a large charismatic church. They stayed there for five years before moving back. Then they floundered for two years, jumping from one church to another, unhappy and unsettled. They also went through serious marital problems, which almost resulted in a divorce. Finally, convinced that they were wrong and humbled by their own personal problems, they returned to North Community, confessed their sin before the pastor and elders, and rejoined the fellowship, where they have been ever since.

Todd and Andrea lasted a little longer in the splinter group. They had high expectations for this new fellowship, but these were soon dashed. Shortly before organizing the group that left North Community, Doug lost his wife in a tragic accident. Within a week he had taken up with a married woman; that relationship soon became adulterous. Todd was alarmed by this turn of events and believed that he was responsible to take action. He sought advice from Jim, the leader of a house church. Jim encouraged Todd to confront Doug, which Todd did, with little result. Jim finally counseled him to separate from the church and to find another. Todd and Andrea did. They began attending Jim's house church.

Todd and Andrea told me that this new church was for a time the most impressive church they had ever attended. "Its leaders," Todd said to me, "were dedicated, unified, mature, serious, fervent and zealous. It was the best fellowship we have ever experienced. It was the closest thing to the true church that we have ever witnessed." After about a year, however, Todd began to notice that not every aspect of the church lined up with biblical standards. The leaders, for example, were giving inaccurate prophecies, and approved of remarriage after divorce. Todd began to raise questions. At first the leaders put him off patronizingly. "You see with a carnal mind," they said. "We see with the Spirit. Give it time and you will begin to see as we do." Yet Todd continued to challenge the leadership. Eventually serious conflict broke out. Attempts at reconciliation failed. Todd apologized for leveling accusations at the church leaders, but he would not back down entirely. He finally announced his departure, but not before the leaders blasted him publicly. "They accused me of mocking God when I prayed," Todd told me. "They said I was of the devil, a troublemaker. One man prophesied, 'The birds of the air will pick out your flesh, for all of Spokane to see.' I wanted to be submissive, but only to men of God. I was profoundly disappointed."

Those prophecies ended up having an ironic twist to them. Three months after Todd left, a scandal broke out that every major newspaper in the country covered. One of the leaders of the church kept spanking his young child because he wouldn't eat. The leader thought that his son was being disobedient, a "spiritual problem" that required physical punishment. He did not consider taking his child to a physician. The child finally died of diabetes. The leader was jailed for child abuse. The church folded shortly after that. It appears that the prophecy pronounced against Todd came back on their own heads.

Bob and Terri believe that they left North Community under false pretenses. "We didn't have a good reason," Terri said. "We were deceived." Bob added, "We can't expect perfection of a church. What we needed was already there—a good church with a faithful pastor and faithful members. What we desired was also already there—a hunger for more of what God wants." They beam when they talk about the church now. They are not naive about it, nor about the pastor. Still, they believe that God is present and at work in their imperfect fellowship.

Todd and Andrea have not been involved in a church since leaving Jim's house church so abruptly. For a while they attended or led Bible studies. Now they do not even participate in those. Their family is their church. They defend their point of view passionately. They believe that most churches are apostate, filled with false believers who have the form of religion but deny the power of it. They claim that they are not looking for perfection. They simply want to find a church whose members seek God, try to obey God's commands and live as disciples of Jesus before the watching world.

I do not believe that Todd and Andrea are self-righteous and arrogant. Their longing for God's blessing kept coming through when we talked. They desire to receive what God wants to give so much that they will not identify with a church that seems to mock him and ignore his promises. They are suspicious of churches that put pastors on pedestals, exalt traditions instead of embrace the gospel, communicate an air of superiority over other churches and tolerate ungodliness among their members.

Though I respect their Christian commitment, I do not agree with their theology. In my mind, they have misunderstood and ignored the mandate of subjection. They expect the church to be something it has never been—perfect. The one occasion in their story when they thought that they had found the "perfect church" turned out to be their most disappointing experience. That was warning enough that it was not simply the church that was in error. So was their theology.

The Church As It Is

Subjection takes the church as it is. It does its work in circumstances that fall short of the ideal. Sometimes, for example, subjection requires good leaders to lead bad congregations. Subjection means that they preach with conviction, teach with clarity, counsel with compassion, confront with hope, exhort with courage and so nudge, push, lure, entice and love the people forward into the fuller life that Christ promises. Sometimes it requires good people to put up with bad leadership. Subjection means that they pray faithfully, volunteer willingly, live as examples of faith and holiness, assume leadership if the opportunity presents itself and, if the situation seems impossible, leave quietly, humbly and graciously to find another fellowship, unless they have the authority, patience and hope to help solve the problem redemptively.

The church is not perfect. Jesus said that it has wheat and weeds. It will until the end of the age. Subjection is the command that keeps us faithful to the church as it is even as we strive to make it better. It therefore keeps pastors from relentlessly pursuing power to "rescue" a troubled congregation, elders from running the church like a business because it seems to run as an institution so inefficiently, choir directors from complaining about choir members who can't sing very well and skip rehearsals for no reason at all, committee members from quitting when they don't get their own righteous way, small group participants from missing meetings because no one else seems committed enough, and ordinary believers from haranguing incompetent leaders and abandoning their churches because one or the other does not meet their ideal. It keeps the imperfect church filled with imperfect people led by imperfect leaders together long enough so that it can become a little less imperfect. It forces us to be humble servants of the perfect

Christ rather than proud masters of the church we want to perfect.

As it is, our attempts to create the perfect church usually have disastrous consequences, yielding suspicion, gossip, judgment, hurt feelings and divisions. I talked with one Christian leader, for example, who is weary of petty criticism, especially when it comes from those who have never bothered to learn all the facts or get to know him as a person. He said that there are reasons why he does not use their theological code words, and he resents that they do not understand and respect what those reasons are. I talked with another leader with a high public profile who feels betrayed by subordinates who have accused him falsely and exposed his weaknesses to the press without first confronting him. I talked with faculty members at Christian colleges who feel slighted by administrators who push through their own ideas without first listening to them. I talked with middle managers of Christian organizations who wonder why entrepreneurial leaders abuse their charismatic power and refuse to share their power with others. I talked with secretaries of churches who feel insulted by pastors who, so careful to be politically correct before the public, treat them as mere conveniences. I talked with members of a committee who are aggravated because, refusing to endorse the ideological orientation of the pastor of their congregation, they were stripped of their power to carry out their assigned task.

I found suspicion, anger, complaints and deep wounds everywhere. The accusations ran along the same lines almost every time. Ordinary church members resent leaders who abuse their power, either by failing to carry out their basic responsibilities or by accumulating power for its own sake. They recognize the need for leadership; that is rarely disputed. But they want to follow leaders who set a clear course, distribute power fairly, welcome ideas from below, listen carefully and respectfully, and serve the common good rather than their own narrow interests. Likewise, leaders dislike church members who whine about petty concerns, criticize without getting involved, complain to everyone but never talk to the leadership itself, expect perfection from imperfect people and come to infallible conclusions about complex issues without first gathering all of the facts and weighing them carefully. Again, subjection turns leaders into servants; it turns ordinary church members into loyal, faithful and discerning supporters. It turns chairs of committees into listeners; it turns members of those committees into active and willing volunteers. It turns pastors into shepherds of the flock; it turns people into sheep willing to be cared for.

The irony—and perhaps the tragedy—is that what we expect from others we are not willing to give, what we often complain about is exactly what we do much of the time. We want understanding but do not seem willing to understand; we want power but are cautious about giving it; we want freedom to function but are slow to give that freedom to others. Subjection enables us to do the opposite. It upholds and transforms the order of the church by forcing us to change the only person we have the power to change, namely ourselves. It makes leaders humble, and thus willing to listen to, serve and empower followers. It makes followers supportive, and thus willing to honor leaders, help them succeed and, when problems arise, address those problems prudently.

Subjection affirms the need for order and then transforms that order through love. It makes all of us dance in church as seamlessly and effortlessly as Astaire and Rogers danced in the ballroom.

4

FORBEAR
ONE ANOTHER

*M*any years ago I ran across an article in the *Los Angeles Times*. Its unusual title caught my eye: "Guilty Only of Stupidity." It told the story of a fraternity prank gone bad. Several members of the fraternity decided that it would be great fun to kidnap one of the pledges and take him on a "ride" to the hills north of Los Angeles. They jumped their victim in the middle of the night, tied, gagged and blindfolded him, then dropped him off in a deserted tract of land with nothing on but underwear and a quarter in hand. They no doubt thought that this prank was mischief at its best. Their victim, of course, had no idea where he was. Removing his blindfold, he wandered around for a while to get his bearings. He was hampered by the overcast sky, which made the night very dark. It was so dark, in fact, that he didn't see the cliff toward which he was headed. He stumbled at the edge and fell to his death. The article said that the students who kidnapped him felt horrible. They disclaimed responsibility, however, saying that they had no idea their prank would end in such tragedy. Police officers decided not to press charges because, as the title of the article announced, they were "guilty only of stupidity."

I have remembered this chilling article over these many years because I have a propensity for stupidity too. If I had been one of those fraternity members I would have participated as eagerly as had the others. My track record confirms that prediction. I have often spoken foolishly, decided prematurely and behaved badly. I too have been guilty of stupidity. Perhaps that is true for you as well.

God knows all about our stupidity and bears with us in spite of it, ever staying loyal to us. He is good at forgiving, putting up with, looking past and loving us through it. God is forbearing toward us.

The Bible mentions the forbearance of God often. In Psalm 78, for example, the psalmist exalts God's patience and compassion. Refusing to trust God, the people of Israel, God's chosen ones, kept putting him to the test, in spite of the many assurances and signs God gave to them of his faithfulness. God disciplined them, to be sure; but in the end he always forgave. He was angered but not put off by their disobedience.

Their heart was not steadfast toward him;
    they were not true to his covenant.
Yet he, being compassionate,
    forgave their iniquity,
    and did not destroy them;
often he restrained his anger,
    and did not stir up all his wrath.
He remembered that they were but flesh,
    a wind that passes and does not come again. (Ps 78:37-39)

The apostle Paul made God's forbearance a foundational principle of his theology. In his pivotal argument of Romans 3:21-26 he used Israel's disobedience to make a point about the character and plan of God. God sent Jesus to be the propitiation for sin, the supreme sacrifice that makes believers right with God, thus canceling their debt of sin. Jesus came in the fullness of time to accomplish this great work. But what happened before Christ came? Paul argued that in his "divine forbearance" God passed over former sins in anticipation of Christ's death on the cross. He looked ahead to what was someday going to happen, much like a storeowner might put up with the indebtedness of a client in expectation of a big payment that some benefactor is about to give. God put up with and forgave them for their sinfulness because Jesus was going to appear someday, and he would pay the penalty for their wrongdoing.

God was forbearing then, and he is now. He suspended final judgment then because Jesus was coming to deal with sin; he suspends judgment now because Jesus has already come and dealt with sin. With the people of Israel, he looked ahead; with us he looks back. In both cases he looks to Jesus, whose triumph on the cross enables God to forbear. It should stagger us to consider how much God forbears. I am not referring now to the terrible things that we do, although God forgives us for those things. I am talking about the little things that we do that God simply overlooks, bears with and loves us through, like our smallness of mind, defensiveness, bad moods, obnoxious personalities, sour attitudes, petty concerns and acute self-consciousness. He forbears like good parents do who recognize that their immature and selfish children will someday become mature and unselfish adults. He is patient with us because he knows that we will someday grow up. Yes, he does discipline and forgive us, when it is needed. But he also forbears when forgiveness is not necessary, when discipline is not appropriate, when only time and experience will do the trick.

We have benefited more than we know from God's forbearance. If we saw ourselves as God sees us, we would fall over dead with shame or fall at God's feet in utter devotion. We would discover how much time, space and opportunity God has given us to outgrow our immaturity. God calls us to imitate him in forbearing one another. He commands us to give each other the slack that he has given us. Forbearance thus requires that we give people room—room to be who they are, to become what God intends, to contribute what they can to the church and the world, in spite of their imperfections.

The word itself is important. A biblical word, it is preferable to two other words that, though more widely used in our culture, do not carry the same meaning or serve the same purpose. The first word is "politeness." It may represent a good quality—I certainly favor politeness over rudeness. Still, it can betray hypocrisy. Behind a polite face can be a disdainful, arrogant, condescending attitude. It is possible for one to be very polite and not be forbearing. The second word is "tolerance," which has become something of an obsession in modern culture. It embodies one of America's ideal virtues. We hurl an insult at people when we call them "intolerant." But tolerance can smack of relativism and compromise. Tolerant people often exalt diversity over the common good, divorce charity from truth and pursue relevance at the expense of biblical absolutes. Ironically, people who make tolerance the chief virtue in the modern world are seldom tolerant of people who disagree with them. Forbearance may at times require politeness and tolerance, but also much more, as we shall see. It is the biblical word, and that is the one we should use.

Forbearance demands consistency. It is what I would call one of the foundational reciprocal commands, as are greeting and subjection. It is obviously not the only command we must obey; it does not, for example, eliminate the need for exhortation and admonition. We should not stop at forbearance in our relationships. Rather, we should begin with it. Rarely will our brothers and sisters in Christ accept our comfort if they have not benefited from our forbearance first; rarely will they allow us to bear their burdens; rarely will they yield to our admonitions. Forbearance builds trust, and trust makes people more willing to let a relationship grow, even when it becomes painful. The long-term vulnerability, openness and strength of our relationships depend upon faithful obedience to this command. Failure to obey it will jeopardize our relationships whenever misunderstanding, wrongdoing or conflict—inevitable in any relationship—arises in the course of ordinary experience.

Oh, but what do we forbear, and how far do we go in forbearing? Should we forbear what appear to be departures from orthodox theology? I have asked many people that question, and I have received a variety of answers. More than half would forbear denial of the virgin birth of Christ and the inerrancy of Scripture. Very few would forbear rejection of the literal resurrection of Christ from the dead. Is this distinction a wise and legitimate one? Is the resurrection more central theologically and historically than is the virgin birth? How do we know what is true?

Again, should we forbear violations of biblical morality? If so, how far is too far? Most Christians in America protest very little, if at all, when fellow believers are materialistic. Not so in the case of adultery or homosexuality, although that is changing rapidly.

Again, to what degree should we forbear obnoxious personality traits and character blind spots? I know some wives who have put up with irresponsible husbands for years, treating them as if they were children. Are these wives patient and forbearing or weak and indulgent? I know some pastors who have endured immaturity in certain members of their congregation for their entire tenure of service at a church. Are they compassionate and sensitive or cowardly and naive?

Learning to discern when and how much to forbear is a little like mastering the art of parenthood. It is difficult to determine when aberrant behavior should be overlooked and when it should be confronted.

Room to Be

The essential meaning of the Greek word is "to bear with," "to give slack to." Forbearance requires that we give people room to be themselves, that we accept them under those terms without communicating a spirit of disapproval or judgment, and that we rejoice in them as a special creation of God. It is a way of saying, "This is who you are in my eyes and I am glad for it."

The apostle Paul commands forbearance of us in Ephesians 4:2 (see also Col 3:3). In that same verse he mentions three character qualities that make forbearance possible: lowliness, meekness and patience (RSV). Surely meekness is necessary if we are ever going to give people room to be who they are. Meek people do not claim the right to remake people into inferior copies of themselves. They do not try to impose their imperious will on them. They are not tyrannical, dominant, judgmental or bossy. They do not use their insights into the character of others as a pretense to force them to submit to their will, nor do they use their concern for others as an excuse to dictate exactly how they ought to believe and live. Meek people let God be Lord of their own lives and therefore of the lives of other people too.

Paul charged Christians to refrain from passing judgment on each other in matters that do not count. He argued, for example, that it was not important whether a person ate or abstained from eating certain foods for religious reasons. Because the issue did not involve a major biblical prohibition, Paul encouraged believers to be forbearing.

Welcome those who are weak in faith, but not for the purpose of quarreling over opinions. Some believe in eating anything, while the weak eat only vegetables. Those who eat must not despise those who abstain, and those who abstain must not pass judgment on those who eat; for God has welcomed them. Who are you to pass judgment on servants of another? It is before their own lord that they stand or fall. (Rom 14:1-4)

Paul applied one basic rule in these circumstances: "Let us therefore no longer pass judgment on one another, but resolve instead never to put a stumbling block or hindrance in the way of another" (Rom 14:13). He was aware of the temptation that "strong" Christians (those whose consciences are formed by biblical principles and not by religious scruples) faced when they considered it a sacred duty to persuade their weaker brethren to give up their admittedly misguided convictions concerning food laws, religious calendar and the like. He charged these strong Christians to "bear with" weak Christians in beliefs and customs that were too insignificant to have ultimate spiritual value. "We who are strong ought to put up with the failings of the weak, and not to please ourselves. Each of us must please our neighbor for the good purpose of building up the neighbor" (Rom 15:1-2).

Paul argued similarly in 1 Corinthians 8—10. In that letter he countered those with "superior knowledge" by claiming that knowledge puffs up but love builds up. Again, he suggested that informed Christians not use their knowledge as justification to flaunt their liberty of conscience before believers who might be hurt by it. It is better to give up such liberty than to abuse it. "Therefore, if food is a cause of their falling, I will never eat meat, so that I may not cause one of them to fall" (1 Cor 8:13). Paul offered this final rule of conduct:

For though I am free with respect to all, I have made myself a slave to all, so that I might win more of them. To the Jews I became as a Jew, in order to win Jews. To those under the law I became as one under the law (though I myself am not under the law) so that I might win those under the law. To those outside the law I became as one outside the law (though I am not free from God's law but am under Christ's law) so that I might win those outside the law. To the weak I became weak, so that I might win the weak. I have become all things to all people, that I might by all means save some. I do it all for the sake of the gospel, so that I may share in its blessings. (1 Cor 9:19-23)

This principle of forbearance still applies today. Many issues that divide Christians and create an artificial standard in the church simply do not count for much. How Christians dress, how they eat, how they entertain themselves, how they talk, how they worship, how they observe (or do not observe) the church year, how they witness, how they serve people in need, how they think politically—these and other areas contain a great deal of room for interpretation and expression. Not that we should cast all standards to the wind. Some standards do apply in dress, speech, worship, witness, custom, ritual, politics, economics and the like. Surely suggestive dress is inappropriate, immoral entertainment unacceptable, insensitivity in witness cause for reproach, unbridled greed and political exploitation blameworthy. But these broad standards certainly break out of the narrow boundaries in which we often force our brothers and sisters in Christ to live. Forbearance prevents us from using our prejudices, tastes and ideologies as a means of controlling people who stand with us in essential beliefs and convictions but depart from us in application, expression and style. As I have said before, forbearance gives people room.

Church music is one of those areas in which it is best to give a great deal of room. Trained church musicians are often galled by the sentimental slop that passes for Christian music today, and theologians are often offended by the egocentric theology in many contemporary Christian songs. Perhaps they are right. Yet many common people, musically untrained but still very opinionated, are intimidated and put off by the sophistication of high church music. As they say, there isn't much beat and swing to J. S. Bach. They want to feel the music, not simply think about it. Both sides have a point. I am impressed by the music director at our church, who has been able to use both kinds of music for congregational singing and choral anthems. He has learned how to defer to *and* challenge those who want nothing but a contemporary sound and those who want nothing but Bach. He knows how to compromise without caving in. He gives people room to have differing musical tastes without capitulating to either side. Our church has livelier and deeper worship because of it.

The command to forbear will require us somewhere along the line to make up our minds about our fellow Christians. We will have to decide whether to accept them in spite of their weaknesses or to reject them because of their weaknesses. I believe that most Christians are basically good people who have a few irritating habits, personality quirks or peculiar beliefs. We all know people like that—self-appointed experts who think that they always have the right answer to every problem, bossy volunteers who take charge even when no one wants to follow, incompetent leaders who make everyone feel anxious because they never seem to get any work done, self-sensitive friends who never seem to stop talking about their personal problems, gifted people who don't seem to care about their obvious lack of goodness and humility. These are the ones whom we are called to forbear—to esteem, love and put up with.

Our fellow Christians will know it. They will instinctively sense the attitude we communicate, whether it be disapproval or delight. Forbearing people impart a spirit of love and create a healthy environment for the growth of relationships. While we lived in Chicago my oldest daughter had the privilege of having a forbearing person as a teacher in her preschool. I know very little about early childhood education, so I cannot say authoritatively if she was an expert. She did not appear to be unusually creative and energetic. In her case, it didn't seem to matter. She had the ability to discern and to value the basic personality of each child. Consequently, she related to each child differently. She communicated a spirit of acceptance and genuine delight. She did not prefer the bright children over the slow ones, the coy ones over the assertive ones, the serious ones over the silly ones. In her eyes, every child was special. To this day, some years later, my daughter still considers her one of the important people in her life. Forbearance has that kind of power.

Still, I do not want to give the impression that forbearance is easy. That is why forbearance requires a mixture of grace, humor and discernment. It requires grace because people can be obnoxious. I am sure that over the course of her career my daughter's preschool teacher had children in her classroom who tested her to the limit and beyond. Over a normal lifetime all of us will meet and have to work with people who make forbearance seem more difficult than martyrdom. My wife, for example, was easily put off by people whose superior abilities and fame seem to give them the right to be insensitive, arrogant and rude. I am bugged more by people whose psychological nerve endings seem to extend ten inches beyond the end of their fingertips. Without the grace of God our best intentions and efforts will fall short of God's command. We will find ourselves tempted to withhold the love of Christ from people who drive us crazy.

Forbearance also requires humor, because sometimes laughter is the best—and perhaps the only sane—way we can respond to people. We will have to learn to say, "Yes, that person bugs me to no end. But I don't know anyone like her." Not everything, of course, is funny. Some matters are deadly serious and we must treat them that way. To do anything less is to overlook God's standards and judgment. But other things are not quite so serious. We must learn to chuckle at inexperience, to laugh at flubs, to smile at foolish mistakes. Most of us have probably heard absolutely terrible church soloists who appeared to have lost a sense of pitch years ago. Too often we have sat in the pew fuming over the bad music instead of laughing about the odd and wonderful nature of the church, which gives average people a chance to test and to use their gifts. Likewise, many of us no doubt know people whose overbearing personality makes us want to hide whenever we see them approach us, knowing, as we already do, that they will push us into a corner and demand our total attention for at least an hour. Too often we have pronounced judgment upon them rather than chuckle at their peculiar way of making friends. I am convinced that forbearing Christians smile a lot.

I have a minister friend who has become a master at remembering, collecting and telling minister stories. Many of these stories relate his own personal experiences as a pastor and his wife's experiences as a musician. On one occasion his wife, Darlene, a very accomplished singer, was invited to be the soloist at a wedding. When she asked who the organist was, the bride assured her that it was a "professional musician." That satisfied her, until she arrived at the wedding and discovered that this "professional musician" was a performer of pop electronic organ music, the kind played, for example, at skating rinks. She played pop tunes for her prelude and waved to people as they were ushered into the sanctuary. When Darlene stood up to sing her first solo, the organist rolled a chord on the organ and tipped her hand toward Darlene, much as a ringmaster would introduce a new act in a circus. Though embarrassed, Darlene managed to make it through the wedding. Her ego was not so large that she could not laugh about it afterward. She has a good sense of humor.

Finally, forbearance requires discernment, because we will have to make judgments. As I have already intimated, not everything is funny. Forbearance implies that we embrace people for who they are. It does not mean that we ignore their defects, weaknesses, immaturity and sin. Sometimes faithful church members insist upon singing solos when they are simply not qualified to perform that service. Sometimes church members make foolish decisions that strain the need for tolerance to the breaking point. Sometimes peculiar behavior cannot be written off as merely idiosyncratic but must be called what it is—irresponsible, obnoxious and destructive. We need discernment to decide when forbearance must give way to exhortation or admonition.

Jesus is our model of forbearance. He gave his disciples lots of room to be themselves. We are surprised to observe how seldom Jesus rebuked his disciples, considering how often he could have. Peter had a habit of making great claims about himself, though he repeatedly fell short of those claims. James and John demonstrated heartless insensitivity on more than one occasion. Yet Jesus continued to forbear. He knew that their puny faith would someday make them spiritual giants. What he did for them then he does for us now. He sees who we are and loves us anyway. He calls us to follow his example.

Room to Become

People change, but not always for the better. It takes a keen eye to trace trends in a person's life so that we can tell whether changes are for the better or for the worse. Forbearance enables us to look for and to affirm a basic pattern of growth in our brothers and sisters in Christ, and it forces us to remember that what people are becoming is as important as who they presently are.

Yet change can be slow, painfully slow. Parents attest to this whenever they say to their children, "How many times have I told you to . . . ?" Teachers betray the same frustration whenever they complain, "I have had to repeat that same point at least twenty-five times, and still you don't know it." Sometimes it seems that people will never get the point, never change, never grow up. Is there no limit to forbearance?

The question itself helps us to understand why the apostle Paul urged that believers be patient, a quality that, like meekness, helps us to be forbearing. Patience is necessary if we are ever going to give people the time and space they need to mature in faith, knowledge and obedience— to become, in other words, a better version of themselves. Such patience is a fruit of the Spirit, a gift that God must give.

There is no easy path to patience. But two disciplines will help to develop it. The first involves our view of God. If we believe in a sovereign God, then we will become ever more confident that he who began a good work in our brothers and sisters in Christ will bring it to completion at the day of Christ (Phil 1:6). It is possible to have too much confidence in people; such confidence will eventually lead to disappointment, because even the best among us fail. But it is impossible to have too much confidence in God. He has the power and the desire to see that our fellow Christians become like Jesus Christ. We don't have to resign ourselves, then, to their imperfections and weaknesses; neither do we have to take on the responsibility of changing them. Our confidence in God will lead us to pray for them and to await the outcome of God's plan to make his strength perfect in their weakness.

The second discipline has to do with how we see ourselves. Patience comes to us more easily when we remind ourselves of what we used to be, and perhaps still are. Impatient people have an inflated view of themselves, having lost the capacity to see themselves as sinners in the process of becoming saints. They also have a bad memory. They have forgotten about all the foolish decisions they made, the stupid things they said to others, the petty concerns that occupied their minds. Every so often we need to be reminded of what we once were and how undesirable it was. Many people have been forbearing toward us—our parents, children, teachers, friends, associates. Is it any surprise that God commands us to do the same for others? A sober view of ourselves will make us much quicker to put up with the immaturity of others.

I have friends who still shudder when they reminisce about their years in junior high, a period in their lives when they gave a whole new meaning to the word *obnoxious*. I know men who still remember what they were like as young husbands, when they were as irresponsible as they were passionate, and more interested in venting the latter than in correcting the former. I have met pastors who cringe now when they relive their early years in the pastoral ministry. They chose then to call their errors innocent mistakes of enthusiasm and inexperience; they are not so generous with themselves now. We will find it less difficult to be patient with people when we remind ourselves of what we once were, and perhaps still are.

We are all in a process. We had to start somewhere, and much of what has happened in our lives since then is a result of what went before. There are reasons why we are the way we are right now. Our background has a greal deal to say about the shaping of our beliefs and actions. Patience implies that we will try to trace the peculiar path that each person's life takes, however much it diverges from our own.

Consider a young woman who has been raised in a rigid fundamentalist home. She goes to college and discovers that the Christian world is larger than her fundamentalist background. She begins to explore new ideas. Her father is horrified and warns her of the evils of her "liberalism." She tries to assure him that she has not deserted the faith, but he considers anything outside fundamentalist beliefs as heresy. His reaction alienates her. She in turn begins to react against his criticism. Soon every discussion turns into an argument. He tries to strong-arm her into submission; she rebels against his authoritarianism. Eventually they can't even talk to each other. The conflict makes him all the more suspicious of liberal ideas and convinces her that all fundamentalists are oppressive and narrowminded.

Forbearance requires that we understand the trajectory of a person's spiritual journey, including our own. All of us have shadows from our past that stalk us, experiences that have shaped how we live today, memories that remind us of what we want and what we despise.

Patience will enable us to give people time to outgrow and overcome their immaturity. Sometimes people change only through a direct confrontation, when pain and conflict seem to be the undesirable though necessary consequences of love. But in most cases people change naturally through the passing of time. Those who forbear keep one eye on what will someday be.

When I was a young pastor in a church in southern California I attracted several products of the "Jesus movement" into my youth group. One person in particular seemed to relish the freedom of the counterculture. He wore cut-offs and sandals everywhere, even to morning worship, where he would sometimes sit next to old-timers who dressed in more churchy clothes. His behavior in worship was quite emotive and expressive, which was typical of those coming out of the counterculture. Some members of the church were irritated by him, but most kept their peace, welcomed him into the church and gave him room to be himself and to adjust to this new religious environment. After a couple of years he fell in love with a young woman in the church. Eventually he married her and entered the work force as a professional. Not surprisingly, his dress and behavior began slowly to change, reflecting the more conservative tastes of the business community and the congregation. He adapted to the old-timers, but they also learned from him. The church allowed him to mature, and he contributed significantly to its gradual transformation. Everyone came out the better for it.

That is a positive example of forbearance. Not every example, however, leads to such a happy ending. What if people will not change, because they are either incapable or unwilling? What if they are too old, too stubborn or too weak to become mature Christians? The passage of time can change people; it can also harden them, making it almost impossible for them, outside of a special demonstration of God's power, to change. In such cases we must exercise wise judgment. Not everything is worthy of confrontation. Some people—infirm, troubled, depressed, embittered—are often best loved as they are with no thought of pressuring them to change, unless their problems pose a serious threat to themselves, to others or to the cause of Christ. A woman of seventy has spent a lifetime in an unhappy marriage and is now resentful and irritable. A man of forty-five has struggled for a lifetime with severe depression. The prospect of either person's changing dramatically is very meager. In these and other cases it seems wisest and safest to forbear in hope, reminding ourselves daily of the wonderful transformation that awaits all Christians in heaven. Sometimes what cannot be done on earth will be done in heaven. Sometimes what people will never be on earth they will become in heaven.

If confrontation is necessary in such cases, it is best done gently and carefully, with only modest goals in mind. We should adjust our expectations so that they fit the people involved and the circumstances they face. As Jesus said, "From everyone to whom much has been given, much will be required" (Lk 12:48). Thus in most cases we would be right to expect more from our children than from our parents, more from close friends than from aquaintances, more from leaders of the church than from marginal members. And we should expect the most from ourselves because ultimately we can take full responsibility only for ourselves. Our commitment to forbear is more fundamental than others' willingness to change.

Room to Contribute

Jesus does not require perfection before he calls us into service. The Bible clearly shows that very fallible people, like Abraham, Moses and David, proved themselves useful to God. Imperfect Christians can still contribute to the work of Christ in the world. Forbearance is the quality that enables us to embrace what sinners have to offer in service to God.

The apostle Paul was often troubled by people who resented his success and wanted to undermine his ministry. They proved to be especially aggressive when Paul was not present to defend himself. Paul often faced just those circumstances when he sat in jail. Yet he was not entirely helpless. He could counter their influence by writing letters to the churches. One such letter he wrote to the Philippians, who were contending at the time with false apostles. These spiritual pretenders were taking advantage of Paul's absence and advancing their own selfish interests. They had to preach Paul's message, however, in order to win Paul's followers. Thus they proclaimed the same gospel that Paul did, though with motives that were antithetical to the gospel. How did Paul react to the crisis?

Some proclaim Christ from envy and rivalry, but others from goodwill. These proclaim Christ out of love, knowing that I have been put here for the defense of the gospel; the others proclaim Christ out of selfish ambition, not sincerely but intending to increase my suffering in my imprisonment. What does it matter? Just this, that Christ is proclaimed in every way, whether out of false motives or true; and in that I rejoice. (Phil 1:15-18)

Paul commended yet a third quality of character to help Christians become forbearing. He charged believers to be lowly, in addition to being meek and patient. We, too, will have to be lowly if we are ever going to accept service rendered by imperfect people. Lowliness will make us open and teachable. We will realize that we can learn from anyone, even from flawed members of the church, and that we must learn from everyone or be left to rely only on our own resources. Lowly people appreciate others for the unique gifts that they bring to the church.

The Greek word that we translate "to forbear" has a secondary meaning, "to listen." The act of listening is indispensable if we want to have true discourse in the church. We learn very little, perhaps nothing at all, from people with whom we already agree. They may help to clarify our thinking and to buttress our opinions; but they rarely stretch us to see God's truth in a new light. If we want to learn and to grow, we must be willing to listen to those with whom we disagree.

Dietrich Bonhoeffer made just this point in his masterful *Life Together*. In his final section on "Ministry" he warned Christians to resist the temptation of scrutinizing and criticizing fellow Christians. This temptation is both attractive and deadly because every believer has a desire to manipulate and to dominate other people. "God does not will," he stated, "that I should fashion the other person according to the image that seems good to me, that is, in my own image; rather in his very freedom from me God made this person in His image. I can never know beforehand how God's image should appear in others." For this reason Bonhoeffer counseled Christians to exercise the "ministry" of listening. He argued that as love of God surfaces in listening to him, love of neighbors finds expression in listening to them. Conversely, he suggested that failure to listen would eventually lead to isolation, narrowness and spiritual blindness.

But he who can no longer listen to his brother will soon be no longer listening to God either; he will be doing nothing but prattle in the presence of God too. This is the beginning of the death of the spiritual life, and in the end there is nothing left but spiritual chatter and clerical condescension arrayed in pious words. One who cannot listen long and patiently will presently be talking beside the point and be never really speaking to others, albeit he be not conscious of it. Anyone who thinks that his time is too valuable to spend keeping quiet will eventually have no time for God and his brother, but only for himself and for his own follies.[1]

Teachableness is especially important in three special cases. The first involves people who do not share our point of view but who nevertheless call themselves Christian. Failure to forbear at this point eventually will lead to impoverishment of mind and spirit, since we will gradually cut ourselves off from those who have the most to give us. I am not suggesting that we embrace alien points of view uncritically; that indeed is as dangerous as not listening at all. But I am urging that we listen to, learn from and struggle with Christians whose points of view depart sharply from our own. Some issues may indeed be clear-cut and do not require prolonged investigation. But many are not so transparent. They demand careful analysis, from many points of view. Such exploration may save us from becoming a prisoner to ourselves, to our unexposed prejudices and uncritical ideologies.

While a chaplain at a Christian liberal arts college, I served on a committee that designed a yearly program of reflection on critical issues. We decided one year to explore the theme of Christianity and politics. We wanted to introduce students to a wide range of Christian political thinking, from far left to far right. We heard few comments from our constituency after a speaker from the far right visited the campus. Such was not the case, however, after a speaker from the left addressed us. One supporter of the college threatened to withhold his yearly financial contribution, which amounted to tens of thousands of dollars, if the president did not apologize for this violation of the college's—in actuality, the donor's—political convictions.

The president did not acquiesce to such pressure. In his reply to the donor he explained that though he did not agree with the speaker's point of view, he did believe that it was important for students to be exposed to such thinking, because it represented an important and influential voice in the church. The president also invited the donor to attend future forums at which similar issues were going to be discussed.

The second case concerns prophets who are called to give a harsh message to the church. If we like what prophets are saying, we tend to approve of their message self-righteously in order to reinforce our own self-serving point of view. Several years ago I read in an editorial about a commencement speaker at Harvard who was called "prophetic" by one liberal commentator for denouncing fundamentalists. I chuckled after reading the piece. What is so prophetic, I thought, about exposing fundamentalists at Harvard? That is self-righteousness, not prophetic criticism. The speaker was only telling people what they wanted to hear! If it had been Jerry Falwell preaching to an audience at a National Religious Broadcasters convention, then I would call such a broadside against fundamentalists prophetic.

But if we recoil from what prophets announce to us, then we tend to use their personal weaknesses as an excuse to dismiss their message. Such has happened over the past few years with Martin Luther King Jr. It has become common knowledge that King had a proclivity for infidelity. Clearly that is wrong from a Christian point of view, and it is not wrong that he be exposed for his sin. Still, King's infidelity does not mitigate the power of his convictions and his criticism of the church. His message of justice, equality and freedom is still valid, regardless of sins that he committed. We cannot require perfection from prophets before we are willing to listen to the word of the prophet.

Forbearance makes us teachable. It gives us the courage to look at what we should become rather than how far short prophets fall of their own professed ideals. Forbearance leads to repentance, not to self-right-eousness or criticism.

The third case centers on the difficulty of dealing with Christians or Christian groups who violate our standards of proper belief and conduct, whether they share the same pew with us every Sunday or attend a church that seems worlds away from our own. The problem with these disagreements is exacerbated because competition and rivalry turn differences of opinion into major showdowns. Christian groups don't just *disagree with* each other, which could lead to fruitful discussion. They also *compete against* each other. They secretly or openly hope for the failure and demise of each other. They think that victory over opponents establishes the righteousness of their cause, assures them that God is on their side and proves that they are superior.

My home church is located in downtown Spokane. It is mainline, big and growing. There is significant diversity among its membership. Abortion is one issue that divides the congregation. The church has sponsored debates, discussed resolutions, talked politics. But no consensus has emerged. Some members have left the church because of it.

I asked the pastor how he handles disagreement and rivalry at our church, since he has to deal with it almost daily. "How do you moderate between different points of view?" I asked him. "How do you present your own point of view without alienating everyone who disagrees with you? And how do you let the Bible speak on these issues without using it as a weapon?"

He said he sees the problem not as disagreement or rivalry, however serious those are, but as lack of perspective and mistaken priorities. He believes that abortion, for example, is an important issue. He is prolife, and he is not hesitant to state his opinion when the occasion seems appropriate. But in his mind it is not an essential issue. The one essential is commitment to Jesus Christ and therefore to evangelism and discipleship. Disagreements and rivalry over issues like abortion tend to distract the church so that it neglects its commitment to the essentials. He added that though his opponents may continue to thump a narrow agenda, he believes that he should not use that error to excuse erring in the same way. As Luther said, in essentials there should be unity, in nonessentials there should be diversity, in all things there must be charity.

I have observed in my own experience that disagreement and rivalry tempt us to reduce our opponents to nothing more than the opinions they hold on some issue. It also tempts us to undermine their influence by speaking ill of them rather than debate the issue itself. We must remember that people are complex, multidimensional. There is more to them than their position on, say, abortion. If we allow them to be real people, we may even be surprised by how much their convictions and interests overlap with our own. Like siblings, church people usually fight the meanest against those with whom they have the most in common. We exercise good judgment when we remember what we share in common with our opponents even as we engage them in debate.

We must also remember what the Bible teaches about the tongue. James says that the tongue is a ruthless, deadly instrument, full of poison. It blesses God and curses opponents, recites creeds and slanders rivals, claims to speak the truth and lies about people. It does far worse damage than mere disagreement does. Too many of us are prone to strain at a gnat and swallow a camel when we aim for theological correctness at the expense of kind speech about our competitors. Does the defense of truth justify the misuse of the tongue?

Still, some issues are foundational, like the authority of the Bible, the divinity of Christ, the historical nature of the resurrection and the saving nature of Christ's work on the cross. In other words, forbearance has its limits. We must give people and groups room to be, become and contribute—but not limitless room. There is more at stake than the need for space. Truth is also at stake, and so is the health of the church. Somewhere along the line we must draw lines—theological and moral lines.

Jesus himself did not always forbear, and neither did the apostle Paul. Jesus was absolutely brutal in his condemnation of the self-righteousness of the Pharisees, and he demanded that sinners repent and "sin no more."

Likewise, Paul announced that God would forgive sinners, regardless of how terrible their sin, but he also insisted that they repent and forsake their sin. No sin was so bad that God would not forgive it; but no sin was so trivial and innocent that believers did not have to repent and change. As Paul said,

> Do you not know that wrongdoers will not inherit the kingdom of God? Do not be deceived! Fornicators, idolaters, adulterers, male prostitutes, sodomites, thieves, the greedy, drunkards, revilers, robbers—none of these will inherit the kingdom of God. And this is what some of you used to be. (1 Cor 6:9-11)

Paul thus commanded the believers in Corinth to pronounce judgment on such evil behavior and to drive out wicked Christians from among them—if, that is, they were unwilling to repent. Obviously Paul put limits on forbearance.

Paul was also critical of those who compromised the basic gospel message. He even confronted Peter when Peter refused to have table fellowship with Gentiles. Paul believed that Peter's behavior made Jewish law binding on Christians, thus violating the true spirit of the gospel. He pronounced a curse on anyone, in fact, who tinkered with the gospel (Gal 1:8-9).

Still, these limits to forbearance leave lots of room, which is exactly what we should give to our brothers and sisters in Christ. Forbearance is where we must start in our relationships with fellow Christians. But as we shall see, it is not where we should end. There is more, much more, that is required if we are to become the loving people that God wants us to be.

_____PART 2_____
SUSTAINING COMMANDS

5

FORGIVE
ONE ANOTHER

Sometimes forgiveness seems heroic. Corrie ten Boom's experience during and after World War II is a good case in point. She suffered unimaginably in a Nazi concentration camp for hiding Jews in her home. After her release she began to speak to Christian audiences about her experiences. At one conference she met one of the brutal guards who were responsible for her sister's death. The guard extended his hand to ten Boom as if, in a gesture, he was seeking forgiveness.

Ten Boom was forced at that moment to make a choice: would she forgive this guard or forever harbor resentment in her heart? Incredibly, she chose to forgive.

Not all stories, however, end so happily. Recently I read Simon Wiesenthal's *The Sunflower*. Wiesenthal tells the story of his torturous years in a Nazi death camp. While doing hard labor near a hospital one day, he was suddenly ordered to drop his work and follow a nurse into the hospital. He was ushered into a dark room where a man lay silent and motionless, obviously near death. The man grabbed Wiesenthal's hand and asked if he was a Jew. Then he told Wiesenthal his story.

He had been a German soldier who, like so many others, had participated in the brutal murder of Jews. On one occasion he had helped to herd hundreds of Jews into a house and then set it on fire. If the Jews tried to escape the inferno, they were shot. As the fire raged, a Jewish man, woman and boy jumped out a window, grasping desperately, pleadingly for life. Their eyes met, the soldier's and the boy's. Following orders, the soldier shot all three.

Later on he was tortured with regret and remorse. Suffering from wounds that drew him ever closer to death, he wanted to find a Jew, any Jew, to whom he could tell his story, confess his sin and ask forgiveness. He could not bear to face death with such horrible guilt hanging over him like an executioner's ax.

"I know that what I have told you is terrible," he said to Wiesenthal. "I have longed to talk about it to a Jew and beg forgiveness from him. I know that what I am asking is almost too much, but without your answer I cannot die in peace."

Wiesenthal listened, pondering what to do. In the end he stood up and walked out without saying a word. The German soldier died without hearing a word of forgiveness.

It is too simple to say that ten Boom was right and Wiesenthal was wrong. Ten Boom forgave the guard for a crime he had committed against ten Boom. Wiesenthal was asked to forgive the soldier for a crime he had committed against scores of Jews. Besides, Wiesenthal was a member of a group of people who experienced such violence and cruelty that normal standards of what constitutes charitable behavior hardly seem to apply. The Nazis committed outrageous acts of brutality and injustice. As Peter Berger suggests in *A Rumor of Angels,* the Nazis' atrocities cry out for an ultimate condemnation, for a sentence of final judgment. They committed acts beyond which even mercy may be able to extend. Perhaps Wiesenthal did what any normal human being would do. As a friend of mine said to reporters after his father was shot dead on a parking lot in Chicago, "Perhaps God will forgive the murderer. But I can't. Not yet, anyway. And maybe never."

These are powerful stories. Some of us have faced similar circumstances, or will someday. The command to forgive will force us, if it hasn't already, to face what appears to be the impossible task of forgiving someone for catastrophic evil. We will have to dig deep to find the resources to forgive the wrong done to us.

Still, most offenses requiring forgiveness are not so sensational. The command is addressed to ordinary believers who must learn to love—and therefore forgive—not-so-lovable and forgivable people in the church, who slander, lie, embezzle, commit adultery and manipulate. It requires the community of faith to return to grace when its unity and peace is jeopardized by human shortcomings and weaknesses. It calls forth obedience when someone else's sin inflicts pain upon an innocent party and breeds mistrust among believers. These occasions may not be as devastating as the ten Boom and Wiesenthal stories, but they are still real.

The reality of such pain is common enough, even in the church. Last year I talked with a friend who recently became the pastor of a big city church. His predecessor had left the church in a horrible mess. While serving as the pastor, he had had an affair with the secretary, then divorced his wife in order to marry his lover. He refused to consider resigning from the church and so forced members to choose sides, to ignore the problem entirely or to leave, which many did.

Just a few months ago I read about a controversy in a large church in Spokane that resulted in a major split. Friendships were ruined, families divided, the church's witness damaged in the community. I know of another church that suffered spasms of betrayal because an elder who made his living by managing people's money squandered the savings of dozens of church members in foolish schemes that promised to make him rich. I heard about still another church that publicly humiliated a young couple who were forced to get married due to an unplanned pregnancy. The church's severe censure alienated family and friends of the couple.

Every one of these situations calls for forgiveness. Every one of these situations makes it very hard to forgive.

I chose to write about forgiveness before confession because forgiveness is a gift that we are called to give even when no confession has been made. Forgiveness is a manifestation of mercy. It is given when it is not deserved. Ideally, it is offered to people who are truly sorry for their sin so that the broken relationship can be mended. But sometimes we must forgive when there is no repentance. As Jesus said on the cross, "Father, forgive them, for they know not what they are doing." Forgiveness is prior to confession because confession does not have to be the condition on which forgiveness is given.

The Difficulty

True forgiveness comes hard, especially in the church. I think that is true for two reasons. First, we tend to expect more from Christians. And we probably should. After all, they are disciples of Jesus. We therefore set higher standards for them. As my wife said once after reflecting on her employment at a Christian institution, "A secular institution would have treated me better." The assumption behind her comment is that Christian institutions should treat people better than secular institutions, simply because they are Christian. Christians disappoint us when we see how far they fall short of the high standards they are supposed to uphold. Our expectations create standards that make failure more inexcusable and unforgivable.

Second, Christians often find it more difficult to admit that they are wrong. That, too, makes it harder to forgive them, for there is nothing worse than having to forgive someone who is unwilling to admit guilt. Christians can be stubbornly self-righteous when they believe that they have God on their side. Their religious self-assurance makes them unreachable, no matter how convincing is the evidence against them.

I have a friend who still feels hostility when he remembers his years in ministry on a university campus. He clashed repeatedly with the leaders of another Christian organization. They considered their organization the pivotal ministry—probably the only legitimate ministry—at the university, as if it were God's greatest gift to higher education. They refused to consider that their aloofness from other ministries damaged the unity of the church and that their hard-sell techniques of ministry trampled people, all in the name of the gospel. Yet they would not admit to wrong; they would not even consider it. They were too sure that they were right. My friend had to forgive them for sin that they would not confess.

I wonder sometimes about people who find it easy to forgive. Perhaps they have not *really* had to forgive yet. Offenses that call for forgiveness inflict deep wounds, tempt the offended party to become bitter, create emotional distress, lead to an obsession with the hurt that another caused. They involve complex situations that take time to unravel and resolve. I have talked to many Christians who speak about such experiences from years past as if they'd happened yesterday. The pain lingers in the soul. It preoccupies the mind, creates anger and outrage, leads to exhaustion and confusion. It has the power to ruin the spiritual life of the strongest believer. It also has the power to deepen spiritual life like few other experiences can. It all depends, of course, on whether we allow God's grace to make us forgiving.

The Occasion

The apostle Paul makes it clear that forgiveness must be reserved for offenses that are truly worthy of forgiveness. "As God's chosen ones, holy and beloved, clothe yourselves with compassion, kindness, humility, meekness, and patience. Bear with one another and, if anyone has a complaint against another, forgive each other; just as the Lord has forgiven you, so you also must forgive" (Col 3:12-13). It is clear in the passage that not all offenses require forgiveness. That is why Paul exhorts believers to forbear one another first (see chapter four). Irritating idiosyncrasies of personality, immature blunders, foolish but well-intentioned decisions, inexperience—these do not call for forgiveness, at least not most of the time. They require forbearance instead. People need lots of slack in their journey toward Christian maturity. There will be unfortunate setbacks along the way. However unpleasant they are, though, they do not really fit the category of sin. Not every bad thing calls for forgiveness.

We must forbear first. Then sometimes we must also forgive. On some occasions forbearance falls short and forgiveness is necessary. Paul used the word *complaint* to establish the criterion that makes forgiveness necessary. The Greek word could be translated "reproach" or "worthy of blame." The offense, in other words, has to be bad enough to merit forgiveness.

What constitutes the "bad enough" is hard to discern, especially in the church. Many people are so excessively sensitive that they take offense at things that do not really require forgiveness. Some people seem to take offense at almost anything. They feel rejected when a friend is merely preoccupied with other pressing matters. They feel angry when they are passed over for praise. They feel hurt when someone fails to acknowledge their presence. They think that every private conversation is about them.

I have a pastor friend who learned one day that a member of his church had felt bitter toward him for two years because he had not greeted her properly at a social gathering. He did not sin against her. If there was any sin involved, it was her own self-preoccupation. We must beware of diluting the meaning of forgiveness. What we might think is someone else's sin may in fact be our own excessive sensitivity.

Forgiveness is required when almost anyone put in the same situation would be as hurt as the offended party was. The offense must violate a universal sense of justice. Sensible people would feel outrage at the injustice. If a lawyer were hired, she would be able to make a good case before a jury and probably win the case. Sadly, such offenses in the church happen frequently. Power is abused, words are used to wound, confidence is betrayed, churches are divided and relationships destroyed over petty issues, marriages are broken through unfaithfulness, money is mismanaged. If the church were a court of law, it would have a full docket of cases to be tried.

The meaning of the Greek word that we usually translate "to forgive" supports this interpretation. The primary meaning is "to give freely" what isn't deserved and cannot be earned. "To forgive" is only the secondary meaning of the term. Forgiveness, in other words, is a gift. When offered, it shocks our human sensibilities and runs contrary to what we consider the moral nature of the universe. It violates our sense of justice and fair play. There is no reason why people should be forgiving except that the grace of God makes them that way, enabling them to wipe the slate clean and to give the offender another chance. We will not be able to comprehend the nature of forgiveness until we realize that logic and justice oppose it. No one has to be forgiving to be a good, just and moral person, and no one really deserves to be forgiven. It is a pure gift, born out of the heart of love.

That is why it often takes awhile for people to forgive an offender. Fred and Esther's story is typical. I talked with them about a year after they had begun to rebuild their marriage. Though active in a local church, they had been struggling with marital problems for years. "Both of us were disappointed with our relationship," Fred told me. "We kept a mental checklist of the faults of the other person, and whenever that person failed to measure up to what we thought a spouse should be, we would add to our mental checklist of disappointments. Each of us had a strong case against the other."

Dishonesty poisoned their relationship. "We did not tell each other the whole truth," Esther said.

Fred in particular felt so much pressure to be perfect and to protect his spotless reputation that he refused to tell me or anyone else about his disappointments, doubts, fears and temptations. I never knew, for example, that on his business trips he would sometimes pick up a *Playboy* magazine and fantasize having sex with another woman. I tended to be more honest, but I communicated my feelings in hurtful ways. I used my feelings as a pretense to get back at Fred for my disappointment in marriage. Consequently, I was not really vulnerable when I was honest. I, too, had hidden parts of my true self from Fred. Fred began to look elsewhere for the love and intimacy that he didn't find at home. He started to spend time with a secretary at work who was also having marital difficulties. Eventually they developed a "soul tie," as Fred called it. That led later to the physical act of adultery. Though Fred stopped the affair months before Esther ever found out, he did not break off the relationship with the other woman. Esther never imagined that Fred would be vulnerable to adultery. Still, she was jealous and suspicious.

A friend advised her to pray intensively for Fred. Within forty-eight hours after Esther prayed, Fred began to tell the truth and to confess his sin, a process that lasted for several months.

It took Esther far longer to forgive. It was months before she was willing even to consider forgiving Fred. Her initial impulse was not to forgive but to blame, strike back, condemn. She kept asking Fred, "How could you do this to me and to the children? How could you do this to God?" She felt betrayed and abused. She was enraged. She wanted justice to prevail. She wanted him to pay a price.

As they eventually discovered, there were factors that made Fred vulnerable to an affair. Still, as he said to me repeatedly, "There are no good excuses for sin. I was guilty. Esther had justice on her side." Fred could not *demand* forgiveness, because he realized that he didn't deserve it. Esther in turn believed that she didn't have to give it. At least that was her initial reaction.

Both of them in one sense were right. Fred *was* wrong; and Esther did not *have* to forgive. Fred learned what many people, including Christians, deny—that people are responsible for their actions, no matter how bad their past, how common the offense, how justifiable the wrong done. Forgiveness assumes that the universe as God designed it is moral, standards of right and wrong are real, and people are accountable before God for how they treat others. People who cause hurt are not merely victims who are acting out the pain of their pasts. They are not sick people who need treatment. They are sinners who need forgiveness.

Forgiveness assumes guilt. If there is no need for forgiveness but only sympathy, compassion, pity, treatment and therapy, then there is also no mercy. Mercy is only mercy when there is sin. Sin is only sin when there is right and wrong. And right and wrong are real because God exists.

Nevertheless, Esther had to learn what many people, including Christians, refuse to learn—that the power to forgive comes from the experience of being a sinner who needs to be forgiven. Jesus taught his disciples that forgiving others will in fact be impossible if we do not realize how much God has forgiven us. In Luke 7:36-50 Jesus said that we will be able to forgive only if we have experienced forgiveness first. The woman in the story loved Jesus much because she knew how much she had been forgiven. As Jesus said, she was forgiven the greater debt, and so showed greater love than did the Pharisee. "The one to whom little is forgiven, loves little," Jesus concluded (see also Mt 18:23-34).

The Cost

Either way you cut it, there is a cost involved. Both forgiveness and unforgiveness exact a price. It is important for us to calculate the cost.

I think about Bill, a seasoned pastor, when I consider the cost of forgiveness. He discovered that cost in the events that led him to offer his resignation as the pastor of the church that he was serving. He had arrived only a short time before, enthused to begin ministry in a church known for and proud of its diversity. On the surface all seemed well. "But what they didn't seem to be conscious of," Bill wrote in a letter to me,

> was the negative spirit of bitterness, of unforgiving avoidance, of petulant criticism which came to characterize the body. When someone is sick long enough, and when the symptoms are easily covered over with fine dress and mascara, or with robust hymn-singing and hearty post-service handshaking, then the sick person doesn't know any longer what it is like to be well. Cantankerous grumbling, spiritual discontent and civil avoidance come to seem "normal."

The diversity of the church, in other words, was "quenching the Spirit," as Bill put it. Not that the diversity was bad. The problem was not the diversity but their response to it.

The members of the pastoral search committee did not tell Bill about the church's problems when they called him to be their pastor. "I didn't know it was a troubled church," he wrote.

The church itself didn't really know. The search committee didn't know at the time of the interviews. At first when grumblings began to surface, I felt deceived. How could these people have called me to minister in a religious community which they pictured as being progressive and together, when in fact it was fractured by party strife and polarized by ideologies?

The conflict became intolerable to Bill. He decided to resign his position and pursue another career. "Never did I dream this kind of defeat could ever happen to me. I was broken and admitted to my board and congregation my failure and my decision to seek other work."

For a while Bill lived under the pretense that the entire problem was the church's, not his. As he discovered later, though, the problem was partly his. The process of restoration began when Bill was willing to admit his own failure. "After my many years of experiencing church growth in various congregations, the loss of fifteen families cut to the quick and left me with a shattered ego and a crisis of self-confidence." He was angry because he felt the church had betrayed him and undermined his success. He eventually discovered that his "shattered ego," as he described it, resulted from an ego that was too big.

There is no room for personal pride, ego-defensiveness, and undue self-confidence in the pastoral role anyway. I needed to learn that. I needed to be taken down a peg to see that without the Spirit of Jesus controlling my life, I was just as much in a carnal fix as the church in its own way. The solution for me was death—death to my prideful spirit and confidence in self.

It was this death that enabled him to forgive.

Forgiveness is costly because it requires us to give up the right to let justice prevail, to get even. The command to forgive confronts our desire to extract payment and to punish the offender. It forces us to let God be God so that his mercy and justice, blended perfectly together, can deal with the offender in a way that both disciplines and restores. God is neither brutal nor indulgent. Only he knows how to punish sin without destroying the sinner.

Forgiveness chooses love and mercy over revenge, and it yields to God the right to punish. The apostle Paul explained:

Do not repay anyone evil for evil, but take thought for what is noble in the sight of all. If it is possible, so far as it depends on you, live peaceably with all. Beloved, never avenge yourselves, but leave room for the wrath of God; for it is written, "Vengeance is mine, I will repay, says the Lord." No, "if your enemies are hungry, feed them; if they are thirsty, give them something to drink; for by doing this you will heap burning coals on their heads." Do not be overcome by evil, but overcome evil with good. (Rom 12:17-21)

The author of Hebrews tells us that God disciplines those whom he loves. Unlike earthly parents, who are often selfish and capricious, God deals with wayward people both harshly and gently. He is committed to helping guilty people repent, be reconciled to former friends and be restored to full relationship with himself. He responds to us out of charity, not brutality.

Still, it is risky to "leave room for the wrath of God," because God might not deal with people as we want and expect. He might not make them suffer as much as we think they deserve. He might not make them suffer at all. He might instead choose to bless them. Thus a former spouse's remarriage may turn out happy, a critic may win a following, an incompetent leader may stay in office.

The prophet Jonah expected as much, and that is why he fled from God when ordered to travel to Nineveh and preach God's judgment. The people of Israel hated the Ninevites and wanted to see them destroyed. Jonah was not afraid that his message would go unheeded or that his life would be threatened. He was afraid that his message would lead to their repentance. Jonah hated the thought that God would show mercy to Israel's archenemy. He wanted revenge, not restoration. He wanted to see them suffer, not repent. That is because he was unforgiving.

95

Certain factors make the cost of forgiveness almost intolerably high. Particularly painful offenses can raise the cost, like a humiliating betrayal of confidence, mismanagement of church funds that forces cutbacks in ministry, slanderous attacks on character emerging from a power struggle in the church. Unforeseen and undesirable circumstances can raise the cost of forgiveness, too, as when an offender isn't aware of wrongdoing and doesn't care when informed, or when offenses go public, thus increasing the complexity of the situation and adding shame to the initial pain.

Fred's affair, for example, eventually went public. He resigned from his job and withdrew from the public eye. Esther admitted with tears that for several months she did not want to leave the house because she felt such shame. That made forgiveness all the more costly. Fred had not only hurt her personally; he had also ruined their reputation, damaged many of their friendships and undermined their financial security. The repercussions of his unfaithfulness never seemed to end. Embarrassment and condemnation kept echoing back to them. Esther wondered if they would ever be able to recover and lead a normal life again. She wanted to run away.

Paying the high cost of forgiveness demands strong faith. Faith enables us to believe that God is still God, able to bring good out of evil, however painful the evil has been. Joseph's brothers sold him as a slave to merchants on caravan to Egypt. Joseph suffered for years from their jealous betrayal. Yet in the end he could say, "You meant it for evil, but God meant it for good." God is a master storyteller; he is able to weave a plot for our lives that uses evil for a greater purpose. God is able to make all things right, however wrong they seem to be. His grace leads to a life of "no regrets" (2 Cor 7:5-12). He is so great that he can turn ashes into bread, a desert into a fertile field, suffering into triumph. It takes time for him to do this great work, of course. Only faith will sustain us as we wait for God to heal and to restore.

Still, however costly forgiveness is, it does not compare with the cost of unforgiveness. The cost of unforgiveness frightened Esther into asking God for a forgiving heart. She began to observe people whom she knew to be holding a grudge, harboring resentment, plotting revenge. She noticed the misery of their lives, their twisted perspective, their sickness of body and soul. She learned that they were slaves to the past, prisoners of their wretched memories, obsessed with getting even. They were angry, anxious, joyless, overly sensitive. Unforgiveness was literally killing them. They could take comfort in being right. They could justify wanting to strike back. But was being right worth it? Did unforgiveness bring that much pleasure? Was their world better because it was empty of mercy?

In *Forgive and Forget*, Lewis Smedes suggests that unforgiveness takes a toll both on others and on the self. In the case of others, it leads to a vicious cycle of revenge.

Vengeance is a passion to get even. It is a hot desire to give back as much pain as someone gave you. An eye for an eye! Fairness! . . .

The problem with revenge is that it never gets what it wants; it never evens the score. Fairness never comes. The chain reaction set off by every act of vengeance always takes its unhindered course. It ties both the injured and the injurer to an escalator of pain. Both are stuck on the escalator as long as parity is demanded, and the escalator never stops, never lets anyone off.[1]

In the case of the self, unforgiveness condemns us to live forever in the dungeon of the past. The memory serves only to remind us of what went wrong, of the hurt we received. We caress that painful memory. We find a strange kind of happiness in thinking about it. It finally poisons us.

Your own memory is a replay of your hurt—a videotape within your soul that plays unending reruns of your old rendezvous with pain. You cannot switch it off. You are hooked into it like a pain junkie; you become addicted to your remembrance of pain past. You are lashed again each time your memory spins the tape. Is that fair to yourself—this wretched justice of not forgiving? You could not be more unfair to yourself.[2]

The apostle Paul described the kind of character that has given in to unforgiveness. "And do not grieve the Holy Spirit of God, with which you were marked with a seal for the day of redemption. Put away from you all bitterness and wrath and anger and wrangling and slander, together with all malice" (Eph 4:30-31). Again, is it worth being right, is it worth getting even, considering what happens to us when we refuse to forgive? Is unforgiveness worth that much? As Paul argues, unforgiveness leads to wrath, which makes us quick to accuse and ready to explode the minute we're crossed. Anger makes us obsessed with the idea of justice. Wrangling engenders quarrelsomeness. Slander is the crude attempt to turn other people against the offender. Malice makes us wish evil on another person. Unforgiveness may get its way. It may cause hurt, inflict punishment, heap blame. Yet its greatest victim will be the unforgiving self. Maybe that's why Jesus was so severe with people who refused to forgive. He understood how destructive it was for everyone involved, both offender and offended.

The Limitations

Forgiveness can't do everything. It has power, but its power is limited. It pushes us in the direction of restored relationships, but by itself it will not get us all the way there. More is needed, much more.

For example, forgiveness does not release offenders from the need to take personal responsibility for the sin committed. That is unjust. Forgiveness, as I said earlier, assumes that people are responsible for their sinful actions and holds them accountable for what they have done. Forgiveness bestows the honor on people of taking their wrongdoing seriously. We must forgive them because they know better.

Forgiveness does not absolve offenders from guilt. That is presumptuous. Only God has the power to absolve us from guilt. Only God is judge and ruler. Only he can ultimately decide the fate of every person's soul. Human forgiveness does not bestow divine forgiveness. A new Christian may have to forgive a father for abuse; that does not guarantee that the father's soul is now secure. A Christian leader may have to forgive a board of elders for stubborn opposition; that does not mean that all things have been made right between the board and God.

We forgive in a relative sense; we have the power to restore the relationship between ourselves and the offender. God forgives in an ultimate sense; he has the power to restore a broken relationship with himself. The Pharisees were furious with Jesus because he assumed a prerogative that belongs only to God. He forgave people for sins they had committed against other people (Mk 2:1-12). That is something only God can do.

Forgiveness does not deliver the offender from the consequences of sinful actions. That is impossible. I remember frequently saying to my mother while I was growing up, "But I thought that you forgave me! Why am I still being punished?" That is a boy's crude theology. Sometimes adults don't do much better. Students who are disciplined at our college for some violation of the rules often say, with wearisome predictability, "I thought that this was a Christian college. You believe in forgiveness, don't you? Then why am I still being suspended?" For some reason people carry this misunderstanding that forgiveness miraculously erases the consequences of the past, breaking the connection between past wrong and present circumstances, as if the law of sowing and reaping no longer applied.

But it still does. Jesus' death on the cross was a real death because there are consequences to sin, no matter how repentant we are. Jesus died to pay the penalty for sin. He took on himself the consequences that we deserved. That is why the cross brings justice and mercy together in one event. Someone had to die; that is justice. Someone died in place of the guilty party; that is mercy.

Forgiveness cannot erase the past. Esther's forgiveness did not get Fred's job back for him. She did not say—and could not have said—to his former boss, "I have forgiven Fred, so you can hire him back." Nor did Esther's forgiveness restore Fred's spotless reputation. The sense of shame and humiliation did not disappear once Esther began to forgive The loss of reputation was a different problem, and it required a different solution. Some decisions we make have permanent consequences—immoral behavior leading to loss of church office, church conflict erupting in a church split, unwise financial decisions crippling the church with severe indebtedness. Forgiveness is a wonderful gift. Still, it cannot save us from having to face the consequences of our sinful behavior, which can pursue us with unrelenting ferocity.

Forgiveness, in short, does not eliminate the real problems we carry with us from the past. That was certainly true for Fred and Esther. Forgiveness sowed good seed in the soil of their lives, but it did not spare them from having to reap the harvest of bad seed that they had sown for so many years. They take great comfort in the new direction that their lives have taken, even as they are reminded daily of the old direction their lives once took. As they testified to me, "There is no neutral seed. We are reaping the harvest of bad seed. But we are convinced that someday we will reap a bountiful harvest if we sow good seed now."

The Possibilities

Still, forgiveness can accomplish good in the church, if we understand its true meaning. Forgiveness means releasing offenders from the consequences of past actions as their behavior affects us. It cancels the debt that they owe us and saves them from having to pay us back. It absorbs the wrongdoing. Forgiveness thus reestablishes the relationship, at least from one end. It restores communication and, under the right circumstances, can restore friendship. It uses the past as a means of strengthening the relationship, not destroying it. Forgiveness is like the growth of a tree that envelops a wound in the trunk, so that what once threatened the tree's life becomes its place of greatest strength and character. Forgiveness ultimately means that we wish offenders well and hope that our relationship with them will grow. We want them to prosper. We pray God's grace and peace on them. We choose to love them, even though they do not deserve it.

Thus forgiveness will enable a woman who desires to hold the office of pastor but is opposed by a vocal minority in her church to understand her opponents' fears, forgive them for their opposition and reach out to them in love, whether or not they are willing to change their minds. Similarly, it will enable a pastor of a large mainline church who feels unfairly criticized by angry feminists in his congregation to view their circumstances with compassion, forgive them for their bitterness and misdirected hostility, and serve them as best he can, whether or not they are open to his pastoral leadership. Forgiveness empowers us to transcend the situation so that we can listen, learn, love and serve even when offenders show no signs of remorse and change.

Forgiveness also takes time. There are no shortcuts. We begin the process by admitting our hurt. We must feel the pain and then voice the outrage. It helps no one, as Lewis Smedes argues, to whitewash the problem. Forgiveness is not the same thing as excusing the offense, or smothering conflict, or accepting the offender, or tolerating the behavior. All these may be good things. But they are not forgiveness.

We must come to the point of stating that there is no reason the offense had to happen, that there is every reason it should not have happened and that there is a good reason for us to feel hurt and angry that it did happen. So again, before women can forgive fellow church members who oppose their calling to church office, they must first recognize and feel the full effects of the wrong done to them. Likewise, before male pastors can forgive angry feminists for attacking them simply because they are male, they must first experience the injustice of the unfair attack.

That is where the journey of forgiveness must begin. But it is not where it should end. Anger is a phase to go through, not a state of affairs that should continue forever. The goal is genuine forgiveness, which always surfaces in love.

Forgiveness in the end is an act of mercy and grace. Eventually Esther wanted to see her relationship with Fred healed. She chose the way of forgiveness over the way of revenge. She gave up the right to punish Fred, extract a payment, relive the ugly details and reopen the wounds. She decided that harmony and wholeness was better than anguish and hatred. She started to invest again in their relationship. She wanted to make it stronger than it had been before. Though she attached no conditions to her forgiveness, she did challenge Fred to search his own soul to discover what had made him vulnerable and how he could protect himself next time around.

Forgiveness does not mean forgetting. If anything, we ought to remember offenses so that we are alerted to similar situations in the future. Remembering past hurts is not bad, depending on *how* we remember them. The memory can suffocate from bitterness or breathe in grace. The memory can relish malice or embrace mercy. Our lives are a story, and our memory helps us to keep that story fresh, to update it when we need to and to draw on it for strength and encouragement when times are tough. The pain of the past can become a chapter in the history of our redemption. We can see the hand of God bringing good out of evil, restoring broken relationships in the church, healing the hurts that other Christians have inflicted on us.

I was deeply impressed by Fred and Esther's story. If they had the power, they would return to the past and live life differently. Obviously they can't. So they have done the next best thing. They have invited God into the past so that it can be made right. Their story has moved many people. It has helped to make peace in other Christians' marriages that were broken by infidelity or hostility. It has inspired husbands and wives to settle old scores, to live transparently, to deal with present and past problems. Their story is leading to a happy ending because Esther chose forgiveness over bitterness and revenge.

Bill chose forgiveness too. His situation was more complex than Fred and Esther's because it involved so many people, some of whom were unwilling to admit any responsibility for causing disunity in the church. Bill had to forgive people, therefore, who did not believe that they were guilty. Very few people at the church, in fact, were willing at first to confess any wrongdoing. Suspicion, dissension and division in the church were always someone else's problem. Yet Bill's forgiveness set in motion a series of events that brought healing to the entire congregation. Forgiveness, as we shall see in the next chapter, led to confession. And confession reconciled relationships. Such is the power of forgiveness. It unleashes the grace of God.

6

CONFESS SIN TO AND PRAY FOR ONE ANOTHER

*O*ver the years I have struggled with a number of specific and obvious sins, as all people do—jealousy, anger, lust, hatred, self-pity. But my struggle has been less as I have matured in the faith. Many of these bad habits have fallen away like dead skin from a molting snake. Surprisingly, I have not responded to this growth in the way I once thought I would, when I was so intent on overcoming these sinful habits in my journey toward perfection. I believe that I am farther from perfection now than I was ten years ago, though I have less trouble with the specific sins that used to torment me. I am more aware of my brokenness, more conscious of my vulnerability and finitude, more sensitive to the dark side of my nature. I may sin less; nevertheless I am more the sinner. I am overwhelmed by the problem of sin that rules my nature. I know now more than ever how desperately I need God, how dependent I am on the grace of God.

Throughout church history Christian thinkers have observed a deep need in the human heart that only God can fill. Human nature has an incompleteness, a feeling of alienation and estrangement that goes to the depth of our being, a sense that something is profoundly wrong inside us. It is the human condition. We were made to become like God; but we were also made to depend totally on God. No one can take God's place in our lives. No one can do for us what God alone can do. If we do not learn this lesson in the course of our life, we will spend a lifetime trying to find a replacement for God—which is as foolish as trying to run our bodies on something besides oxygen, water and food.

The whole world is groaning because human beings have tried to find this replacement for God. It has not worked. It never will. But still we try. We see the effects of this vain attempt everywhere—strained marriages, rebellious children, perverse imagination, smallness of spirit, injustice and violence in society, sickness of body and mind, addictions of every kind. The leaders of the Reformation used the phrase *total depravity* to describe the extent to which sin reaches; it touches every area of life. We might not be as bad as we could, but every part of us has some degree of badness in it. There is something fundamentally wrong with us. We may know the problem is there, but we can't seem to solve it. There is no unstained area of our lives to which we can appeal to save us from our sin. We are fallen creatures.

I am concerned that the self-help movement in modern American culture has raised the expectation in many people that they have the power within themselves to overcome the dark side of human nature, to take control of their lives and to reach perfection. It has only reinforced our obsession with power and control. Self-help seems to imply that if people learn the right philosophy and practice the right techniques, they will become masters of their own lives, able to manage time, money, diet, thoughts, feelings, people, circumstances and problems, until they reach the point where they have complete mastery.

We can gain much from the self-help movement. Who doesn't stand in need of conquering bad habits and overcoming nagging problems? I for one have benefited greatly from books and seminars that have taught me how to manage my time better, how to budget my limited financial resources, how to work with problem people, how to turn negative circumstances into positive opportunities for personal growth. Self-help empowers people to live more creatively, responsibly and happily.

But there is a problem in human nature that self-help can't touch and solve—the problem of sin. Sin runs deeper than the surface problems that techniques can help us to overcome. If anything, self-help can actually exacerbate this deeper problem of sin by deluding us into thinking that we have the power to solve it. It is possible to become a child of hell by thinking ourselves too self-sufficient, strong and powerful for God. If self-help makes us think that God is unnecessary, then it is worse than the problems that it helps us to conquer.

The Fellowship of Sinners

The mutuality command of confession and prayer addresses the debilitating effects of sin in human life, whether it be our own sin or someone else's. Confession exposes us for the sinners we are and opens us to the grace of God. Confession makes the church a community for sinners instead of pious saints. It gives us the freedom to be vulnerable and honest rather than pretentious and hypocritical. Prayer in turn enables us to receive God's healing power so that we can become whole and healthy human beings, not because we have mastered self-help techniques but because we have learned to seek God, to trust God's goodness and to embrace God's gracious provision for our lives.

In *Life Together* Dietrich Bonhoeffer argued that mutual confession constitutes the "break-through" to fellowship. Sin divides and isolates from fellowship; confession unites and builds community. He writes:

In confession the break-through to community takes place. Sin demands to have a man by himself. It withdraws him from the community. The more isolated a person is, the more destructive will be the power of sin over him, and the more deeply he becomes involved in it, the more disastrous is his isolation. Sin wants to remain unknown. It shuns the light. In the darkness of the unexpressed it poisons the whole being of a person. This can happen even in the midst of a pious community.[1]

Confession brings sin to light, where it is exposed for what it is and then covered by the grace of God. Where sin goes unacknowledged, grace remains untapped, an abstract idea that does not touch and transform our experience as the church.

In confession the light of the Gospel breaks into the darkness and seclusion of the heart. The sin must be brought into the light. The unexpressed must be openly spoken and acknowledged. All that is secret and hidden is made manifest.[2]

According to Bonhoeffer, we must confess our sin in the presence of a brother or sister in Christ. Confession makes us sinners before one another, breaks us of our self-righteousness and enables us to become a fellowship of sinners. Thus we become the true church that is founded on Christ's righteousness, not our own.

Since the confession of sin is made in the presence of a Christian brother, the last stronghold of self-justification is abandoned. The sinner surrenders; he gives up all his evil. He gives his heart to God, and he finds the forgiveness of all his sin in the fellowship of Jesus Christ and his brother. The expressed, acknowledged sin has lost all its power. It has been revealed and judged as sin. It can no longer tear the fellowship asunder. Now the fellowship bears the sin of the brother. He is no longer alone with his evil, for he has cast off his sin in confession and handed it over to God. It has been taken away from him. Now he stands in the fellowship of sinners who live by the grace of God in the Cross of Jesus Christ. Now he can be a sinner and still enjoy the grace of God. He can confess his sins and in this very act find fellowship for the first time.[3]

Of all the mutuality commands, confession and prayer pose the greatest risk to ourselves and perhaps the greatest hope for the church to become a loving community in its diversity. Controversy, conflict and enmity engender a spirit in the church that makes us defensive and accusatory. We criticize our opponent's weaknesses and applaud our strengths; they of course do likewise. Thus both sides become intransigent in the face of opposition, protective of their own position and hungry for power over others. The righteousness of one's cause is assumed, the evil of the other side forcefully proclaimed. A balanced perspective is lost in the shuffle of competing interests.

We forget what sinners we are, however right our particular perspective might be. We forget that it is entirely possible to be right for the wrong reasons, or wrong for the right reasons. We forget that being right does not stand as the only worthy goal that Christians should pursue, though it *is* of course a worthy goal. Too often Christians have, for the sake of being right, involved themselves in a conflict that led them deeper into sin. In the heat of battle they forgot that they were sinners. They used the conflict as an excuse to overlook their own sin, because they were too intent on combating the supposedly worse sin of their opponents. They neglected to pursue humility, kindness and joy because they were too busy gaining the advantage over the other side. Being right is important, but not at the expense of Christian virtue.

Confession forces us to own up to our own sin and not to use the wrongness of the other side to excuse our own. Confession reminds us that we are sinners who desperately need the grace of God. It makes us weak and vulnerable, exposing the underside of our bellies to the rest of the church and revealing that we are not the high and mighty people we want others to think we are. It thus undermines the unassailable position that controversy tempts us to assume. That is very risky, because it yields ground to our opponents. It puts us at their mercy and gives them the edge over us.

Still, it is a risk worth taking. Confession may put us at the mercy of our opponents, but it also puts us under the mercy of God. In my mind it is better to lose power and gain our own soul than to have power at the price of our soul. Confession gains the soul, for it leads us to the cross, where we can find forgiveness and hope.

Confession levels the playing field of the church. It displays us as the sinners we are, mitigates conflicts that threaten to destroy the church and disarms our opponents by demonstrating the way of humility to them. It reduces us to the needy people we are, regardless of where we come down on the issues. It reminds us—everyone, really—that weakness in the presence of God has dignity and integrity that human strength cannot comprehend and match.

I once witnessed the power of confession in a church that was embroiled in a controversy. A leader of the church had followed a philosophy of ministry that put pressure on laypeople to do the work of ministry. His philosophy troubled a number of older church members, who had different ideas of what clergy and laity ought to do. Their disagreement was aggravated because the personality of the leader was strong and demanding. His critics accused him of dominating his followers, from whom he extracted almost outrageous commitments of time, energy and loyalty. They also said that he acted like a messiah. How people responded to him appeared to be tantamount in his mind to how people responded to Jesus Christ. The accusation and acrimony threatened to force the two parties toward a showdown.

One evening during a period of prayer at a worship service, the leader took the microphone, as was the procedure for anyone who wanted to request prayer, and told the congregation of his personal struggle against the sin of pride, of the enormous ego that had created anguish in his life and of the drive for control that made it easy for people to dislike him. He admitted his loneliness and pain, and he expressed his longing to be gentle and humble. Then he asked the members of the congregation to forgive him and to pray for him. His act of confession exposed his own need to the church and invited the church to see him as a sinner in need of grace. And it gave his opponents the freedom to admit that they were at fault too.

Journey to Wholeness

This mutuality command is found in the book of James. It comes at the end of a series of injunctions that James gives to his readers. He presents a variety of life situations and then tells his readers that, no matter what the circumstances, they are always to seek God. God in turn will respond appropriately by meeting their need. A call to confession and prayer concludes the series of exhortations and sums up what Christians should do in order to become spiritually healthy.

Are any among you suffering? They should pray. Are any cheerful? They should sing songs of praise. Are any among you sick? They should call for the elders of the church and have them pray over them, anointing them with oil in the name of the Lord. The prayer of faith will save the sick, and the Lord will raise them up; and anyone who has committed sins will be forgiven. Therefore confess your sins to one another, and pray for one another, so that you may be healed. (Jas 5:13-16)

The passage assumes a definite connection between spiritual health and physical health. Sin causes sickness; confession and prayer lead to healing. The kind of relationship we have with God determines the quality of life we live in the world. Sin has consequences, just as forgiveness does. Those consequences are physical as well as spiritual.

There are no secret sins. Sin that is done secretly always has public consequences, not only in our lives but also in the lives of others. Sin perverts character, lowers standards, hurts other people, destroys relationships, ruins our health, poisons the spirit. It mars the image of God in us.

The Bible is very clear in linking sin with sickness. The lame man whose story is told in Mark 2 had to be forgiven before he could be healed; the implication is that his sin was at least partly the cause of his sickness. The apostle Paul argued that some of the believers in the church at Corinth had become ill and even died because they had sinned by taking Communion in an unworthy manner (1 Cor 11:27-30). David believed that unconfessed sin erodes the human spirit; it causes exhaustion and anguish.

While I kept silence, my body wasted away
  through my groaning all day long.
For day and night your hand was heavy upon me;
  my strength was dried up as by the heat of summer. (Ps 32:3-4)

As mental health professionals have shown, guilt often undermines good health, leading to such physical maladies as asthma, sleeplessness, nervousness, arthritis, ulcers and headaches. When the spirit is not right with God, the body ends up paying the price.

The link between sin and sickness does not imply, however, that sickness is always the consequence of one's own sin. Sickness is a result of the world's sin in general, not necessarily the result of one person's sin in particular. Jesus did not imply that sick people deserved to be sick because they had sinned. In one instance he refused to agree with the verdict that blindness was the result of sin; he said instead that it was for the glory of God (Jn 9).

James links sin and sickness together. Sin undermines what God designed for human life and causes sickness of body, mind and spirit. But the way to reverse the destructive cycle is through mutual confession and prayer. Confession admits wrongdoing. Prayer asks for restoration and healing. God then acts to make us whole. Thus just as sin leads to sickness, so confession and prayer lead to forgiveness and wholeness.

Confession and Restoration
The obvious application of this mutuality command involves confession to the people whom we have offended and from whom we need forgiveness. Confession implies that we are willing to take responsibility for our wrongdoing and that we want to restore the relationship. As Jesus said, "So when you are offering your gift at the altar, if you remember that your brother or sister has something against you, leave your gift there before the altar and go; first be reconciled to your brother or sister, and then come and offer your gift" (Mt 5:23-24). Confession in this case holds the promise of reconciling broken relationships, thus healing wounds in the body of Christ. Jesus commands us to confess our faults to those hurt by them, regardless of whether they too are guilty and intend to respond in kind. There are no conditions attached to this command. That makes Jesus' words difficult to obey, because where wrongdoing goes both ways we are inclined to wait until the other party

is willing to admit fault as well. Such unwillingness to act first often keeps Christians from obeying this command at all.

In the last chapter I told the story of a pastor, Bill, who faced the difficult task of forgiving the members of his congregation for divisiveness and criticism. He also realized that he had failed them and needed to take responsibility for the sins that he had committed. He finally decided in his discouragement and brokenness to admit his failures openly and resign from the church. As he wrote:

So it happened. The day came I decided to leave the ministry and take a position in teaching. Never did I dream this kind of defeat could ever happen to me. I was broken and admitted to the elders and congregation my failure and my decision to seek other work.

Strangely, his decision to confess his sins charged him with new energy and boldness.

Along with my brokenness came a strange new courage, boldness to tell the council and congregation how I saw the whole situation in all its tragedy. Never had I dared be this honest. What would they think? I had nothing to lose anymore. I had already given over this job and my career. Reactions didn't matter anymore. What freedom!

Freedom for him; repentance, as it turned out, for them.

What an amazing response from the people: one by one dropping to their knees. They were dying, too! One by one getting up out of their pews and going over to someone with whom they sought reconciliation. Forgiveness was happening! In the church! God Almighty, could it be!

Forgiveness happened because confession had gone before. And healing followed.

The explanation was simple. It was a miracle of healing brought by a fresh outpouring of the Holy Spirit, sparked by brokenness, absolute honesty, confession and forgiveness. On all sides. God led me to stay with this church and ministry.

The miracle continued for some time. Relationships were restored, membership loss stopped, undercurrents of discontent and criticism were stilled. Bill's preaching became more honest, simple and direct, the congregation's response more genuine. The church became a community of sinners for the first time. And it all started because someone was willing to risk everything by confessing his sin.

The more general application of this command involves confession of sin before brothers and sisters in Christ who are in a position to impart grace to us, to support us in our weakness and to help us overcome our sinful inclinations. Confession in this case forces us to be honest about ourselves, makes our faith authentic and leads us into the light of the gospel.

But we recoil from exposure. We fear being known as sinners and tend therefore to hide behind a front of false piety. We project an image of ourselves as strong and pious Christians, though looming behind the image are doubts, addictions, fears and failures.

Christian leaders in particular face enormous pressure to perform as models of perfection before their adoring congregations or organizations. As a consequence they feel profound loneliness, wanting desperately to be known for the sinners that they are but feeling terrified by the prospect of being found out. So they feel pressure to demonstrate that they have conquered all sin and stand before the people of God as examples of faith and obedience. They deny their own raw humanity for the sake of their ministry.

That impulse to be perfect before the world only increases their vulnerability to sin, which they can't admit to anyone else and maybe won't even admit to themselves. Until it is too late. Over the past few years the church has witnessed the moral failure of many prominent Christian leaders whose secret sins were finally exposed after months and even years of deception. They might have followed a different path if at least a few of their friends in the church had known of their struggles and had helped them to face their weaknesses squarely. Their heroism isolated them from the church and forced them to face their weaknesses alone or to deny them altogether. Appearance became more important than truth, image more important than authenticity.

Henri Nouwen has observed this fear of vulnerability in Christian leaders and writes of it in his book *In the Name of Jesus.* "Often I have the impression that priests and ministers are the least-confessing people in the Christian community. The sacrament of Confession has often become a way to keep our own vulnerability hidden from our community."[4] Nouwen wonders how Christian leaders can know that they are loved and cared for if no one knows them for who they are.

I am not at all surprised that so many ministers and priests suffer immensely from deep emotional loneliness, frequently feel a great need for affectivity and intimacy, and sometimes experience a deep-seated guilt and shame in front of their own people. . . . It is precisely the men and women who are dedicated to spiritual leadership who are easily subject to very raw carnality. The reason for this is that they do not know how to live the truth of the Incarnation. They separate themselves from their own concrete community, try to deal with their needs by ignoring them or satisfying them in distant or anonymous places, and then experience an increasing split between their own most private inner world and the good news they announce.[5]

Nouwen believes that Christian leaders, like other members of the church, need a safe place for themselves where they can admit their problems and receive grace through the ministry of the body of Christ. They, too, are called to be full members of the church, even though they may be leaders of it. They, too, are accountable to others, need their support and love and require the ministry of compassion when they are broken. They, too, must confess their sins. "Through confession, the dark powers are taken out of their carnal isolation, brought into the light, and made visible to the community. Through forgiveness, they are disarmed and dispelled and a new integration between body and spirit is made possible."[6]

I celebrate the recovery movement because it has created a safe place for wounded people to admit their problems and find help. The movement itself grew out of the Twelve-Step philosophy of Alcoholics Anonymous. The first step is confession. "My name is Bill, and I am an

113

alcoholic." "My name is Mary, and I am an alcoholic." We can apply this principle universally, not just in the case of alcoholism but in the case of any habitual sin—rage, bitterness, drugs, food, sex, gossip, lying and so forth. Confession places wrongdoing on the table, frees us from the bondage of hidden sin and submits our problems to the counsel and accountability of the church.

Several years ago a student came to see me. He told me that he had a secret to tell. When he was in junior high he had a serious acne problem on his back. His classmates used to tease him about it. One day he returned from football practice later than his teammates. When he entered the shower, only a few others remained. They congregated in a corner, whispering to each other. Suddenly they jumped him, wrestled him to the ground and, taking a safety pin, began to prick the acne on his back. They told him that they were going to help him get rid of it. They laughed gleefully, making jokes about his back and claiming to be his only true friends. Then they left him lying on the shower floor. He was overcome with rage and shame. He never told anyone about his humiliation until the day he entered my office. He sobbed through the story. Then he confessed his deep bitterness toward his assailants. Once the truth was out, the emotion spent, the confession made, he stood up as a new man, having received the healing grace of God.

Confession, nevertheless, needs to have limits. While Christians must confess their sin, that doesn't imply that they should be indiscriminate with whom they talk and lurid in how they tell it. Not everything should be said, and not everyone should be told. Confession should get to the point and focus on the real problem, sparing the gory details that awaken curiosity and sidetrack people. If adultery is the sin, then adultery should be confessed. But that doesn't mean the person doing the confessing should take twenty minutes to describe every detail. Nor should that person announce the sin to the world. The circle of those who hear should include only those who have the right or responsibility to hear—spouse, support group, pastor. Not necessarily the whole church. Private sins require a small circle privy to the confession, public sins a large circle. Confessing sins of small consequence should involve a few people; confessing sins of significant consequence will probably involve many people.

Confession also needs to have a goal: to restore the sinner to full fellowship with God and the church. That requires the community to zero in on the root problem, not the surface sin, so that confession leads not only to forgiveness but also to insight, self-knowledge, discipline and victory. We sin for a reason; we struggle because we have needs and desires. We need to learn the why after we have admitted the where, when, who and how. Confession mandates that we not only repent of a past misdeed but also pursue a future plan of action. Confession "puts off" past sins; restoration engenders a new mind and "puts on" new behavior (Eph 4:22-24 RSV). The old way of sin must yield to the new way of godliness. Confession should eventually lead to transformation.

Finally, confession may uncover problems that require the expertise of mental health professionals. Confession assumes personal responsibility for sin. But the root of the problem may involve more than a rebellious will. It may also involve a bad background, past traumas, genetic defects, even mental illness. Therapy does not eliminate the need for confession; it supplements confession by probing the reasons for the sin and by exploring new strategies for healing and growth. The church and the mental health community should be allies, not enemies, in the quest for spiritual wholeness.

Prayer and Healing

James tells us to confess sin and to pray for one another, that we may be healed. Full restoration requires prayer as well as confession. If confession exposes our sin and brokenness, prayer gives us access to the healing power of God.

Prayer is perhaps the greatest service that we can render to our fellow believers. That may surprise activists who insist that Christians serve broken people best through concrete acts of justice and mercy. They take their responsibilities as followers of Jesus seriously, just as they take the

Bible's criticism of apathy seriously. They do not want to be guilty of sinning like those who, on seeing obvious need, simply dismiss the problem with a casual "God bless you. Go on your way now. Be warmed and filled. I'll be praying for you" (Jas 2:15-16). They recoil from the sin of indifference.

But prayerful people are cautious about overestimating the powers that they have to meet the deepest needs in people. They do not want to be presumptuous. That does not mean that they neglect their God-given duty to serve, to bear burdens and the like. Still, they recognize that some needs run so deep, some problems become so severe, that God and God alone is the only solution, for God alone is sufficient. People need to know God, to receive the grace of God, to experience the healing power of God. No human ministry is adequate to touch people at the deepest levels of their being. That is why we must pray. Prayer does not replace practical ministry; it is the most effective expression of practical ministry. Prayer lifts people into the presence of God.

My own experience over the past two years affirms the importance of prayer. I have benefited in many ways from the church's practical help since my wife and daughter died. People have served me, comforted me, borne my burdens and encouraged me. But over time I have appreciated the ministry of prayer the most. I can manage my life well enough on one level. I don't need the practical support I once did. But on another level I am more needy now than I have ever been. I am faced with the daunting responsibility of raising three young children and of having to make major decisions alone. I struggle with profound questions, nagging doubts, erosive depression. I worry about the future. I sometimes feel lonely and restless, like a caged animal that can't quite shake the memory of its life in the wild. I have needs that no human being can fill, problems that no practical advice will solve. That is why I now tell people to pray for me when they ask how they can help. I need people to believe for me when I can't muster the faith myself, to intervene before God on my behalf, to pray the grace and love of God into my soul.

A number of members at our church have been called to the ministry of prayer. They are devoted to this ministry. They pray for hours every week and meet together regularly for prayer. At their meetings they pray for each other, for needy members of the congregation and for the church around the world. Sometimes they sit in silence and listen to God until God gives them the prayers to pray. They pray as a community for one need at a time until there is discernment and agreement among them. They keep in regular contact with the people for whom they are praying. They consider prayer their most important ministry in the church.

We must pray even for our "enemies," especially for our enemies in the church, not for their destruction but for their salvation. They need the grace of God, as we do. They need God's help, as we do. They need to know God's truth, as we do. Sometimes prayer is the only ministry we can do for our Christian opponents because it is the only ministry that they will receive from us. They may reject our greetings, service, encouragement, admonition. They may avoid us altogether. But they cannot spurn our prayers. Since prayer appeals to God on behalf of someone else, its effectiveness does not depend on how well we get along with that person. It depends only on God's grace and power.

Prayer for enemies is a profound act of love. Jesus said:

You have heard that it was said, "You shall love your neighbor and hate your enemy." But I say to you, Love your enemies and pray for those who persecute you, so that you may be children of your Father in heaven; for he makes his sun rise on the evil and on the good, and sends rain on the righteous and on the unrighteous. (Mt 5:43-45)

As I have argued elsewhere, ministries like prayer remind us that our opponents in the church are human beings with problems like our own Regardless of their position on an issue, they battle sins of flesh and spirit, find it hard sometimes to believe, fight a losing war against mortality and wonder occasionally whether their faith is real and God is true. They are more complex than the opinions they hold, more needy than the way they appear to us, more vulnerable to sin and evil than they would ever let on. They are our brothers and sisters in Christ, whether we like them or not, whether we trust them or not, whether we get along with them or not. They need our prayers, just as we need theirs. We must be as generous with our prayers as God is with rain and sunshine, which he sends to everyone regardless of their worthiness. Conversation in the church may fail sometimes, negotiations break down, affection dissipate in the heat of conflict, mutual respect deteriorate. We may not get along with everyone in the church, however hard we try. But we can always pray for them, because we know how much they need God.

Confession exposes; prayer heals. Confession takes responsibility for wrongdoing; prayer asks God to help us do what is right. Confession acknowledges the human condition; prayer draws upon the transcendent power of God. Confession addresses our sin; prayer leads us to righteousness. The two belong together as one mutuality command. Confession challenges us to risk being weak and vulnerable before our brothers and sisters in Christ. We can of course choose to do otherwise, and in many cases no one will ever know, since many sins can remain hidden for a long time. But in the long run we will suffer loss, for we will not be known and still loved for the sinners we are, nor will we receive the grace of God through the ministry of others. Prayer, in turn, requires us to intercede on behalf of those who have been weak and vulnerable before us. This mutuality command is the one command that appeals directly to God, who alone has the power to forgive, restore and heal broken sinners such as we all are.

7

SERVE ONE
ANOTHER

*I*first heard about Habitat for Humanity when we moved to Chicago to begin my Ph.D. program at the University of Chicago. The executive director of the Chicago affiliate was a member of our church. From time to time he would inform the congregation about the work of Habitat in the Chicago area. Eventually he challenged the church to do its own Habitat project. The elders endorsed it enthusiastically. Suddenly we found ourselves engaged in a hands-on ministry that altered our entire view of missions. It was no longer at some far-off place, done by paid professionals whom we supported financially. It was local, carried out by lay volunteers. The whole church was caught up in the excitement of serving a cause that actually put ordinary church members to work. It took the church ten months to rehab a two-flat in inner-city Chicago. That project changed the church forever because it united the members together in significant service.

Habitat is a Christian ministry that was started in the 1970s by Millard Fuller. The goal of Habitat is to provide decent and affordable housing for the working poor, who invest in their own home by putting in five hundred hours of "sweat equity" and then purchase the home through an interest-free loan from the "Fund for Humanity." The ministry has exploded around the world, especially in the United States. The vast majority of work is done by volunteers; the money comes from donations and grants; each affiliate is controlled by a local board of advisers. Habitat has grown so dramatically that it has become, in its short history, one of the leading organizations in providing affordable housing for low-income families. It is one example among many of how groups of people in local communities are trying, against all odds, to make life a little more livable for the needy.

I believe that most people in Western societies today misunderstand how to solve social problems. They think that money and bureaucracy alone can solve social problems. Of course it is always the government's money and the government's bureaucracy. The assumption is that social problems can be solved without individuals' having to make real sacrifices to solve them. That is simply not true. Money and bureaucracy are necessary. But they are not sufficient. We will not be able to address social problems at home or abroad unless we are willing to take personal responsibility for these problems. That requires a courageous commitment to service.

To serve one another in the body of Christ is to commit our resources—time, money, energy and expertise—to meet the practical needs of fellow believers. Two different words are used in the Greek New Testament for the English expression "to serve." We can translate one word "to be a slave of"; the other word "to wait on." Service implies that we wait on other people, as if we were choosing to be their slave. It means that we are willing to devote ourselves to meet the needs of people most easily overlooked or exploited in our society.

Service is necessary for two groups of people in particular. The first group comprises people who would not otherwise be able to function as productive disciples if they did not receive help. Some Christians are kept from doing the will of God not because they don't want to but because they aren't able to. They lack basic necessities—steady income or transportation or child care or medical attention—that would allow them to make their contribution to society. Service takes care of these practical needs. While burden-bearing (chapter ten) enables people to get back on their feet and discover what God wants them to do, service meets the ongoing needs of people so that they can stay on their feet and do for Christ what they always wanted and intended to do.

Suppose a young woman has an accident that causes deafness. This physical disability might precipitate a spiritual crisis that plunges her into severe depression. She would then need someone to get her back on her feet again, help her to make peace with her disability, and challenge her to discover what God wants to accomplish in her life. She would need someone, in other words, to bear her burdens. But her deafness might also strengthen her spiritual commitment, causing her to go deeper, grow wiser and become tougher than she was before. However changed for the better, she would still need practical help to proceed along the course she has set for herself. She would need to learn sign language, and she would need help in school. This kind of practical help for people who want to carry on is the essence of service.

The second group of people needing service includes those who, without the help of others, would not be able to survive at all. Unwanted children in orphanages and hospitals need service. Old people in nursing homes need service. Severely disabled people need service. When I was an interim pastor during my graduate years in Chicago, I met a woman who took care of her invalid husband for ten years. He was completely incapacitated and therefore unable to move, eat, talk. He was as motionless and expressionless as a block of wood. Yet she fed him every day, massaged him and moved him so that he would not get bedsores, invited visitors into his room, played him music and talked to him throughout the day. She had little hope that he would ever recover. That did not keep this remarkable woman, so happy and carefree and contented, from serving him faithfully and without complaint.

That All Things Be Equal

Service means sacrifice. It requires us to give what we have so that, as we learn to live with less (time, money, energy, opportunity, advancement), others in need will have more. But it must be voluntary sacrifice. In Galatians 5:13-14 Paul enjoins believers to use their *freedom* in Christ to become servants of one another. The Bible commands us to be servants as a way of living out the liberty we have in Christ. Freedom, then, should be the primary motive for service. Not having to serve is the starting point for service. Gratitude for God's gifts will lead us to use our gifts for others, and freedom from compulsion will make us eager to sacrifice for somebody else's sake.

Paul suggested that the goal of such service is equality. In his second letter to the Christian community at Corinth, he encouraged them to fulfill the promise that they had made at an earlier time to collect money for the poor in Jerusalem. He admired their willingness, but he wanted them to match that willingness with action.

For if the eagerness is there, the gift is acceptable according to what one has—not according to what one does not have. I do not mean that there should be relief for others and pressure on you, but it is a question of a fair balance between your present abundance and their need, so that their abundance may be for your need, in order that there may be a fair balance. (2 Cor 8:12-14)

In Paul's mind, the gospel inspired those who had much, to invest it in those who had little, until all things became equal.

This quest for equality has the potential for uniting a pluralistic church. If we see ourselves as stewards of God's gifts to us rather than owners of what we consider rightfully ours, we will be more willing to invest what we have in the church, striving to help those with less get more—and not simply more money, but more knowledge, more compassion, more wholeness, more opportunity. The advantages some Christians have due to natural endowment, background, opportunity and hard work can and should be used as resources to lift other Christians up, not to put them in their place. Thus those made more sensitive to suffering in the world through their study and travel should not complain about insensitive and compassionless people in their local churches, but should instead spearhead programs that will expose them to the world's needs. Likewise, those made more aware of the brokenness of humanity through their own journey toward wholeness should not condemn self-sufficient and self-righteous people in the church who scoff at dysfunction, but should instead enable them to recognize their responsibility to contribute to the healing of broken humanity. The ministry of service promises to unite the church in the greater purpose of creating a healthy body.

It Shall Not Be So Among You
The Bible teaches that servanthood is every Christian's duty. But it speaks most forcefully about servanthood when it addresses leaders. When his disciples began to argue about who would be the greatest among them, Jesus said:

> You know that among the Gentiles those whom they recognize as their rulers lord it over them, and their great ones are tyrants over them. But it is not so among you; but whoever wishes to become great among you must be your servant, and whoever wishes to be first among you must be slave of all. For the Son of Man came not to be served but to serve, and to give his life a ransom for many. (Mk 10:42-45)

Jesus himself set an example of servanthood when, the night before his crucifixion, he washed the disciples' feet (Jn 13) and then commanded them to follow his example. Peter must have gotten the message. He exhorted the elders of the churches "to tend the flock of God that is in your charge, exercising the oversight, not under compulsion but willingly, as God would have you do it—not for sordid gain but eagerly. Do not lord it over those in your charge, but be examples to the flock" (1 Pet 5:2-3).

Jesus envisioned a community of disciples who would dare to move downward instead of upward, who would dare to retreat from selfish ambition so that others could get ahead. Jesus of course was the quintessential example. As the apostle Paul wrote, "For you know the generous act [grace] of our Lord Jesus Christ, that though he was rich, yet for your sakes he became poor, so that by his poverty you might become rich" (2 Cor 8:9). Though Jesus was in the form of God, Paul wrote to the Philippians, he did not count equality with God a thing to be grasped but emptied himself and became a servant, even to the point of sacrificial death (Phil 2:5-11).

Jesus set a pattern for his followers. If anyone had the right not to sacrifice himself, Jesus did. Yet he offered his life for our sake. We too are to count others as better than ourselves and seek the welfare of our brothers and sisters in Christ.

The Bible recognizes that church leaders in particular face the temptation of exempting themselves from servanthood. They are more interested in seeking power, accumulating power and clinging to power, either for its own sake or for some ostensibly greater purpose. They easily forget what power is for and how perilous power is. In the end it corrupts them. Like money, power is not unequivocally bad. But also like money, desire for power corrupts the soul and does great evil in the world, even in the name of good. It can intoxicate and delude and destroy. The best protection against this temptation of power is to live according to the biblical principle of servanthood, even and especially before one ever has power. Then, if power ever comes to us—say, by achieving high office in the church, or by contributing lots of money to a church building project, or by becoming the pastor of a large and prestigious congregation—we will not have to live with the burden of having sacrificed biblical principles to get it or keep it. Moses' meekness and Joseph's prudence demonstrate the possibility of being both leaders and servants. But the latter must be our aim; the former must be left to God's guidance and plan.

Like leaders, gifted people in the church—musicians, preachers, writers, scholars, managers—are not exempted from servanthood either. Lynda and I were in the final stages of adopting a special needs child when the accident occurred. Adoption would have given us a fifth child, and Lynda had not eliminated the possibility of a sixth, even though she was forty-two at the time. Some people raised questions about this decision, especially as it would have inevitably affected Lynda's schedule and career. She was a gifted musician who could have gone in a number of different directions, giving her an even higher profile in the community.

"Why another baby?" they asked. "Couldn't you use your gifts in a better way?"

Lynda always replied the same way: "I can't think of a better way to use my abilities than in service to my children."

Service and sacrifice are not intended just for those who don't seem to have much to contribute except their unused time and average abilities. Some assume—I believe wrongly—that gifted people have a good excuse for not serving and sacrificing themselves for others. For some reason we assume that people of outstanding abilities are obligated to develop and use their abilities as much as possible, no matter what the cost to others. It is unthinkable that they might choose to neglect their abilities for some ostensibly lesser cause. Yet that is what servanthood sometimes requires. A father might sacrifice advancement in a career to care for his children; a prominent leader in the church might take a sabbatical from leadership in order to teach Sunday school to first-graders; a busy executive might give extra time to a long-range planning committee in her church; a coach might sacrifice a lucrative job opportunity at a major high school to start a recreation program at an inner-city church; a superior student might sacrifice enrollment in the best graduate program in order to continue a relationship with the needy kids in his youth group. Jesus said that we will be judged by how we use our resources in caring for "the least of these," the one group of people usually overlooked as we climb our way to the top. Sometimes we will find opportunity to employ our gifts in service to the needy; at other times we will have to let some of our abilities and opportunities lie dormant as we seek to serve people in need. The two of course are not mutually exclusive; but neither are they exactly the same.

Time, Money and Expertise
Service begins when we are willing to give our time to people in need.

George Barna argues that time, not money, has become the most important commodity in modern Western culture. Recently I talked with a man who installs underground sprinkler units. He said that people don't complain about the cost, however expensive those systems can be. Instead, they mention the amount of time it saves. Saving time is more important than saving money.

I can testify to the value of time. As a single parent, I find incredible demands put on my time. It takes time to manage the home, work as a professor at the college, teach Sunday school at church, coach soccer for my son's team, sit in on my children's music lessons and take care of endless chores at home. My time is in short supply. I am careful about what I choose to give my time to, and I must battle resentment when a responsibility or a person takes too much of my time, especially when, in the case of an interruption, I had not planned it into my schedule.

Servanthood takes time. Mowing the lawn of a widow takes time, visiting the sick at a hospital takes time, volunteering at a clinic for low-income families takes time, spring cleaning at church takes time, organizing a Vacation Bible School takes time.

What do we do when we don't have the time to serve? First, we must consider the impact on our schedule of every decision we make. Purchases, commitments, responsibilities, hobbies and projects all contain hidden costs, some of which common sense will reveal to us. We must be ruthlessly realistic about those hidden costs. Every home improvement project I have begun has taken triple the time I had anticipated it would take. Leisure activities that I enjoy take far more time than I often estimate. I have friends who bought a cabin as a family getaway. As a vacation spot, the cabin has been wonderful. As a piece of property requiring upkeep, it has been a drain on time and resources.

Second, we must simplify our lives as much as possible. Renting a cabin may be more convenient than owning one, providing needed rest without adding the responsibility of upkeep. Saying no to all but the essential commitments may release time in our schedules for more service. Careful planning of the calendar may protect us from getting too busy at the wrong times of year—say, during late summer when we need a rest, or around the holidays.

Third, we must make service a habit and build it into our weekly schedules. One big decision eliminates having to make lots of little ones. Service will fit into the rhythm of our lives only if we make it a regular priority, such as when we volunteer to teach Sunday school for an entire year or tend the nursery once a month. All the board members of Habitat for Humanity in Spokane are required to volunteer half a Saturday a month to help build a house. Every month the sign-up sheet is passed around at the board meeting, and each board member signs up for Saturday service. That is one example of how service can become a regular part of the schedule. If service is kept optional, it will be the first thing to go when our time is pinched.

Time is not the only important commodity for those who want to serve—so is money. Most forms of service require money. Money is necessary for transportation, supplies, education, child care, salaries, administration. However willing, however committed, however organized, we will not succeed in serving on a large scale without money.

The wealthy have the greatest resources at their disposal but have the most difficulty giving it up. The most parsimonious people in the world are the rich, who demonstrate an appallingly low level of generosity. That is true for rich Christians, not just rich pagans. And by rich I mean rich according to a global perspective. If we take into account how people in India, Nigeria, Bangladesh and South America live, middle-class Christians in America are rich.

The Bible warns us to be wary of wealth. Paul exhorted Timothy:

But those who want to be rich fall into temptation and are trapped by many senseless and harmful desires that plunge people into ruin and destruction. For the love of money is a root of all kinds of evil, and in their eagerness to be rich some have wandered away from the faith and pierced themselves with many pains. . . . As for those who in the present age are rich, command them not to be haughty, or to set their hopes on the uncertainty of riches, but rather on God who richly provides us with everything for our enjoyment. They are to do good, to be rich in good works, generous, and ready to share, thus storing up for themselves the treasure of a good foundation for the future, so that they may take hold of the life that really is life. (1 Tim 6:9-10, 17-19)

The Bible says that we are stewards of our wealth as one of many resources that God has given to us. It calls us to invest it in other people, thus laying up for ourselves "treasures in heaven."

Stewardship demands careful planning. If we live by conviction, we will limit what we spend on ourselves, budget our income and live in order to give. More money can mean a bigger estate, vast ownership, excessive entanglement. It can also mean fruitful ministry. John Wesley provides us with a good example. He made a great deal of money, but he died penniless, choosing to give all of it away. He believed that money should be made so that money can be shared. Again, the best way to use our money for service is to develop a habit of giving, to build it into our budget so that the money we invest in service is not left to spontaneous decisions at the end of the month, after our paycheck has been eaten up. The money we devote to service should be viewed on the same level as the money we set aside for house payments and food.

Expertise joins money and time as the third essential element in service. It is easy to think that service is a volunteer activity we do when we are not working in our area of expertise. We may work in high finance during the week, but on Saturdays we don overalls and grab a paintbrush in order to perform our weekly service. Of course there is nothing wrong with giving time and energy to forms of service that lie outside our area of expertise. But service should also tap our areas of expertise, so that we see our service as an avenue and extension of what we do best.

The Habitat project our church took on in Chicago tapped the expertise of many of our church members. A committee of leaders organized the project. Bankers helped raise the money. General contractors supervised the construction. Subcontractors helped to organize novice work crews, and skilled laborers supervised and trained those crews. Other people packed lunches, provided snacks, watched children, took photographs, cleaned up at the end of the day, scraped, painted, pounded nails, sanded floors, wired walls, stuffed insulation. Still others spoke to the community about the project, wrote articles, recruited more volunteers. The project required a broad spectrum of skills, from common laborer to money manager. Everyone was important because everyone had something to contribute.

Person to Person

In its simplest form, service means that one person serves another person in need. It is direct and personal, unmediated by larger institutions.

Alice is one such person who gave herself unselfishly to care for another. For two years she served a good friend of hers, Tricia, while the two attended college together. Tricia is a bright, happy, friendly professional woman who is about the farthest from being "needy" of anyone I know. She is competent and successful in her work, active in her church and busy every day of the week. She also has muscular dystrophy, which has left her severely disabled since birth. She has some use of her arms and no use of her legs. She has lived in a wheelchair her whole life. Though her disability has made life more difficult for her, it has not kept her from excelling. She was a very good student through college and now works as an elementary school teacher.

Alice roomed across the hall from Tricia during her freshman year and saw firsthand what Tricia required of a roommate, who took care of many of her personal needs. At the end of that year a mutual friend suggested that Alice room with Tricia. Alice proposed the idea to Tricia. Though surprised, Tricia accepted the offer.

Much of Alice's service was routine. Every day she had to dress Tricia, comb her hair, make her bed, wash her clothes, turn her from back to side during the night, give her a shower, take her to the bathroom, help her get exercise and maintain her motorized wheelchair. Such service was demanding, but it became a part of Alice's daily schedule.

It was not always easy. "There were days," Alice told me, "I did not feel like serving. These feelings were usually followed by guilt. Tricia was dependent on me and could not function without my help. I had to put aside my selfish feelings and meet her needs first. If I did not change my attitude, but rather went through the motions to help her, Tricia would sense that through the way I handled her. I soon learned that serving is not only what you do, but it is an attitude of the heart."

Alice went beyond the call of duty. She carried Tricia up flights of stairs in a residence hall so that she could attend a friend's surprise birthday party. She even took her sledding, an activity that Tricia had never done before. "In a push and one big whoosh," Alice told me, "we were speeding down the hill. I'm sure Tricia had never experienced anything quite like that before. The event ended with a wipe-out at the bottom of the hill and snow in our faces. We had never laughed so hard! Going down was quick. Carrying her back up the hill was a task, but well worth it!"

I know Alice, and I consider her one of my heroes. She helped make it possible for Tricia to earn a college degree and prepare for a meaningful vocation. Tricia had all the abilities she needed; she had a winsome personality and a happy heart. But she needed someone to meet her basic needs. Alice volunteered to be that person.

Alice's example is extraordinary. Still, I have observed many people in the church—to say nothing of the larger community—who need to be served. They need lawns mowed, houses painted, errands run, children watched, wheelchairs pushed, books read to them, meals provided, appliances repaired. Over the past few months I have talked with several young widows, and their stories bear a striking resemblance. After the initial shock of the loss and rush of support, their friends returned to life as usual and forgot about the widows' needs. They did not realize or care that young widows cannot return to the same normal life. They told me of their loneliness, of their need for a surrogate father for their children, of the difficulty of finding good child care, of the inconvenience of having to do the household jobs that used to be divided in half.

My experience has been different, and I have often wondered why.

Perhaps people have the opinion that widowers are much less capable of managing the home than are widows. Or perhaps women are more sensitive to the needs of children and therefore quicker to step forward to meet those needs when, as in my case, the children are deprived of a mother rather than a father. Whatever the reason, I have been helped greatly by my friends. One friend in particular has served my family with exceptional sensitivity and consistency. She watches my preschooler five mornings a week and refuses to accept payment. She picks up bulk food items for me when she makes a run to a wholesale outlet. She initiates special events, like picnics in the summer. Another friend brings her two sons over to my house so all the kids can play together, and she occasionally takes my daughter out to lunch. Still another friend drives my kids home from school, and she also keeps an eye on them at school when she volunteers in the classroom.

This kind of direct and personal service comes from a heart of sympathy. I have asked these serving women on more than one occasion, "Why are you doing this for me?" They have usually responded the same way. "All I have to do is think about what it would mean if my own husband were in your shoes," they say. "I think about how he would respond, what he would have to do just to maintain the home, where he would go for help, whom he could depend on. That is all it takes for me to help you as much as I can."

Sympathy comes from looking at life from the perspective of another person. Sympathy for widows and widowers arises when we think about what it would be like for us to lose our spouse, for single parents when we think about what it would be like to raise children alone, for the infirm when we think about what it would be like to feel interminably sick, forgotten and alone, unsure of health and safety, and unable to do the chores that used to come so easy. Sympathy makes us sensitive to what life is like for the people who are unable to do what comes so naturally to us. Sympathy makes us servants. It motivates us to throw our lives in with "the least of these."

Of course the least of these could easily become any one of us. As I suddenly discovered, what separates a happily married man from widower-hood can be simply being in the wrong place at the wrong time. All of us are closer to being vulnerable and needy than we could ever imagine. What separates the competent from the disabled, the independent from the dependent, the strong from the weak usually has very little to do with ourselves but is more a matter of the accidents of birth, place, time, opportunity and chance. A birth defect could have crippled our children. Cancer could have ravaged our body. Unemployment could have plunged our home into financial insecurity. There is little rhyme or reason to much of what happens in life. Servants recognize the capricious nature of life, realize that it could have happened to them, and thus throw themselves into helping the people to whom it happens.

Advocacy
Sometimes it isn't possible to meet a person's basic needs, though that person may be our best friend. Some needs require direct and personal service, as we have just observed. Other needs can't be met that way but demand a different strategy—advocacy. Advocacy requires servants to line up on the side of the needy and intervene on their behalf before the people and agencies that are in a position to help.

My friend Peter is an exceptional advocate. For several years now he has worked for the Mennonite Central Committee. Though involved in community organization and bureaucracy, he has never lost touch with individual people whose needs he is devoted to meet. He met Marianne on the street several years ago. Marianne, just forty-eight years old, had a college degree. But she was on the verge of homelessness, spared only by the generosity of her mother, who lived on a subsistence level herself. Marianne also had medical problems. She suffered from insulin-dependent diabetes, heart disease, liver disease, alcoholism and blindness. Despite these severe maladies, she was ineligible for welfare because she did not have a medical statement certifying that she was unable to work.

Peter could not ignore her plight. "I became her friend and advocate. I raised a ruckus on her behalf at the county hospital, the county welfare office, the social security office and boarding houses. Marianne and I laughed together, shared burdens together and won a few small victories. Not long after we won our biggest victory—a medical statement verifying that she was legally blind, which guaranteed that she would receive social security disability—Marianne died. The cause of her death was malnutrition and lack of medical care."

Peter served Marianne by representing her before the powers that be. However willing to serve, he could not address her medical needs or her unemployment. Some needs are so big or complex that individuals alone cannot meet them. At such times service becomes advocacy—advocacy for minimum-wage increases, job training, health care, affordable housing, legal aid, protection of the unborn, day-care programs, nursing home improvements. Advocacy belongs in the church, too, to draw attention to the special needs of widows, the unemployed, single parents, troubled youth and so forth. Advocates function as society's conscience for the forgotten.

Community

Peter discovered that service also requires community, because community can look out for people in a way that individuals can't. For several years he lived in an intimate community—"a group of folks who were seriously looking to follow Christ." It was an unusual group comprising ex-cons, ex-drug dealers, recovered alcoholics. They called themselves "the brotherhood," and they met every morning for prayer and Bible study. They experienced an unusual degree of mutuality. "These folks became my family. The group looked out for each other."

This inner-city group served each other as counselors, spiritual guides and financial aides. "One morning one of the brothers shared that he was short of groceries for himself and his dependents. We left the prayer meeting and together went shopping at the grocery store. There was no feeling of someone giving and someone receiving. We knew beyond explanation that we were all equally receivers and beneficiaries. Perhaps that is why we never said 'thank you' to each other. Acts of mutual compassion were only what we were supposed to do for each other. A thank-you somehow cheapened the relationship."

Apart from community, service can become patronizing. Sleek, smooth fat cats bankroll programs for the needy and assume that they have the right to control those programs; self-righteous activists think that their zeal for good deeds gives them the right to impose their ideology on the people they're helping; faithful volunteers make the recipients of their service feel indebted to them and guilty if they are not overwhelmed with gratitude.

Peter said to me that service can be harmful if it is done apart from community. "Those of us who do the serving can convince ourselves of our own selflessness, and we can become arrogant and condescending in a provider-recipient relationship. Such a relationship builds dependency, breeds resentment and continues powerlessness. This problem results because of broken community. Service within the context of community is a mutual giving and receiving as time and circumstances change."

Community links giver and receiver together, forces them to see how similar at heart they really are, and thus blurs the distinction between those who have and those who don't. As Alice discovered, what appeared to be a one-way relationship of service to Tricia became a two-way relationship of love. Alice realized that the disease could have been hers. She saw the beauty, strength, courage and freedom that characterized Tricia's life, born out of suffering and struggle. She learned that servants receive something that only the needy can give—an understanding of what it means to be dependent on others, to embrace the undeserved concern of others, to live in grace. She grasped that being truly needy is the human condition. What separated her from Tricia was her inability to recognize her true state of need before God. She began to realize her own self-delusion.

As many Christians have learned, the "haves" really have far less than they think, the "have-nots" far more. Every three years a group of students from Whitworth College spend a semester in Central America on a study program. These students come largely from middle-class backgrounds. They are usually horrified by the poverty and suffering they see, and they become more aware of their own material wealth. But they learn something else too. They discover their own spiritual poverty as they witness the spiritual depth of many Christians in Latin America. As these students become the recipients of Latin hospitality, kindness and generosity, they begin to recognize the depth of their own greed and selfishness. They return to the United States with a very different idea of what constitutes true wealth and spirituality.

Organization

I served for two years on the board of directors for the Spokane affiliate of Habitat for Humanity. We had little trouble recruiting volunteers to donate time and materials for our building projects. People welcomed the opportunity to do hands-on work. We had difficulty, however, persuading people to serve on the board. They were wary of taking ownership for the ultimate success of the ministry, cautious about making an open-ended commitment and suspicious of institutionalized forms of service. To many people service means doing a concrete activity—pounding nails, cooking meals, visiting the sick, becoming a big brother. They do not realize that these expressions of direct and personal service require an organization that sets it up, administers the program, raises the money and provides the training.

Americans are suspicious of institutions, and with good reason. Bureaucracies often become bloated and self-serving, consume enormous amounts of money and time to perpetuate themselves, and lose their original sense of purpose. They become an obstacle to service instead of a channel for service. Many service organizations—private and Christian as well as public and secular—that were started with the best of intentions have become the worst offenders. They waste money, time and energy to keep themselves alive and accomplish less and less of the purpose for which they were created. Reports of scandals only undermine the confidence the American people have in these institutions. Fraud, waste, greed and mismanagement in these organizations disillusion the very people who are most willing to help.

Still, some needs are so massive and complex that person-to-person ministry is not enough. Sometimes potential givers are too far removed from needy recipients, as in the case of the wealth of Americans and the poverty of Indians, and a relief organization is therefore necessary to bring the two worlds together. Sometimes the needs are so complex that an organization is necessary to break the needs down into manageable parts. Sometimes the resources required are so extensive that an organization is necessary to manage and distribute those resources so that they have the most impact. How often are we frustrated by reports of shipments of food that rot because the relief effort lacked an efficient organization to get the food to the people who needed it? How often are we angered by stories of homeless people who are willing to work hard to help rehab a home if they would only be given an opportunity?

However prone to corruption, organizations are necessary if Christians want to serve on a massive scale. Mechanisms are needed to channel resources from those who have to those who have not. Committees are needed to begin and to oversee vital ministries, whether local or international. Bureaucracies are needed to manage money, materials and people. What we need are better management, expertise and commitment, whether in a committee organizing service projects for a local church or in a large and sophisticated bureaucracy.

Christians in America have many good organizations from which to choose. Though my knowledge and experience are limited, I believe that organizations like World Vision, Compassion International, Prison Fellowship and Habitat for Humanity do a commendable job of matching resources to needs. Their overhead is low, their staff members are dedicated, their vision has remained true. They have made it possible for millions of people to do their small part in serving Christ around the world. We need more organizations like them.

Such organizations will win support if they remain true to their original purpose, stay as streamlined as possible, resist becoming top-heavy, attract broad leadership and representation (women as well as men, people of color as well as European Americans, poor as well as rich, ordinary people as well as well-known people), and require their leadership to get involved in practical service rather than remain sequestered in the safety of board rooms.

The Servant as Paid Professional

Organizations require people to run them. Many of these people are paid professionals. The necessity of using professionals in service organizations exposes us to a problem that clergy have always had to face: how should we view service if it is our profession?

When I was a pastor of a church I never really succeeded in distinguishing between my Christian duty and my professional responsibility. I was unsure of where the one stopped and the other started, how to draw the line between when I was doing my job and when I was simply being an ordinary Christian. A handful of members from the church exacerbated the problem by suggesting that since I was a "paid" Christian, I was always on duty as pastor, always required to play the role of professional minister.

The growth of service-oriented ministries over the past few years has created a similar problem for many others. I suppose that all Christians face the problem in that all Christians ought to see their vocation as a form of service to Christ and must therefore make some kind of distinction between service to Christ on the job and service to Christ as a volunteer at church. That is true whether one is a plumber, banker, business owner, public-school teacher or fireman. But the people who work directly for Christian organizations—church as well as parachurch—have the additional problem of working for an organization that most other people serve as Christian volunteers. They are paid to do what most people volunteer to do. Thus, in addition to regular clergy, other professionals like Christian counselors; business managers of churches and Christian organizations; choir directors; teachers, office workers and custodians at Christian schools and colleges; and nurses and physicians at clinics for the poor face a similar problem.

137

There is no easy solution. I believe, however, that professional "servants" should be paid well, protected from overwork and given adequate time off for rest and education. But they could help solve the problem by finding some form of voluntary service outside of their formal job that allows them to live like most other Christians, who must divide their time between job and Christian service. Thus clergy, for example, could volunteer to work at a rescue mission one Friday night a month, business managers could volunteer for child care in the church's nursery a few times a year, Christian counselors could volunteer to prepare meals for the elderly poor occasionally. This voluntary work might even motivate them to do their job better, once they saw from the volunteer's side how important their job is. It might also show how demanding it is to be a serious Christian for people whose jobs and Christian service appear to operate in completely separate spheres.

Should Strings Be Attached?
The modern welfare society embodies a model of service that departs radically from earlier models. Welfare gives a handout to people in need; it does not enable them to overcome that need. It tends, therefore, to keep people in that same state of need. It perpetuates the problem it is supposed to solve.

Service used to come with strings attached. People who needed help were required to work for it. As they received help, they learned to help themselves. The needy thus washed dishes, chopped wood, gleaned fields. They contributed to their own release and redemption. There was no free lunch, in other words. People in need still had to contribute something for the help they received.

The gospel is not a message about self-help but about unmerited grace. Still, the gospel itself tells us to work out our own salvation with fear and trembling, even as it assures us that God is working in us. Self-help is good because it makes us partners with God. We can't earn our salvation. But we can grow up into it and allow God to transform us by it. However needy, people still have to realize that they are responsible before God, bearers of God's image, and charged to use what God has given them to live as good stewards.

Habitat for Humanity is only one of many ministries that come with strings attached. As I mentioned before, the people accepted into the program must put in five hundred hours of "sweat equity" before they can move into their home. This Habitat philosophy is based on the gleaning principle of the Old Testament. In that system landowners were mandated to leave some of the grain in the fields after harvest; then the poor had to go out and gather it themselves.

Other programs follow a similar philosophy. I know of churches that run programs to teach reading, to help people find jobs, to support single parents, to offer child care, to run clinics. All come with strings attached. Those strings announce that the goal of service is to help people function as productive disciples. It weans them from dependency and forces them to take responsibility for their lives.

Still, it is inevitable that our service will fall short of what we intended and hoped for. People are people. They don't always measure up to what we want them to be. They don't always turn out the way we had hoped. The results of service are usually mixed. Servants should beware of expectations and avoid making the needy feel indebted. However much they receive, the needy will not always show gratitude to those who helped them. They might not even change for the better. They might continue to drink or live in poverty or abuse their children or collect unemployment or fail to pay their bills or complain incessantly about how difficult life is.

It all comes down to motives. In our service we must remember that the needy don't owe us anything, and it is not right to make them think that they do. We serve for their sake, not our own. We serve to obey God, not to get them to obey us. As Peter said to me about his years with the Mennonite Central Committee, "Service is love for our neighbors. We serve because it is right. We serve because we are being made new in Christ. We serve because it is who we are and we cannot do otherwise."

8

ENCOURAGE ONE ANOTHER

A society can survive only if a high percentage of its citizens live responsibly and fulfill the duties of citizenship, without threat of punishment or coercion. Once that high percentage begins to drop, social order comes to rely solely on the stick and the carrot. Resources are diverted to force or lure people into obeying the laws and doing their duty. New laws have to be passed, the police force grows, courts are overwhelmed with cases, jails are overcrowded. Soon the society collapses because it could no longer rely on the majority of its citizens to abide by the law and do their duty simply because it is the right thing to do.

Societies can survive only if we can assume that most people will live responsibly, that most parents will raise their children well, that dentists will fix our teeth and doctors will diagnose our sicknesses and prescribe the right treatment for them, that salespeople will tell us the truth, that mechanics will know how to fix our automobile engines, that teachers know their subject matter and how to teach it.

Like secular society, the church assumes that most of its members will live responsibly, fulfilling the basic requirements of discipleship. Some church members are going to be hit-or-miss, here one Sunday and gone the next, unwilling to volunteer for service because they're too busy, frequently late to meetings (if they show up at all), inclined to jump from one church to another every two or three years. The church exists for them, too, as Jesus demonstrated in his ministry. But it is able to exist for them only if most of its members function dependably, showing up week in and week out to teach Sunday school, bake cookies, rock crying babies in the nursery, run the sound system, sing in the choir, pay their tithes, show up at committee meetings, type the newsletter and visit shut-ins. The church needs ordinary, faithful people like that to survive. We rarely realize how dependent the church is on such ordinary people until they are gone.

Encouragement is the mutuality command that meets the needs of these faithful people. Encouragement is to people in the church what maintenance is to trucks and washing machines. We service our vehicles and household appliances to keep them running for a long time. Toyota trucks may drive for 300,000 miles, but only if we change the oil every 3,000 miles. Maytags run well for years if we take care of them properly. Things like engines require maintenance if we want them to keep going. Their performance depends on both the quality of the product and the quality of our care. Likewise, we encourage people to help them function as disciples over the long haul. Encouragement helps ordinary Christians to keep going. It is the maintenance ministry of the church.

One Truth, Many Angles

The New Testament uses one basic word to describe the many aspects of encouragement. The Greek word translated "to encourage" can also be translated "to exhort" and "to comfort," depending on the context. Other expressions, like "to build up," convey a similar meaning. All stress the need to help fellow believers to persist in faith, to keep going as disciples. If believers flag in zeal and their desire for godliness wanes, we exhort them. If they struggle with a problem and stumble in their walk with God, we build them up. If they face loss and disappointment, we comfort them. There are many angles to this command, because there are many ways our spiritual engines wear down. But the truth is one. We need encouragement when we're discouraged. We need maintenance to keep going.

As I mentioned before, I teach an adult Sunday-school class at my church. There are many encouraging people in that class who invite me for coffee, send me notes, cheer me on, affirm me for my teaching. But one person stands out. Charlotte is an eighty-four-year-old widow. She emotes grace and quiet and sophistication. She reads widely, entertains elegantly and communicates warmly with everyone she meets. She embodies the spirit of this command. Never have I met someone who encourages people as naturally, sincerely and extravagantly as does Charlotte. She cares about many people. But she is especially sensitive to ordinary people in the church who do their duty without fanfare and complaint. She has devoted her life to keeping them going.

Charlotte is extraordinarily effective. In a note she received from a widow friend of hers who is trying to raise four young children—a note that she kindly let me read—she received some indication of how her encouragement affects people who are trying to carry on. "It is important to me," the note read,

> for you to know that your supportive comments about my family meant a great deal to me. At this point in my life, my children consume most of my time and energy and, of course, my money! Expensive little people they are! I'm trying very hard to give them the very best start I can, and when you notice it, it means that, just maybe, I'm on the right track.

I asked Charlotte to tell me the secret of her ministry, what made her such an encouraging person. She began by telling me the story of her family background. When she was still young her father invested in a farm, and the investment went bad. Though he worked hard, he never escaped the consequences of that one bad decision. "I can still see his suffering and regret," she said to me. "It lasted his whole life. That left a strong impression on me." She had her own disappointments along the way too. For example, she never had children, though she wanted them desperately. She never attended college, though she had the intelligence and desire to. She endured years of financial difficulty. Her own disappointments, however, did not make her self-pitying, as they often do to people; instead, they made her sensitive to other people and to the struggles they face. She turned outward rather than inward. She had to endure her own troubles, often with very little encouragement from others. She does not want other people to survive as she had to, working hard without receiving much support. She wants now to recognize and affirm people for their hard work and faithfulness when it takes everything they have just to keep going.

Charlotte is also grateful for and feels indebted to the faithful service of others. She has a sense of wonder when she considers what others contribute to her life—a moving anthem on a Sunday morning, a polished sermon, a good Sunday-school lesson, a reception after worship that has plenty of coffee, punch and cookies. She appreciates the average people who do their jobs without receiving much attention for it. She is aware of how much she gains from them.

She expresses her gratitude to them and affirms them for their service. She encourages them to keep going. She speaks directly to them, often while holding their hand; she writes them notes; she calls them on the phone and invites them over for coffee. She speaks specifically about their ministry to her. "I appreciated so much your selection of the anthem this morning. It fit perfectly into the worship service." "You sang with such a peaceful countenance." "Your children look like they are doing so well right now. You're doing an excellent job of raising them." "You have used your time and talents so wisely in serving other people." "Thank you so much for helping out in this project. I don't know what we would do without people like you who volunteer for this kind of work." "Your Sunday-school lesson made that story so applicable to my life." She makes me want to teach better, raise my kids better, live for Christ better. Charlotte keeps me going. She keeps lots of people going.

Occasions for Encouragement

People like Charlotte nudge ordinary Christians along the path of discipleship. She helps faithful people to do their jobs and fulfill their callings in life. She knows that people need and ought to be told that they are doing well, honoring God, following his will. She believes that all Christians—especially the many faithful ones who are most easily overlooked—need that kind of encouragement.

We need encouragement all the more when we find it most difficult to persevere. We need encouragement, for example, to continue practicing spiritual disciplines when we're distracted, busy and under pressure. The apostle Paul was aware of this need, so he encouraged believers to pray faithfully, set their minds on spiritual reality, train themselves in godliness: "Therefore, my beloved, just as you have always obeyed me, not only in my presence, but much more now in my absence, work out your own salvation with fear and trembling; for it is God who is at work in you, enabling you both to will and to work for his good pleasure" (Phil 2:12-13).

In another letter he wrote, "Therefore, my beloved, be steadfast, immovable, always excelling in the work of the Lord, because you know that in the Lord your labor is not in vain" (1 Cor 15:58). The practice of spiritual discipline puts us into postures to receive the grace and love of God. Paul encouraged his fellow believers to keep up the disciplines. "Train yourself in godliness," he wrote. We too should encourage one another to pray, study, meditate, worship and seek the face of God. If we are attentive to this need for encouragement, we will find countless opportunities to meet it, whether through personal example, telephone calls, notes or goal-setting at a Bible study.

Sometimes we need encouragement to remain steady in difficult circumstances, such as we face in opposition and persecution, in rejection and failure. The hostages held in Beirut needed encouagement from each other to keep going when everything in their world screamed darkness and death. *Newsweek* reported on what the hostages did to support each other during their terrible ordeal.

They sustained one another. After beatings, John McCarthy would mimic his tormentors "with a precision and zaniness that reduced their sometimes brutality to insignificance," said his former cellmate Brian Keenan. Over dominoes in their six-foot-by-six-foot cell, McCarthy imitated Sigmund Freud and Peter Sellers. Six years ago U.S. hostages formed "The Church of the Locked Door" and began holding twice-daily services. Spirited arguments and thousands of push-ups have helped keep up their minds and bodies. When they could, most read voraciously.

Each man tutored the others in his own profession, according to a newly published memoir by former U.S. hostage David Jacobsen. His group of cellmates embarked on joint projects, including a satirical "Hostage Cookbook" that includes a dish called "Hint of Chicken"—rice that a chicken has walked across, leaving behind its droppings. They sang to one another, recited poetry, talked of their travels. Still, many of the 21 Western hostages held for extended periods struggled with black despair, especially after their captors promised to free them, then reneged. The others would comfort them. "Choose joy," McCarthy would say. "We had to work very hard between us to keep our spirits up, to keep ourselves happy, determined to carry on," McCarthy said. "We have done that very well, I think."[1]

Their circumstances were unusally distressing. Yet many people face hardships that, though less difficult, still press them to the breaking point. I have friends who work in jobs where the atmosphere is so rabidly secular that it grinds down their spiritual zeal and confidence. Students at secular colleges take courses from professors who delight in expressing cynicism and hostility toward the Christian faith. Christian parents raise their children in neighborhoods where the pervasive system of values undermines the Christian convictions that they want to nurture in their children. Dedicated church workers try to move their church toward greater biblical fidelity, only to face opposition at every turn. Many quiet Christians face the daily torment of problems that seem unconquerable.

All of us face the pressure of living in a fallen world that erodes faith and squelches spiritual enthusiasm. It wins more than we would like. Survival under such conditions seems victory enough.

Encouragement helps us to do more than survive. It keeps us going and growing, struggling and resisting, so that, as J. B. Phillips puts it in his translation of Romans 12:2, we do not let the world squeeze us into its mold. Encouragement enables us to stand strong and true and stable, in spite of the pressures we face.

We also need encouragement to develop Christlike character and convictions, to grow daily in the grace of God. Encouragement helps us to be conformed to the image of Christ, who shows us what we will someday become. Hebrews 12:1-2 tells us to keep running the race set before us, following Christ, who for the joy set before him endured pain and suffering until he reached the prize.

Personal Example

The best way to encourage people to grow in grace is to grow in grace ourselves and thus set an example of faith, as Jesus himself did. Paul exhorted Timothy to set believers an example of faith and purity and righteous living. It is tough to be Christian in the modern world. We bump into so many unpleasant and unhappy people—crabby, angry, ungrateful, selfish—who make us feel almost obsolete, as if we were curious vestiges of the medieval world, because we want to be loving, kind, grateful and giving. Avoiding the bad is only half of the battle. We must also embrace the good. That is the business of developing character. The best way to overcome ingratitude is by becoming grateful. The best way to overcome selfishness is by serving needy people. One person of Christlike character can set the pace for everyone. One person can start a chain reaction in which a growing number of people desire God and godliness.

Setting an example requires that we consider the impact of our actions and attitudes on other people. Don't be a stumbling block, Paul warned in Romans 14. We must use freedom to build up, not tear down. We need to weigh what we eat, where we go for entertainment, how we talk, what we give our time to—all according to its potential influence on fellow believers. If it trips them up, however justified we are in doing it, we should refrain for the sake of our Christian friends. Love builds up; love removes stumbling blocks to the growth of other Christians. (See also 1 Cor 8—10.)

Conversation has peculiar power to tear down or to build up, depending on its subject and tone. I work in an academic environment that values quickness, cleverness and humor. Colleagues and students alike win points by showing their superiority in repartee. But too often our conversations put down, intimidate and embarrass. James says that the tongue holds great power. We had best wield that power wisely. Paul cautioned believers to refrain from letting evil talk and levity come out of the mouth. Good encouragers do not put people on the defensive. They speak with grace and peace. Their conversation creates an atmosphere of kindness and love rather than of competition and cleverness.

Finally, we need encouragement to stay true when we are tempted to make small and easy compromises. Turning the steering wheel of a car only one degree to the left or to the right will eventually, given enough open space, turn that car completely around so that it is headed in the opposite direction. We need nudging, challenge, exhortation—all expressions of encouragement—when we gradually wander off course. Encouragement draws the best out of people. "Let's not go to that movie tonight. I read reviews of it yesterday that made me wonder if it's the kind of movie Christians ought to see." Or: "Let's stop the insults for a while. I'm defensive and don't feel free to let my guard down." Or: "You didn't seem prepared tonight. That's unusual for you. Is everything all right?"

I received an anonymous letter a few weeks ago, written by someone who had attended a conference that I helped to organize. He said that he appreciated my leadership and organization. "It was one of the best conferences I've been to," he wrote. "But," he added, "I think that your humor approached being base. It was funny to most, offensive to a few.

I believe that the opinions of those few matter." In his mind, that kind of record was not worth it. His exhortation nudged me to keep learning how to be a more gracious leader.

Perhaps the church would have fewer major problems if it were more attentive to the small ones. Encouragement keeps people on course before they wander too far off course. It provides positive reinforcement rather than negative criticism. Diversity becomes divisive when we fail to stay on the common course of ordinary and healthy Christian discipleship. Nudges in the right direction work far better than major course corrections.

Encouragement as an Art

I believe that encouragement is a medium that provides opportunity for artistic expression. Of all the commands, this one calls for careful attention to detail, elegance of style, beauty and sophistication. If done well, encouragement as an art can make people feel like they are the most extraordinary people in the world.

Writing letters is one such artistic medium for encouragement. Lovers labor for hours to write letters that communicate the deep respect, affection and longing that they feel for each other. They ponder every word, strive to give the right nuance in every sentence, share their hearts by polishing their prose.

The telephone has replaced the letter as the major medium of communication between friends, colleagues and lovers. Of course something is gained in the replacement. Telephone conversations are more spontaneous and immediate. They provide the opportunity for an exchange of ideas and feelings, because the telephone allows for two-way conversation. But something is lost too. Unlike the telephone, letters pay attention to the medium of communication—the words themselves—thus allowing for rich and meaningful expression. People can take hours to write them or read them. They can be high expressions of creativity, something that telephone conversations rarely are—if ever.

I received perhaps three thousand cards and letters after the accident.

Some of them conveyed profound sentiments and insights. They were works of art, masterpieces of writing. One friend wrote at length and with deep feeling about his own divorce. Another explored the Puritan view of suffering and quoted extensively from the journal of a Puritan who had lost his wife of ten years. These letters encouraged me. I read them and reread them. I pondered every word. The people who wrote them took their time. They gave extravagantly of themselves to communicate their sympathy.

In my mind there is no better medium for encouraging fellow Christians than letter writing. Words have power. They convey insight and feeling. Words can lift the spirit. Words on a page work themselves in the memory and the heart. What would we do without the words of the Bible? What would we do without letters of encouragement to keep us going?

Another artistic medium for encouragement is entertaining. I have heard people make a distinction between hospitality and entertaining, as if the former embodied Christian humility and the latter secular sophistication. Perhaps the distinction is fair. Our homes should be open to people when they are dirty as well as clean, when the dinner fare is leftovers rather than filet mignon, when toys are scattered everywhere instead of stacked neatly in the closet. Hospitality at its best is unpretentious and natural. The home becomes a livable space that anyone can enter and where anyone can feel immediately comfortable.

Still, on some occasions entertaining is appropriate. The ministry of encouragement fits in such a category, because entertaining treats people as if they were honored and special guests. I was invited recently to the home of friends and fellow members of my home church. They are both professional psychologists whose children have grown and left the home. They live in a comfortable house in an upper-middle-class neighborhood in Spokane. As the wife said to me in her invitation, she wanted me to join the two of them for an elegant dinner and an evening of conversation. My evening with them was wonderful. I felt like royalty. That evening encouraged me.

Good food, carefully prepared and served in the right setting and in the right way, has the power to bring people together. The film *Babette's Feast* tells the story of two sisters who, though beautiful and talented, choose to remain single to serve their father and his small church. After his death they take in a fugitive from France, Babette, who works as their housemaid and cook. To show her gratitude, she spends her entire life savings on one dinner, to which she invites the sisters and the members of their small church. The meal becomes a sacramental event. Divisions are healed, relationships restored, past misdeeds forgiven. Every person sitting around the table receives the grace of God. The lavish meal serves as the medium of that grace because it is far beyond what they expect, deserve and understand.

One final artistic medium for encouragement is humor. Humor can be base, cutting and cruel, as we have witnessed many times, I am sure. Yet humor in the right setting can build people up too. It can communicate affection, gratitude, respect and indebtedness. A colleague and friend of mine in the psychology department at the college once put an announcement in the bulletin for the students in his experimental class. It said, "Students have until the last day of exams to pick up their brains. After that they will be donated to the religion department, which needs brains desperately." He would only dare to mention a department that included members he knew well and respected enough to tease. He really believes that the religion department is perhaps the best department on campus. That is why he dared to put in that announcement. It was a subtle—and humorous way—of encouraging us.

Even "roasts," as they are called, can make people feel significant. The assumption behind a roast is that the honored guest—the recipient of the insults—is important enough to the institution or group to merit that kind of attention. Ironically, it is the ultimate compliment for someone to be given a roast. Roasts are reserved for those few who have endeared themselves to the many, who have served well over the long haul, who have carved out such a distinctive place for themselves that they have become irreplaceable.

The humor at a roast is intended to make fun of the honored guest's idiosyncrasies. It exaggerates faults, pokes at odd habits, draws attention to peculiarities. It celebrates what makes that person unique and valuable. We aim this kind of humor only at those who can take it, at our friends, at those who have earned the right to receive it. Such humor encourages. It keeps people going by telling them how significant they have been and still are to everyone.

Encouragement in the Life of the Church

As I said earlier, Charlotte is one individual who has devoted her life to encouragement. Churches can devote themselves to encouragement too. They can pursue a course of action that will encourage a whole congregation to keep going. That requires churches to identify and honor the quiet, faithful majority of people who help the church to fulfill its mission in the community and in the world. Too often this silent majority of people are assumed, used and neglected, while a disproportionate amount of energy and attention is given to a few high-profile people, whether they be the rich, famous, opinionated, angry or needy.

I know of such encouraging churches. One such church calls, commissions and supports people who function as encouragers for the congregation. Another church takes seriously Paul's injunction that Christians should "outdo one another in showing honor." That church looks for any excuse to honor members for faithful service, whether they be custodians, nursery attendants, wedding hostesses, youth sponsors or pastors. Many churches encourage members by commissioning them before they begin service in, say, teaching Sunday school, leading small groups or coordinating service projects. My home church, for example, plans two banquets every spring, one for primary and secondary Sunday-school teachers, another for adult teachers. At the adult banquet members of the Christian education commission express their gratitude to the teachers for their past year of service.

It takes a great deal of energy to keep a church going. Much of that energy must come from paid staff who go beyond the call of duty and from volunteers who do their duty without any financial support at all. Encouragement affirms these dedicated people for their hard work, makes their contributions known to the whole congregation and cheers them on as they try to live out their commitment to Christ at home and church, in the neighborhood and the world.

Encouraging churches don't wait for faithful people to burn out or drop out before they pay attention to them. They don't take them for granted. They help them to keep going.

Encouragement in Friendships

I believe that the best setting for encouragement is personal friendships. Friends above all have the ability and opportunity to keep each other going. The book of Samuel tells the story of the friendship between Jonathan and David. Jonathan kept David going when David, driven into the wilderness as a fugitive, needed to be propped up. The Bible says that Jonathan "strengthened David in the Lord."

I know of a modern Jonathan-and-David kind of friendship. I first met Stan and Peter when they were freshmen at the college that I served as chaplain. Stan was a bright student and cocky athlete who came to college to study, compete in sports and party. In his first football game as a freshman he made a spectacular seventy-yard run. Stan was used to friends who maneuvered for power, destroyed others with cutting comments and elevated themselves by putting others down. He expected that they would somehow mock or disparage his first college football success, which they did. Peter, however, was different. He left a simple note on Stan's door. It read, "Great job, Stan. Nice run!" That was it. As Stan said to me, "From that day on I realized that Peter had a unique gift of building others up, rather than tearing them down. He could encourage others without it being a threat to himself."

They soon became fast friends, and still are to this day, some fifteen years later. They started to share a room together in the middle of their freshman year. They learned to be honest without being brutal, supportive without being indulgent. They kept each other on course. Peter, for example, once told Stan, who was going through a period of vocational indecision, to begin a time of daily prayer and devotion. As Stan said, this "pushed me to become what God wanted me to be. He understood that God does not call us fundamentally to do something, but rather to be someone. He always encouraged me to persevere in my faith and continue to obey God's commands."

Out of their deep friendship they decided to begin a ministry to the students on their wing in the residence hall. "Guys," Stan said, "would wander into our room just to talk. We would listen primarily, but doors were opened to share the joy that we have in Christ as well. We began to work as a team. As Peter would talk, I would pray silently; as I would talk, Peter would pray. We had a common cause. We were both working to further the kingdom of God. We were bound together in Christ to serve God's purpose, not our own. This was a very big step in our friendship." The next year they started Bible studies with their friends and began to introduce them to the Christian faith. Those friends in turn began similar ministries.

Their deep commitment to each other caused them to want the best for each other. They tried to help each other to hate sin, not savor it. Stan observed:

I did not delight in his mistakes, nor did he delight in mine. To see Peter fall was very painful for me. It was not a joke or something to kid him about in the future. Also, we worked together to strive for purity. It is very easy to lose your convictions when you are with friends in order to win acceptance. But Peter and I tried to help each other maintain our faith. We attempted not to compromise on what others may have considered little, insignificant things. For example, both Peter and I returned hospital scrubs that we had pilfered in the past. Purity in all things was the goal, not always achieved to be sure. But still the goal.

They grew to trust each other almost completely. "I began to trust Peter's judgment about my character flaws," Stan told me. "I knew that he had my best interest in mind. I felt like my spiritual growth was as

153

important to him as his own. He corrected me because he loved me, not because I was wrong and he was right."

They moved to different regions of the country after graduating from college. For many years now they have been able to see each other only twice a year, if that. But they talk on the phone once a week and have continued to deepen the friendship.

The commitment to each other's spiritual vitality remains. It allows us to move beyond superficial conversation. I believe God continues to shape and mold the vision of godliness he began in us in college. Some would say what we had during our years in college was only so much youthful idealism, and that it will fade as the realities of daily life overtake us. But I'm confident that what appeared to be idealism is really a hope in Jesus Christ for this world.

I can testify to the unusual depth of their friendship. Still, I am not convinced that it has to be as unusual as it appears to be. Their depth can be anyone's if we are willing to make the same basic commitment that they have made. The center of their friendship is Jesus Christ. They want to keep each other going and growing in faith. They provide each other with needed maintenance so that faith, hope and love do not wane. They have learned to encourage each other. If they can do it, so can the rest of us.

PART 3

CRISIS COMMANDS

9

COMFORT
ONE ANOTHER

Sooner or later every human being loses someone or something important. That is one of the inevitabilities of life that no one, however powerful, can avoid. Every human being suffers loss, faces disappointment and feels pain. Every human being is forced to reconsider and readjust expectations—a long and healthy life, a happy marriage, a successful career—that unfavorable circumstances dash to the ground. Grief is a school every human being must enter.

The New Testament uses one word in particular to describe the experience of loss: *affliction*. It connotes the circumstances—trouble, distress, difficulty, suffering—that press us down, squash us underfoot and hem us in, as if we were forced, like a baby being born, to pass through a channel that is not big enough for convenient and easy passage. According to the Bible, these afflictions can be both external and internal. External afflictions are outside forces such as political oppression, the scourge of war, exile, mortal danger, slavery, imprisonment, sickness, death and persecution, which gets special attention in the Bible because of the experience of the first Christians. Internal afflictions are the distress, anxiety and fear that accompany such painful experiences. The Bible teaches that affliction is inescapable, especially for Christians, who not only suffer loss like the rest of humanity but also struggle to reconcile their suffering with the sovereignty of God. Affliction symbolizes the reign of evil and death in the world. It forces a decision: to accept our mortality as final and fall into despair or to believe that there is more to life than meets the eye and that affliction, expecially the affliction of persecution, will eventually give way to glory.

Clearly the apostle Paul knew something about affliction. In his second letter to the Corinthians he describes his many sufferings. He lists labors, imprisonments, beatings, whippings, dangers, deprivations, hardships and miseries. He also had to endure internal struggles. "And, besides other things, I am under daily pressure because of my anxiety for all the churches. Who is weak, and I am not weak? Who is made to stumble, and I am not indignant?" (2 Cor 11:23-29). Even Paul's mature faith did not spare him from experiencing suffering. If anything, his faith brought on the suffering.

Facing the Grim Reaper

Modern culture has multiplied the occasions for grief and compounded the problem of grief. Even the most familiar form of grief—death of a loved one—is vastly more complex than it used to be. And other forms of grief—mobility, divorce, abuse, long-term sickness, loss of job, rejection—have exploded on the scene. Never before have people needed so much comfort. Never before has comfort been more difficult to give.

The grief that comes from loss of a loved one is bad enough. Rarely does it happen that an elderly person dies a timely and peaceful death and leaves behind a family that is sad for the loss but grateful for the memories. My uncle John died at home in his sleep when he was in his eighties. His wife and son grieved but celebrated the fifty-plus years they'd had together. His kind of death is the exception these days, even for an elderly person. More often than not people do not die at home but in hospitals, where they are engulfed by technology that makes their life—and death—appear antiseptic, cold, impersonal. Then they are whisked away and made to look "peaceful" and "nice" in the casket. So death itself, even when we expect it to happen, has become unfamiliar, distant and artificial to us. And that is under the best of circumstances.

The circumstances of life of course are not always at their best. Death causes grief and leaves a vacuum of loss, however expected and natural. A simple death is bad enough in itself. A simple grief is still grief and must be endured. Yet death is rarely a simple affair; it so seldom happens when and how we expect it to happen. It usually finds us unprepared and ends up being ugly and messy.

Death can leave us with overwhelming responsibilities. Tragic death in particular often does that. Shortly after moving to Chicago, we learned that a backyard neighbor had lost his twenty-nine-year-old wife by a bizarre heart attack; he was left with three small children. Five years later I found myself in similar circumstances after I lost my mother, wife and daughter in a drunken-driving accident. The unexpected loss plunged me into catastrophic grief. But the loss itself was not the only problem I faced. I also inherited the new and pressing responsibility of being the sole parent of three young children who had their own grief to work through. I had to shop, cook, clean, pay bills, repair broken household items, visit schools, drive to activities, keep the master schedule—all without the aid of spouse or family. I discovered that busyness and exhaustion threatened to sabotage my grief by preventing me from facing the terrible darkness that my loss thrust on me. As we shall observe, my experience is not as unusual as it seems. Literally millions of single parents must deal with the same problem daily.

Death can also leave us with guilt. The brokenness of relationships today has made grief a bitter experience. Guilt darkens our memory of the past. It fills us with regret for what we did and cannot now undo. "If only . . ." keeps ringing in our ears. Memories do not comfort; they only torment. We not only miss the loved one, we miss the chance to make right what we did so wrong. Guilt also makes the future seem even more foreboding than it already is. How can we press on, burdened, as we are, with the mistakes of the past? How can we redeem what has been permanently lost? How do we know that we will be able to do otherwise the next time around?

Other kinds of death lead to what mental health professionals call "disenfranchised grief." This kind of grief often goes unrecognized by the public. It remains hidden, sometimes a source of embarrassment, always a source of bitter pain. A miscarriage can lead to this kind of grief. So can the death of a distant but still significant friend or relative, the loss of a pet that functioned like a member of the family, and the loss of someone through suicide or AIDS. So can the loss of a "nontraditional" relationship like a live-in lover or a homosexual partner. Disenfranchised grief can be just as deep as any other kind, but it lacks the public empathy that makes grief legitimate.

The Many Faces of Grief

Death is perhaps the most catastrophic loss we can face. But it is certainly not the only loss. Modern culture has enlarged the range of potential losses we can experience and forced us to expand our understanding of grief. The most common by far is loss through divorce. Roughly 50 percent of the people who are being married today will get a divorce. Neither husband nor wife expects or plans to get a divorce when they vow before witnesses to be faithful to life's end. But life doesn't always lead to the end we had planned. Bliss easily turns into indifference or hostility. What begins with so much promise can end in immense pain. Divorce is a loss that leads to profound grief and leaves one bewildered, broken and disillusioned.

Take Sue Ellen. She met Matt on a blind date. He was studying to be a research scientist, she a nurse. He was a recent convert, she a lifelong Christian. After marriage their spiritual commitment cooled rapidly. She refused to take on the role of spiritual leader in the relationship, and he did not seem to be interested in filling the vacuum. Soon they dropped out of church altogether. Matt meanwhile became increasingly critical of Sue Ellen. She tried to teach him the meaning of love and to salvage the relationship by accommodating to his wishes, but the harder she tried, the more distant and sarcastic he became. His emotional inaccessibility and constant criticism undermined her sense of self-worth. She gained weight and plotted revenge. She also decided not to have children, since she refused to bring children into such an unhappy, tense and loveless relationship. That sacrifice only compounded her grief. Sue Ellen became so desperate that she even contemplated suicide. Finally Matt filed for divorce. Sue Ellen was free of him but not free of the regret, guilt, shame, confusion and brokenness that those years of marriage had caused.

Sue Ellen chose not to have children, so she was spared the pain of seeing them go through divorce. Not everyone is that fortunate. Recently I talked with a woman who divorced her husband to escape emotional and physical abuse. Her two young children were rescued from the unhappy and unhealthy home environment. But now they have to make sense of their traumatic past and make peace with their dad. They were delivered from one kind of suffering. Now they must endure another, the suffering that comes from living in a single-parent home that has limited financial resources.

Unfulfilled desire leads to loss. One out of twenty-five married couples in our country cannot have their own children. Many of them experience a quiet grief that few people understand. So do the many single men and women who want to marry but have never found a suitable spouse. Both groups may strive to change their circumstances but come up short. A close friend of mine, Rebeccah, lost her husband in a tragic accident over thirty years ago, leaving her with two young boys. She endured the terrible grief and rebuilt her life. But then she had to face another, unexpected loss. She began to realize that she might never remarry and thus never again experience the intimacy of marriage or find a father for her sons. The second loss was different from the first, but equally painful.

There are still other examples of death—the death of health, the death of friendship, the death of dreams, the death of an organization (like a church) to which we belong, the death of a business that we owned, the death of a job. All of us have experienced some of them; some of us many of them. We have survived, but not without profound hurt.

Then there are special kinds of losses more applicable to life in a pluralistic church. The departure of a popular pastor, the splitting of a once prominent church, denominational controversies that polarize and embitter factions within it, theological conflict that divides believers, and failed programs are just some of the many losses that can erode enthusiasm and commitment. They make it hard to stay true to a church body that seems to have too many unsolvable problems.

Yet grief of whatever kind can serve as a catalyst to unite a pluralistic church into a comforting and healing community of broken people. My own experience has shown me that the body of Christ is a community of suffering. Many Christians, however different from us, live with pain similar to ours. I have met many people who have responded to my tragedy by telling me their own stories of suffering. These stories have created a special bond between us, though previous to that we appeared to have little in common. For example, several months after the accident a coach from the college approached me to express his sympathy, and we fell into a brief conversation. Suddenly he said that when he was a teenager he lost his younger brother in a drowning accident for which he was responsible. Though the tragedy happened thirty-five years ago, he still wept as he retold the experience. The pain was that fresh.

I am convinced that we have allowed differences in the church to divide us because we have neglected to let our common experience of suffering unite us. The gospel speaks to the broken, the weak, the lost, the lonely. It speaks to those who have suffered loss. It speaks to all of us.

A Willingness to Be Changed

Every person's grief is different. Grief is a solitary journey; no two people go through it the same way. What takes years for one person may take months for another. What creates guilt in one may cause resentment in another. What brings tears to one person's eyes may engender blank stares in another's eyes.

Yet I have observed that, however unusual the grief, the comfort that the grieving desire is relatively uniform. It provides a special opportunity for believers to show love—to strangers as well as friends, to opponents as well as allies. People suffering loss are temporarily immobilized by it, and even when they begin to function again, they find it impossible to return to the life that they lived before the loss occurred. The world as they knew it stops revolving. They enter a different dimension of time that distorts their understanding of the past and future. An event in the distant past, like a marriage ceremony or the birth of a baby, seems as if it happened yesterday, while an event that happened just a month ago seems as if it occurred in another century. Everything changes; nothing remains the same. The world becomes a strange place, and they feel like strangers in it.

Good comforters must be willing to be changed by the ones who need the comfort, however uncomfortable the situation, such as a person's dying of AIDS. Good comfort requires commitment, empathy, suffering and ultimately change. Comforters must be prepared to let the pain of another become their own pain and so let it transform them. That decision will never leave them the same. Their own world will be permanently altered by the presence of one who suffers. It will mark the end of detachment and superficiality. It will prevent them from ever thinking again that the world is a nice place, full of nice people and nice experiences.

Time and again I have heard the same comment from my closest friends: "You have no idea, Jerry, how much your experience has changed us." They talk about the impact of my tragedy on their marriage, their children, their view of life, their schedules, their quest for meaning, their conversations late into the night. They have been changed, as they say, because they chose to get involved. They allowed my suffering to become theirs. They refused to give me a week or a month and then return to the same life they had before. Since life cannot continue to be the same for me, they decided that it won't be the same for them either.

I have heard many similar stories from others who were willing to get involved, whether it was with Christian friends going through divorce, new church members working through their abusive background or declared homosexuals who have lost family and jobs. Good comforters make room in their lives for broken people. They cook an additional meal every week for someone else; they open their home to a motherless child; they help a friend find another job; they listen week after week, month after month, even year after year to the same stories, the same complaints, the same problems; they visit shut-ins after everyone else has stopped; they set another place at the table for Sunday dinner; they provide support to a friend going through divorce. Comfort demands sacrificial change. If it is safe and convenient, if it is offered on one's own terms, it isn't comfort.

The Enormity of Grief

Good comforters encourage the grieving to face the enormity of their loss. People who have lost someone or something special will bear witness to the major impact that the loss has had on their life. It changes everything. Loss poses a major threat to what we have come to expect out of life. Peter Berger uses the term *anomie*—which means literally "against order" or "disorder"—to describe the effects of loss. Suddenly we find ourselves living in a capricious world without safe boundaries and givens. We are pushed to the margins of life, as if, standing on the edge of a cliff that plunges into absolute oblivion, we felt the ground beneath our feet begin to shake and realized that we were going to fall into the horrible abyss below. Loss creates uncertainty, anxiety, fear, bewilderment. It strikes terror in the soul. It is anarchic.

I liken loss to amputation—not like the amputation of a limb, but more like the amputation of the self from the self. It is the amputation of the self as professional, if you have lost your job. Or the self as husband, if you have lost your spouse. Or the self as an energetic and productive person, if you have lost your good health. Or the self as prominent leader, if you have lost your office in the church. It is the loss of a self you once were and knew, the self you can no longer be. I still think of myself as a husband to Lynda, as a father to Diana Jane, as a son to my mother. But the people who defined me that way, who played the role opposite me as wife, daughter and mother, are no longer there. The self I once was cries out for them, like nerves still telling me that I have a leg or an arm, though only a stump remains.

Loss thus leads to a confusion of identity. We understand ourselves in large measure by the roles we play in society—husband or wife, parent or child, doctor or teacher. We find ourselves in a vertigo when these roles are changed or lost. "I used to be in sales until I lost my job," a woman says to a new acquaintance. *Until I lost my job.* The words blare in her ears as she says them. She is unemployed now. She isn't what she used to be, though she still thinks of herself that way. The same could be said of other phrases. "I am divorced." "We don't have any children." "I am terminally ill." "I lost my husband last year." These words imply loss of identity. They say that what we used to be we are no longer. It requires that we get to know ourselves all over again under very different terms. It means that we must discover a new kind of identity.

The loss of identity is only one aspect of the enormity of suffering that the grieving discover and must endure over time. Grief plunges those who have suffered loss into deep and terrible darkness. My own tragedy pushed me into a darkness from which I longed to escape. Shortly after the accident I dreamed that I was running west toward the sun, trying to catch what was gradually slipping away from me over the horizon. Suddenly I stopped and glanced with foreboding over my shoulder to the east and to the vast darkness that was closing in on me. I longed to keep running after the sun because I wanted to remain in the light, though I knew that it was futile. Then I realized that the quickest way to reach the sun and the light of day was to plunge into the darkness until I came to the sunrise.

Those who suffer loss must face that darkness. They must grieve. Good comforters allow them to grieve, however long and bitter the grief is, because they know that true grief leads to true healing. It is both bitter and redemptive. Grief is hard and long and exhausting. It is also creative and healing and powerful.

As I reflect on my own experience, my own capacity for pain has grown immeasurably. But so has my capacity for peace and joy. I have never felt more apathetic; I have never been so full of purpose. I have never been so tempted to hate; I have never felt such love. I have never felt so dead; I have never been more alive. I have learned that sorrow and joy, apathy and purpose, anger and love, death and life are not mutually exclusive but strangely complementary. Grief can enlarge the soul, if we are willing to face loss squarely and experience its full effects. That enlargement goes both ways, since both grievers and comforters can experience the deepening of faith and growth of character that accompanies loss.

Understanding

Those in grief welcome a visit if it comes without too many words, conversation if it comes without too much advice, initiative and invitation if they come without too much pressure to accept. Grievers do not like it when they are required to make conversation to put everyone else at ease. They do not welcome people who use their concern as a pretense to tell them what to do. Too much advice—and sometimes any advice at all—is needless and presumptuous. The people who are able to give advice—that is, those who have listened well before speaking or who have suffered a similar loss—usually feel least qualified to give it. As Sue Ellen told me about the people who comforted her after her divorce, "What comfort means to me is knowing that whoever I was talking with listened intently enough to understand what I was feeling. It is impossible to bring much comfort without knowing the situation. You can only know by listening. Understanding allows the comforter to give out more than superficial one-liners." She appreciated Christian friends in her church who offered advice only when she asked for it.

The people who were successful in giving me a real sense of inner peace amidst the turmoil were people who offered very little advice unless I requested it. They gave me a sense of control when things seemed out of control by having confidence in any decisions I had to make. At times I did ask my friends and family for advice, but in these situations I asked people who I knew would not be offended if I did not act on their advice.

Loss that involves a moral issue—a divorce, for example, or a job loss due to a deserved termination—often tempts would-be comforters in the church to make unsolicited, uninformed and unfair judgments. Sue Ellen found this form of comfort irritating, however well intentioned. Sometimes the judgment was directed toward her. "People who hurt me were folks who judged what I did in agreeing to a divorce when they were not aware at all of any details of the situation." At other times the judgment was directed toward her husband. "I was also not helped by the people who said hurtful things about my husband as a way of identifying and sympathizing with my bitter feelings. I had much anger and bitterness toward him, but deep within me was an amazing sense of loyalty." She realized that healing requires forgiveness. Her bitterness blocked that forgiveness for a time. The people who helped her did not take sides; they did not therefore pass judgment on her husband or on her but encouraged her to live in God's grace, find healing and eventually forgive her husband.

Practical Help

Those who have suffered loss need practical help. As I mentioned earlier in the chapter, my friend Rebeccah was so overwhelmed with the loss of her husband that she was incapable of carrying out many of the responsibilities that she had done before. She told me that the meals provided by friends and relatives saw her through the first month of devastation. A neighbor took care of her boys while she kept vigil at the hospital. A good friend helped her with her financial affairs. Her husband's boss spent time with her boys. Her pastor functioned as the hub of a complex communication network involving hospital, funeral home, church, community. He also stayed with her dying husband during the last twenty-four hours of his life and witnessed his death in the early morning hours.

Other people who have suffered loss told me about lawns mowed, leaves raked, meals provided, plumbing problems fixed, babysitting offered, transportation and hospitality made available. Good comforters realize that, though the world seems to stop for those who have suffered loss, it in fact keeps going and requires that everyone keep going with it. Loss does not keep the lawn from growing, stop the bills from coming, prevent the house from getting dirty. Responsibilities do not end. If anything, they may increase.

People in grief appreciate expressions of kindness and sympathy. They remember the number of people at the funeral. They count the cards. They treasure the personal notes that bring to mind old memories, express appreciation and offer comfort instead of advice. I was comforted by the people who sent long letters months after the accident, and especially by a close friend who wrote me fortnightly for the first year, after most people seemed to have forgotten. Other friends, a couple whom Lynda and I had known for years, called me every Sunday night for a year. Sometimes the conversations lasted three minutes, sometimes over an hour. They realized, as good comforters do, that grief goes on for a long time. They were willing to go through it with me without cutting off support when they thought enough time had lapsed for my recovery. Still another couple planned on having my children and me over for dinner every Sunday for the first year. We rarely accepted; but that did not prevent them from inviting us nearly every Saturday. They also decorated our home for every birthday during that first year and helped plan surprise birthday parties and other special outings.

The First Death Is Bad Enough

Loss of any kind provides the church with the opportunity to become a healing community that enables grieving people to become stronger and wiser than they were before, leading them to ever higher levels of spiritual maturity. Good comforters do more than understand and serve; they also caution and challenge. They know that one death can easily lead to a second and worse death. So they are vigilant as well as sympathetic. They challenge the grieving to be death-hating and life-affirming.

The death that comes through loss of spouse, friend, job, health or dream is not the worst kind of death. Worse still is the death of the spirit, the death that comes through bitterness, hatred and despair. The first kind of death happens *to* us, the second kind of death happens *in* us. We bring it on ourselves. Those who suffer loss face the temptation of confusing the two, allowing the first to cause the second and to justify the second. Still, these two deaths are not the same thing, however closely associated they seem to be. Thus divorce may tempt us to hate an ex-spouse; yet the hatred itself is the result not of the divorce but of the way we choose to respond to the divorce. The death of a child may tempt us to become self-pitying; yet self-pity is the result not of the death but of a decision we make about the loss. Hatred, bitterness and despair are temptations for anyone who suffers loss. They conquer and control us, however, only if we allow it to happen. That choice will lead to the soul's death, which is a worse death by far than the death of loved one or job or health.

In the past months I have met people whose losses ennobled them, largely because of the decisions they made in the face of their loss and because of the support and encouragement they received from friends in their church. I met one woman whose simple and gracious presence caused me to weep, though I had never met her before. There was something about her spirit that moved me. Later I found out why. She had lost two children at birth and an eleven-year-old daughter to cancer. She suffered profoundly but chose nevertheless to embrace life. She became an extraordinary human being. On the other hand, I have met people whose losses turned them sour. Their presence depressed me, snatched away my fragile hope and made me think that there will never be life for me in the future.

A New Story

Loss of any kind alters the story that we had assumed our lives would tell. It forces us to write a new and unfamiliar story in which we must play a role that we did not choose and do not want.

Every human being imagines how life will turn out. Children day-dream that one day they will be athletes, singers on the stage, tightrope walkers, writers, presidents, firefighters. As they become adults, this imagination does not fade but changes, falling into line with what appears to be more realistic and appealing to them. We like to dream about what the story of our lives will tell. Then we try to live out that story, because we want our dreams to come true.

Loss means that the dream has died, the story as we imagined it has ended. Suddenly we face the difficult task of readjusting our expectations. Our change of circumstances is not what poses the problem; rather, the loss of what we had hoped the future would be causes the problem. Loss of one's future creates deep wounds in the spirit. We think often about what would have been if the death had not occurred. We find it hard to give up the dream. We long to live the story that will no longer be told, and we fall into depression when we realize that it will never be.

Those who suffer loss must eventually decide to live a new story. They must decide to readjust their plans and head into the unknown, discovering what that new story will be. Such a decision is risky and frightening.

In a dream that I had about a month after my loss, I was sailing a ship on a huge ocean. My three children were on board. I wanted to steer the ship back into the safe and familiar harbor that I had just left and could still see behind me. But the prevailing wind wouldn't let me. So I sailed onward, into an ocean with no sign of land or ship on the horizon. I felt overwhelmed with the vastness of it all, as if I were an atom lost in infinite space. The next morning my sister reminded me in a phone conversation that the earth is round, not flat. I could therefore not see what was ahead of me as I sailed my ship toward the empty horizon. I realized that in time I would discover new lands and adventures, though they were still hidden from view by the curvature of the earth.

A future is there for those who grieve. But they must choose it. Twice now in this chapter I have mentioned a dear friend who lost her husband over thirty years ago. Rebeccah was living in a small town at the time. After the accident her husband lived for two torturous weeks, though he never recovered from the coma into which he had slipped. During the months following his death she gradually discovered the obvious—that life would never be the same. "I had to face the fact that my life would be different. My marriage relationship had ended. The man I loved so deeply would not come back. I could not share with him or be touched by him. He was no longer a part of me. I was alone. I didn't want to believe this was true. It all seemed like a dream."

Still, Rebeccah embraced the future, though it was uncertain and repulsive to her. For example, she began to meet with a lawyer about her financial affairs. She involved herself in church and community activities. She tried to establish a stable and loving home for her two boys and channeled them into activities that would expose them to good male role models. She became increasingly independent. Four years later she moved to a bigger city in another state, where better jobs and social opportunities were available. She decided to believe that she had a meaningful future. As she said to me:

I looked into the mirror one day and talked with God. I told him that I was through with my struggle. I would resign myself to him and accept whatever life would bring. From that day on my life began to change. I began to establish a new identity. I accepted my present and let go of my past. The wonderful memories still remain. I will cherish them forever. But I had come to the place of acceptance, of knowing and believing I would be okay after a long journey of grief.

A Community of Comfort

Comfort is best given and received in the community of the church. As I said before, the body of Christ is really a community of suffering. We may disagree strongly in matters of belief and style, but we are one in our experience of loss and pain. Suffering visits all of us.

Like most mainline churches, my home church has had to learn to live with diversity. The lessons have often come hard. There is more than enough suspicion and disagreement. My own tragedy in 1991, however, had a unifying impact on the whole congregation. As I have said, Lynda and I were both visible people in the church. Naturally my suffering was visible too. I started to teach Sunday school again a month after the accident. The class became a community of suffering and comfort. Suddenly prochoice and prolife, Democrat and Republican, traditionalist and progressive, mission-minded and social activist found each other in brokenness, both theirs and mine. It altered the atmosphere of our public conversation without necessarily changing the opinions of the people involved. We became finite, fragile, weak people. We became more than our diverse and sometimes divisive opinions had allowed us to be. We became a community of fellow sinners and sufferers who desperately need God's love and grace.

Good comforters never forget that friends and enemies alike are more than their acceptable or suspect opinions. They are mortal creatures who struggle with problems, suffer in a fallen world and will face certain death.

The apostle Paul understood what this suffering community could be. He wrote about it in his second letter to the Corinthians, a book that has helped me perhaps more than any other over the past months. Paul had a rocky relationship with the believers in Corinth. They had strong disagreements, as evidenced by the number of controversial subjects Paul had to address in his first letter to them. In spite of these disputes, Paul began his second letter not by disputing a point but by describing his suffering.

> We do not want you to be unaware, brothers and sisters, of the affliction we experienced in Asia; for we were so utterly, unbearably crushed that we despaired of life itself. Indeed, we felt that we had received the sentence of death so that we would rely not on ourselves but on God who raises the dead. (2 Cor 1:8-9)

Paul believed that his own suffering belonged to the community of suffering. Fellow believers were given an opportunity to comfort him; he was given an opportunity to comfort them. Suffering allowed them to recognize their need for grace and to impart God's grace to each other.

> Blessed be the God and Father of our Lord Jesus Christ, the Father of mercies and the God of all consolation, who consoles us in all our

affliction, so that we may be able to console those who are in any affliction with the consolation with which we ourselves are consoled by God. For just as the sufferings of Christ are abundant for us, so also our consolation is abundant through Christ. If we are being afflicted, it is for your consolation and salvation; if we are being consoled, it is for your consolation, which you experience when you patiently endure the same sufferings that we are also suffering. (2 Cor 1:3-6)

I believe that the quest for power in the church causes division; the experience of suffering creates unity. Not that power is a bad thing. Sometimes the quest for power is legitimate, however arduous and divisive the process. I have a hard time believing that the debate over abortion rights or homosexuality is going to go away even if we admit that we are all suffering sinners in need of God's grace. Still, acknowledgment of weakness does introduce another dimension to relationships. We come to know each other in the depths of our humanity, as fragile creatures who are subject to sickness, brokenness, grief, confusion and ultimately death. We see each other as people with feet of clay easily toppled over by life's savagery. Even enemies can join and weep together when they discover that they face another and greater enemy, their own frightening mortality. Many of our conflicts and divisions may appear trivial and trite in the face of the terrible reality of suffering, evil and death.

The Hope of Glory

The apostle Paul understood the ambivalence of faith that suffering creates. In his mind, that ambivalence is resolved through Christian hope. Paul believed in the power of the gospel; but he also recognized the problem of living in a fallen world. His life experience did not always measure up to the promise of the gospel. If anything, it appeared sometimes to contradict it.

But we have this treasure in clay jars, so that it may be made clear that this extraordinary power belongs to God and does not come from us.

We are afflicted in every way, but not crushed; perplexed, but not driven to despair; persecuted, but not forsaken; struck down, but not destroyed; always carrying in the body the death of Jesus, so that the life of Jesus may also be made visible in our bodies. (2 Cor 4:7-10) What made the gospel wonderful to Paul was not simply what it promised for the present, for present experience in his mind was always tinged with the reality of death, but also what it promised for the future.

So we do not lose heart. Even though our outer nature is wasting away, our inner nature is being renewed day by day. For this slight momentary affliction is preparing us for an eternal weight of glory beyond all measure, because we look not at what can be seen but at what cannot be seen; for what can be seen is temporary, but what cannot be seen is eternal. (2 Cor 4:16-18; see also Rom 8:18, 24-25) Good comforters offer hope. They keep pointing to a time when life will not be miserable any more but will be good again, alive with meaning and purpose and joy, even if that time will not arrive until we enter eternity. They believe in the God who gives hope, and they believe for sufferers who have no hope. They carry them into the future without pushing that future onto them. They let them go through the process of grief, never minimizing, never exaggerating, never trivializing. They also have hope that the process will have an end.

Hope gives meaning to suffering. People who have suffered loss don't always want answers right away and may even be repulsed by the premature and trivial answers they receive. But they will eventually want—and need—to make sense out of their suffering. Why is there suffering? Where does it come from? Why does God allow it? Every person asks these questions sooner or later, because every person suffers sooner or later. They are forced to find meaning in the madness of pain. Good comforters help them find it when the time is right. They help them build a biblical view of reality.

Rebeccah joined a grief support network and found friends who helped make sense out of her loss. Others I interviewed talked with pastors, counselors and mentors who helped them to reflect on their experiences. I met with a small group of men once a week and had lunch frequently with friends who joined me in finding perspective on my own suffering and, as it always turned out, on theirs as well. Together we found meaning in the cross, that the almighty God became a human being, shed tears of pity for those in pain and eventually died for sinners. He suffered loss in a way no one will ever comprehend. We also found meaning in Bible stories, like the story of Joseph, which shows that redemptive history continues to unfold even when we can't see it and don't understand it. Finally, we found meaning in the love of God, a love so great that nothing—not even death—can separate us from it.

The greatest hope of all, however, is the hope of the resurrection. People who suffer loss want the loss reversed. The problem with that desire, however, is that eventually they will have to lose it again. The great enemy we face is death itself, which claims everyone and everything. In his earthly ministry Jesus performed signs and wonders. The deaf were made to hear, the blind to see, the dead to live again. But sooner or later the deaf lost their hearing again, the blind their sight, the living their life. Death in the end won out. Jesus' great victory was not any of his miracles but his resurrection. The grave could not hold him. He conquered death and rose to a life that would never die again. The hope of the gospel is the promise that sin is forgiven, death is defeated, eternal life is ours through Jesus Christ. Easter tells us that the last chapter of God's story will be wonderful. Jesus' resurrection guarantees it. All tears and pain and sorrow will be swallowed up in everlasting life and pure, inextinguishable joy.

What sets the Christian community apart, therefore, is not absence of suffering but hope in suffering, if we are willing to help each other live in that hope. We know that life has defeated death as surely as light conquers darkness. Jesus Christ is the great victor. Those who know and love Jesus Christ will live with him for an eternity of glory. For this reason the apostle Paul encouraged believers to press forward in humble and faithful service. "Therefore, my beloved, be steadfast, immovable, always excelling in the work of the Lord, because you know that in the Lord your labor is not in vain" (1 Cor 15:58). For this reason also Paul charged believers to comfort one another with the assurance that, though we grieve as the world does, we grieve in the hope that death will not have the final word—the resurrection will. As the first fruits of the new creation, Jesus has already gone before us to show us the way—to provide the way—to eternal life.

10

BEAR ONE ANOTHER'S BURDENS

W hile speaking at a conference in New Jersey several years ago, I met an energetic and engaging woman, Marie, who told me her story. A mother of eight, Marie had recently lost her husband to alcoholism and was trying to survive on a small income. She appeared to have enough problems of her own, although, as she said to me, it was in just those circumstances that she always seemed to inherit someone else's problems too. That was exactly what happened when she met Sally.

Marie's daughter first introduced her to Sally. Pregnant, unmarried and alone, Sally was searching for someone to help her through the biggest crisis she had ever faced, an unwanted pregnancy. She turned to Marie immediately for support. At first Sally believed that abortion was the simplest and easiest solution to the problem, though Marie gently encouraged her to consider other options. Sally even made an appointment to visit a local abortion clinic and went there with the intention of following through on her decision. But when her name was called in the waiting room, she decided that abortion was no answer. Leaving the clinic, she drove at once to Marie's house and in tears asked Marie what to do. Marie had an idea. She invited Sally to move in until, as she put it, Sally could "get back on her feet again." Sally lived at Marie's house for four years.

Marie redecorated a room for Sally. She helped her to apply for Medicaid, arranged for her to see a Christian counselor and helped her to get a job. She was Sally's coach during the delivery and sometimes cared for the baby when Sally worked. She drew Sally back into the church, where Sally became active as a Sunday-school teacher and as a volunteer in a crisis pregnancy program. She also introduced her to a new set of friends, one of whom eventually became her husband. She treated Sally like her own daughter.

The Bible calls what Marie did an act of bearing burdens. Her story is a moving one, complete with a happy ending. It is an exceptional story, the kind one uses in inspirational sermons and magazine articles. For most of us, however, it is simply too unrealistic, too impractical and, well, too radical. How many of us have ever had an opportunity to do what Marie did? Probably not many. How many of us want to? That is the real question.

Bearing burdens is inconvenient and disruptive. It requires that we be flexible, spontaneous and available. It is costly, even when we are called to do something far less sacrificial than Marie did, although Marie refused to label her deed as anything extraordinary. "No matter how difficult reaching out to others and carrying their burdens may seem to be," she told me, "it ceases to be a burden when the Lord turns it to love."

The Bible tells us a story about just how costly burden bearing can be. It is the story of the good Samaritan. The account is a troubling one to me. Jesus hardly gives us adequate information. For all we know, the Samaritan could have been unemployed or on vacation; he could have had the time, in other words, to care for the poor man at the side of the road. The priest could have been rushing to an emergency meeting that had been called to discuss the dangerous conditions on the Jericho road. The Levite could have been wearily returning home to his wife and children after spending a week doing good deeds in a nearby city. We simply don't know. The story lacks that kind of mitigating detail. It is simple, direct, clear. There are no qualifications given, no conditions and exceptions. Jesus leaves us with nothing but a question and a command. He asks, "Who proved to be neighbor to the man on the side of the road?" Then he commands, "Go and do likewise."

If Jesus told a story to make the point, the apostle Paul gave a clear mandate. "Bear one another's burdens," he wrote, "and in this way you will fulfill the law of Christ" (Gal 6:2). Like comforting, bearing burdens is a command that helps us to deal with people who want to progress on the journey of faith but find it difficult because of crises they are facing. As we have already observed, to comfort fellow believers is to stop at the side of the road and stand beside them while they grieve over a loss so great that they cannot continue on the journey, at least for a time. We know, however, that they will eventually recover and resume the journey. The same cannot be said of people with severe burdens. They may not be able to resume the journey unless we lift them up, carry them along for a while and eventually get them walking again.

To bear burdens requires us to stop at the side of the road with our fellow believers, just as we must do for those needing comfort. But in this case the goal is to help our brothers and sisters in Christ, immobilized by undesirable circumstances and accompanying sin, to get back on their feet so that they can continue growing in faith. Bearing burdens thus demands that we focus on two problems simultaneously—the suffering that people do not choose and the sin that they do.

The Occasion
The apostle Paul was probably dealing with an actual situation in the church at Galatia and used it as an opportunity to give instructions to the fellowship there (see Gal 6:1-5). Burden bearing is required on those occasions when Christians are unable for some reason to walk free and

unhindered with Christ on the journey of faith. Paul used two important words to make his point. The first word, *overtaken* (RSV), is in the passive voice, which means that it entails action that is being done to a person, not action that a person is doing. The implication is that sin is doing the chasing and a person has been overrun by it. We don't know what conditions Paul actually had in mind that make believers weak and vulnerable. He was probably referring to difficult circumstances, unanticipated problems or, as William Barclay put it, "the chances and changes of life." But we do know what the effects of these circumstances are on the behavior of people—capitulation to sin. Our own experience confirms what Paul was describing. We have seen it happen too many times. People often make adversity worse by the foolish ways they respond to it.

Paul's use of the word *trespass* reinforces this basic idea. The Greek could be translated as "unwitting deed," "mistake," "slip." It is clearly a category of sin. But a trespass is different from willful, rebellious sin. Paul is talking not so much about a plunge into sin as a slide into it. He is addressing the problem of people who keep tripping over obstacles that life sometimes puts in their way. These obstacles make them susceptible to temptation. And temptation turns into sin by the foolish— and sinful—choices people make in response to them.

It is possible, then, to make a distinction between a leap into sin and a slip into sin, between willful rebellion and weak acquiescence, between sin as aggressor and sinner as victim. The problem in the latter case is the circumstances that make Christians easy prey to sin. Such circumstances are the major—but not the only—problem. Poor choices aggravate the problem brought on by those circumstances.

Take two families. One is upper-middle-class. The husband and wife have enjoyed financial prosperity their whole lives. Their children have had a privileged upbringing—private education, music lessons, sports camps, exotic vacations. Though active for many years in a local church, they have recently drifted away. They like the weekends free to pursue other activites, especially at their new cottage. Besides, they are fed up with what they perceive to be their church's legalistic, narrow-minded and judgmental atmosphere. They don't like to be told what is right and what is wrong, which they believe their church does with a vengeance.

The other family has only recently reached the middle class, and then barely, after many years of struggle. The husband and father, uneducated but hardworking, has two jobs, as a janitor and, on the weekends, as a night watchman. The wife and mother cleans houses. Their children are making it in school, primarily as athletes. One is excelling in basketball and hopes to win an athletic scholarship to pay for her college education, which would be the only way she could pay for it. They, too, have drifted from the church. They don't feel comfortable anymore in the church they attended for years, and they haven't had the time or interest to search for a new church home. They are often just too tired to do much of anything on Sundays except rest and spend time together as a family.

Both families should return to the church. Their priorities need to change. But there is a difference between the two. Paul describes this difference in Galatians 6.

There are desperate people in the world, and many are our fellow church members, for whom we have a special responsibility. Every day a woman just like Sally discovers that she is pregnant, either against her wishes or against someone else's. Every day a young man finds out that he has cancer and must decide whether it is worth the pain to undergo treatment that may be worse than the disease. Every day a teenage girl is mercilessly mocked just because she has a homely face or stringy hair or fat legs or an obvious lisp. Every day a baby is born into abject poverty and will have to grow up in a community that has none of the privileges and pleasures that most people in America enjoy. Every day a middle-aged, middle-class woman contemplates suicide because she feels trapped in an abusive marriage, unhappy home or unfulfilling job. Every one of these people may attend a church just like ours, sit in a pew next to us, sip coffee in the fellowship hall after morning worship, participate in a small group with us and maybe hide his or her problems from us, as we do ours.

Bad things often happen to decent people who do not choose these things but get their fair share of them anyway. Is it any wonder that so many people live in hopelessness, struggle against bitterness, wallow in depression or tremble with rage at the slightest offense? Is it any wonder that they yield so readily to sin? Not that their sin is justifiable. I reject the idea that people are merely victims and nothing more. Still, some circumstances make sin understandable, though not excusable.

The apostle Paul commanded Christians to bear the burdens of people like that. It is a universal command, applicable for all times and to all people, because there has never been a time when or a place where Christians did not have burdens that needed bearing. We have been out of the Garden for a long time now. Thistles, pain and death are our lot in life. We need help to make it on our journey to the new garden that we call heaven.

Yet the modern world has made burden bearing more complicated. There are several reasons for this. The enormity of modern social problems, for example, has created a culture of apathy and despair, both of which are expressions of the feeling of powerlessness. Social problems like unemployment and poverty are one thing in a small town, where community spirit, neighborliness and simple social organization make it relatively easy to rally people to come up with solutions, if they are willing. They are another thing altogether in cities like New York, Cleveland, Kansas City and Los Angeles.

While attending the University of Chicago I lived in a suburb twenty minutes south of campus. Life was relatively safe and serene in our community. To get to the university, however, I had to drive through south Chicago, which contains some of the poorest living conditions in America. Every week I made my way through miles of ghetto wasteland. I saw long lines at the unemployment offices. I scanned vacant lots filled with trash. I looked everywhere at empty apartments, run-down houses and abandoned storefronts. The problems seemed so vast and complex that I began trying to look straight ahead and to pretend that they weren't there. The magnitude of the problems contributed to my apathy.

The people living in south Chicago, however, could not dismiss these problems so easily, because they were surrounded by them. They could not escape them as I could. The magnitude of the problems contributed to their despair.

Many of these social problems are chronic. People do not always choose them. They are rooted in the very system. They have become a part of the way things are. Like babies born with addictions, many people living in the inner city have little to say about the life they inherit. It is a part of the environment, like an ugly background on a portrait that was put there even before the artist had a chance to take brush in hand and paint the subject's face. Thus welfare is no longer a short-term answer to a solvable problem. It is a syndrome, a habit. People inherit a welfare mentality and pass it on, like genes, to the next generation. These social problems are not deviations from a cultural norm; they have become a way of life.

Mobility and dislocation have also added to the problem of burden bearing. We move on the average of once every five years, and not just down the street but across the country. We lack a sense of place, commitment to community and feeling of permanence and belonging. Our mobility often prevents us from developing the networks of relationships that make burden bearing possible. To find jobs for the unemployed, to connect troubled families with competent counselors, to locate decent housing for the poor, to provide affordable or free health care for the sick and destitute—all practical examples of burden bearing—requires familiarity with and extensive contacts in a community. These can be developed only if one lives there for a long time.

Still another characteristic of modern society makes burden bearing difficult. That is our knowledge of and interest in modern psychology, which has given us new powers to comprehend human personhood. It has equipped us with tools to describe, diagnose and sometimes solve problems that one hundred years ago did not exist or were largely ignored and misunderstood. It has also given us the power to understand ourselves, especially how the past influences the present, how background, parentage and early experiences shape our identity. It provides us with knowledge to explain how we became the persons that we are and how we developed the problems that we have.

Yet in explaining the origin of our problems, psychology can also explain them away, giving us an excuse to assign the responsibility to someone or something else. Now it is not the devil that makes us do it; it is an absent father or suffocating mother or domineering teacher or mean friend. Though certainly not intending this, modern psychology has helped to create a whole class of victims who can describe their problems in great detail without having to take responsibility for them. However unwittingly, modern psychology has thus given people the means to justify all sorts of sin, like bitterness, anger, self-pity, passivity and selfishness.

The influence of psychology in the modern world has obvious and significant implications for the life of the church. On the one hand, it can give us tools to help people who used to be ignored, condemned or at best tolerated. Many churches now employ a counselor on staff who helps troubled people to understand themselves and to handle their problems and who equips the members of the congregation to become a healing community for the many broken people the church attracts. On the other hand, it can create a whole new category of burdens. It is one thing when Christians have burdens that can be overcome, assuming that they want to overcome them. It is another thing altogether when fellow believers have burdens but do not want to overcome them because they have become addicted to them. They often demand much but give little or nothing in return. They eagerly share their problems but resist solutions. They use the church as if it were a bottomless pit of love but they never replenish the supply. Every Christian organization—church, college or whatever—has people like this in it. It makes burden bearing itself a heavy burden.

I asked one professional people-helper, Alice, about this problem, and she agreed that it represented a formidable challenge to Christians who want to bear burdens. Alice herself has worked with several cases involving just such people. In one case she began to counsel a young woman, Lori, who struggled with depression and bulimia. Lori was a master at explaining why she had problems but was not interested in learning how to solve them. If anything, she seemed to derive a strange pleasure in her disorders and developed a dangerous dependence on them. In a letter to me Alice observed, "I began to notice after several months that Lori was making no progress. Her words gave me very subtle indications that perhaps she did not want to make progress. She knew how to be depressed and bulimic, and she did them well. So why change?" As Alice put it, Lori did not *have* a burden; she *was* a burden.

The Fulfillment

There is a prerequisite to fulfilling this command. We are charged, first of all, to *restore* wayward Christians gently, lest we too be tempted (Gal 6:1). Then we are commanded to *bear their burdens* (6:2). This prerequisite requires that we address the problem of sin, if and when it is appropriate. Not all burdens are the result of sin. But when they are, as is often the case, we must be courageous and compassionate enough to address it. No matter how bad the circumstances, if sin is involved it must be confronted. It cannot be excused as a justifiable response to a bad situation.

Yet sin of this kind must be dealt with gently. Paul uses the word *restore* to make the point. The Greek word could also be translated "cure," which says something about the manner with which we should confront burdened people. Paul is not telling us to treat them as sick people, as if they were mere victims, for that would deprive them of one of the essentials of being a human being—personal responsibility. He is telling us, however, to conduct ourselves with the same kind of kindness and sympathy as a physician displays when working with a frightened child. We are to woo them back to Christ, not yank them back. Our confrontation should be padded with compassion.

Restoration implies that we must get burdened people back on their feet *spiritually*. We must deal with their sin, which is usually—though not always—part of the problem, challenge them to take responsibility for their lives and call them to repentance. We must remind them that there are ultimately no excuses for their unforgiveness, jealousy, self-pity, immorality or whatever sin theirs happens to be. No one, in other words, is just a victim to whom bad things happen. Even victims are free agents who have at least some power to change their lives and determine their destiny. We must therefore help them to stand before God and become accountable for their attitude and actions. They were made in God's image. However marred that image is, vestiges of it are still there. As loving friends, we must call that image forth in them, expecting the best. Such is the spiritual work that is a prerequisite to burden bearing.

Then, as Paul says, we are ready to bear their burdens and so fulfill Christ's law of love. Paul enjoins us to stand under, hold up and carry along our brothers and sisters in Christ. At this point we must address not the sin but the circumstances that made them vulnerable to sin in the first place. We must get them back on their feet physically, emotionally, socially, economically, politically. If restoration addresses personal responsibility for sin, bearing burdens addresses the conditions that make sin easy to yield to. This task may require us to help them find a place to live, get a new job, straighten out their personal finances, heal a broken relationship, build an adequate self-image, solve deep psychological problems, secure their political rights, change unjust structures, feed them healthy food, reform the criminal justice system or change bad habits.

A gospel story shows us how to proceed. The setting is important: Jesus was teaching a huge crowd of people in someone's home. When four men came, carrying a crippled friend, they could find no way to get their friend to Jesus, who they believed could heal him. Their ingenuity led them to hoist their friend onto the roof, where they removed enough tiles to make a hole for the stretcher. Then they lowered the man into the middle of the room, right at the feet of Jesus. They were no doubt eager to hear those powerful words of Jesus, by this time familiar to many people, "Rise, take up your bed, and walk." But Jesus did not say those words, at least not at first. Instead, he said, "Your sins are forgiven," much to the surprise and disappointment of the man's friends, who had sought out Jesus for a different reason. Then, when Jesus perceived that the Pharisees in the crowd were questioning how he, as a human being, could presume to do something only God can do—forgive sin—he proved that the man's sin was in fact forgiven by showing the effects of forgiveness in his life. He then told him to rise, take up his bed and walk.

Jesus thus addressed both the man's sin—the more fundamental problem—and his physical sickness—the more visible problem. The point of the story is that it is always harder to forgive than it is to heal, although both are necessary for real wholeness. Jesus restored the man to a right relationship with God, the prerequisite to burden bearing, and then he bore his burdens by making him well.

Bearing burdens is a mandate given to the whole Christian community, not to a special class of professional people-helpers or to an exclusive group of supersaints. Some people may devote more time to the task of burden bearing than others; some may pursue vocations more in line with the work of burden bearing, like counseling or social work; some may be more naturally suited by temperament, interest or skill for burden bearing. All Christians are nevertheless called to bear the burdens of their brothers and sisters in Christ, however natural or awkward, convenient or inconvenient it is.

Burden bearing requires a balanced strategy. First, there must be balance between individual initiative and corporate responsibility. Sometimes location, opportunity and need put a special demand on certain people to shoulder the burdens of fellow Christians. As I mentioned before, three weeks after our family moved to the Chicago area we heard news that a neighbor, whom we had met only once, had lost his wife to heart disease. She was twenty-nine years old, and she had left behind three young children. A week later the grieving husband visited our home and asked if we would be willing to care for his youngest son, Mark, then three years old, while he was working. We looked after Mark for the next two years. Though we provided most of the support, many other people—friends, neighbors and especially family members—helped as well. It was a ministry to which a whole community of believers contributed.

Marie's story follows a similar script. She was the one who opened her home to Sally; yet she was by no means the only person who helped get Sally back on her feet. Members of her church donated a crib and baby clothes, supported Sally financially and welcomed her into the church. Men from the church came forward to spend time with Daniel, her new son. Marie played the major role, but it was not a one-person show. A large cast of characters appeared onstage in supporting roles.

Those supporting roles are often as important as the leads. No Christian has everything that it takes to bear all the burdens of needy Christians. We must learn to draw on the rich resources of the whole church to get the job done. Deeply troubled people need trained mental health professionals to give them good counsel; they also need ordinary friends at church who are willing to listen without comment or judgment for hours at a time. Poor people need money, jobs and housing; but they too need ordinary friends at church to help them in the little ways. Whatever our skills, connections, wealth, training or interests, we are responsible to bear burdens in the body of Christ.

Second, we must strike a balance between engagement and distance Bearing burdens demands a sacrifice of time, money, energy. We have no choice in the matter. We do have a choice, however, in determining how much time, money and energy we can give. Choices of this kind can be difficult, even torturous. Always saying no engenders guilt; never saying no leads to burnout and creates resentment.

Jesus appeared to teach that true disciples should never set limits; it is an all-or-nothing proposition. Yet Jesus himself took time off from his ministry. He chose not to preach in some areas, and he did not heal everyone. He disappointed the crowds on more than one occasion.

It is simply impossible to bear the burdens of every person in need that we know. It is also unhealthy. For every Saturday that someone gives in volunteer service, a Saturday is taken away from family, friends and other responsibilities. For every dollar that someone donates to a worthy cause, a dollar is taken away from other causes that may not be as critical but are still important, like the church's operating budget. Granted, too many members of the body of Christ give too little of themselves or their resources to alleviate burdens in the world; their problem is indifference and selfishness. But some members give too much; their problem is busyness, distress and anxious concern.

Alice told me that she had to deal with this latter problem. Her identity was so wrapped up in helping other people that she could not set limits on her ministry. She was addicted to bearing burdens. Though she found every reason to justify her fanaticism—she *was* doing good, after all—she discovered in time that much of her concern for others was motivated by a "need to pad" her own self-image. She was afraid of disappointing people, or of being misunderstood. She needed to be needed. Alice had to learn that it is right and necessary to set limits.

All of us are responsible to shoulder burdens; but none of us is responsible to shoulder them all, and to do it alone. Sometimes we are most obedient when we say no.

Finally, there must be a balance between short-term and long-term burden bearing. Some burdens demand immediate attention from the church. People lying bloody on the side of the road require quick action—postponement may mean death. That is why we must be available and flexible if we want to fulfill this biblical command, for people in crisis cannot afford to wait for our help; they need it right away. Yet some burdens cannot be dealt with adequately unless we devote ourselves to the task over a long period of time, perhaps a lifetime. Burden bearing of this kind isn't nearly as spectacular and obvious; but it is certainly as important. For every wounded person lying by the side of the road who needs a good Samaritan to stop and help, there are many unsafe streets that need protection and unjust social structures that need transformation. For every dying cancer patient who needs immediate care from church friends, there are thousands of cancer patients who need experts in medical research to discover cures. For every victim of poverty who needs generous donations of food and clothing given in Sunday morning food drives, there are cities, even whole countries, that need just laws and good government. For every person who needs a competent counselor to enable him to overcome deep personal problems, there are many ordinary Christians who need to read popular books on counseling written by professionals in the field.

Scholars holed up in libraries, executives working. in board rooms, scientists sequestered in labs, politicians debating issues in legislative chambers can be burden bearers too, although the effects of their work might not be immediately evident. We must realize that our usefulness in the body of Christ is determined by how we serve Christ over the long haul. Spontaneity and availability are important qualities that must be cultivated; but they cannot replace careful study, good management, precise research, political involvement. The urgent cannot always be allowed to put off the important.

The Peril

The apostle Paul issued two warnings in his passage on bearing burdens. He gave the first in Galatians 6:1: "Take care that you yourselves are not tempted." We must beware that in bearing burdens we don't overestimate our own strength. None of us is invulnerable to sin—any sin, even sins that seem now to offer no attraction to us. However self-controlled and stable we are, none of us is above temptation. We should never delude ourselves into thinking that it will never happen to us, because it can.

Much of our supposed strength of faith is often the product of time, place and environment—a good background, a happy home, freedom from major problems. A change of circumstances could easily put the strongest among us flat on our spiritual back, where we would suddenly find ourselves looking up at temptations that we never even imagined before. Husbands who at one time never considered adultery have committed adultery. Women who appeared at one time to be inextinguishably joyful have grown bitter. Business leaders who at one time followed the strictest moral code have cheated on their income taxes. A sudden change of circumstances can throw us into a vertigo, exposing our supposed virtue for what it really is, a product of our environment.

So we must be constantly self-critical, always vigilant, never presumptuous. As the famous phrase goes, "There but for the grace of God go I." What separates most of us from the people at the bottom of the social barrel is not who we are but what we have, where we live, whom we know, how we have been treated. We have the same capacity for sin as anyone does.

Paul issued the second warning in Galatians 6:3-4. "All must test their own work," he wrote. The peril in this case is in our tendency to overestimate—or to underestimate—our own importance. The ministry of bearing burdens brings two groups of people together. One group consists of relatively healthy Christians who assume the dominant and supposedly superior role; the other comprises relatively needy people who assume the subordinate and inferior role. One does the helping; the other needs the help. One is strong; the other is weak.

The former group will face the temptation of pride. They will tend to inflate their sense of self-importance when they compare themselves—as they inevitably will—with those who depend on them for help. They will find it easy to feel as if they are better Christians. The latter group will face the opposite temptation. They will tend to diminish their importance in the church when they compare themselves with those who seem to do all the giving and never seem to do any receiving.

Not that self-evaluation is a bad thing. It comes naturally to us, and it can serve a healthy purpose. The problem is that we usually use other people—their appearance, their accomplishments, their wealth, their intelligence, their personality, their interests—as the standard against which we measure ourselves and determine our self-worth. That is good news for the few people whose extraordinary gifts seem to make them rise to the top. It is bad news for most people whose average abilities keep them in the middle of the pack, no matter how hard they try. Most of us will always find some people, sometimes many people, more accomplished than we are.

Paul advises us to "test our own work." We are to evaluate ourselves according to standards most appropriate to us alone. We must discern what God expects of us and fulfill our calling, although that may depart radically from what he wants of our friends. Common sense should convince us of the soundness of Paul's counsel. Contrary to what the Declaration of Independence says, we were not all created equal. No two of us look the same, have the same abilities, come from the same background, get the same opportunities. Every one of us is different. What is easy for one is hard for another. What is interesting to one is boring to another. We would expect a graduate student to read at least twenty-five books over a summer; we would not expect the same from a high-school dropout. We would expect a journeyman carpenter to build flawless cabinets; we would not expect the same from a novice. We would expect incredible productivity from a ten-talent person, as Jesus himself taught; we would not expect the same from a one-talent person. There are no superior or inferior people in the body of Christ, just different. God only expects that we serve him faithfully with everything we are and have.

The problem of pluralism in the church is exacerbated by our inclination to make everyone just like us. But the body is a body because it has different parts, each one having a unique function. That applies even to burden bearing. We won't always respond to a need in the same way, and we're not supposed to. We must therefore "test our own work," fulfilling our responsibilities as God has called us, neither depreciating nor inflating our work in the light of what others do. The social activist lobbying politicians in Washington should do her work to the glory of God; so should the church member who volunteers in an inner-city soup kitchen. The counselor should use her education and experience to help heal broken people; so should the evangelist who calls people to commitment to Christ. Burden bearing is best done in community, so that all resources of the church contribute to the task at hand.

The Goal

The apostle Paul concluded the passage by stating the goal of burden bearing. "For all must carry their own loads." He used the same verb—*carry* or *bear*—but a different noun—*load*. The goal of burden bearing is to enable our brothers and sisters in Christ to discover, pursue and carry out their own particular purpose in life, however burdened they have been or will continue to be. The burdens that weigh them down do not excuse them from doing their God-given duty. Thus the goal is to get them back on their feet so that they can serve God in the church and in the world.

They may not, literally speaking, have feet left to stand on. Joni Eareckson Tada, for example, suffered a serious accident when she was a teenager and has been confined to a wheelchair ever since. After the accident she became very depressed and doubted the goodness of God. People bore her burdens until she got back on her feet and began to discover what God wanted her to do as a quadriplegic for the kingdom. She has had a fruitful ministry ever since, as an artist, writer, speaker, advocate. She has followed what Paul prescribed; she has learned to bear her own load.

Sometimes the "load" will correspond to the burden. Problems that have been conquered often prepare people to help others do the same. Once again, that is true for Joni, who has helped other disabled people to find hope and purpose in life. That is also true for Chuck Colson, whose year in prison made him sensitive to the needs of prison inmates and led him to launch Prison Fellowship, which serves inmates and their families around the world.

Past struggles often lead people into ministries that correspond to them. Thus couples who have survived unfaithfulness are often the most effective in helping other couples heal broken marriages. Recovered alcoholics are often the best counselors for other alcoholics. People who have overcome the pain of abuse are often the most capable of helping the victims of abuse. If grace leads to a life of "no regrets," as Paul intimates in 2 Corinthians 7, perhaps it is in our sin and struggle that we may find our purpose in life. Old burdens will turn into blessings for the body of Christ. Our weakness will build strength into others. God will use our brokenness to bring healing to the church.

Yet getting people back on their feet does not imply that all needs have been met, all problems solved, all adversity overcome. Burden bearing gets people back on their feet. Once on their feet, they may still have troubles that remain. When bearing burdens is no longer called for, service may still be. Recovered alcoholics may still require support and accountability, sometimes for the rest of their lives. Cancer patients may still need care even after the crisis has been averted and they are on the road to healing. Elderly people who have found the courage to face their mortality may still require assistance in cooking, cleaning, dressing. Service, as we have seen, deals with the ongoing needs of people—as we find, for example, in illness and old age—that demand time and attention.

But what if people don't want to bear their own load? What if they don't want to get back on their feet? It may be necessary in such cases to forbear or serve them first. The church is not called to be like Nazi Germany, a homeland only for the strong, perfect and pure. It was brought into being for the sake of outcasts and nobodies. Paul said it so well: "Consider your own call, brothers and sisters: not many of you were wise by human standards, not many were powerful, not many were of noble birth" (1 Cor 1:26). Moses told the children of Israel that God made them his people because they were inferior to the peoples surrounding them. God seems to have a special concern for people at the bottom, for the ones most easily and frequently trampled by everyone else. God is not a Social Darwinist. In his kingdom the least fit survive and prosper.

Those who bear burdens should also remember that their burden bearing ultimately must be a matter of obedience to God's command, not a matter of utilitarian service to others. Not everyone with burdens is going to respond as we would like. They might take longer to overcome their problems than we would like to allow. They might not overcome them at all. They might even take advantage of our helpfulness, exploit our good intentions and use our resources to advance their selfish interests, like the proverbial alcoholic who asks for a dollar in order to buy a loaf of bread when his real purpose is to buy another drink. Burden bearing always carries the risk of failure. Careful though we may try to be, there are no guarantees that we will be spared from being used.

We cannot allow that risk to harden our hearts to needy people. But neither should we let it make us indulgent. Foolish obedience—say, giving a dollar to an alcoholic—is not much better than no obedience at all. The best option is to obey this command intelligently. In the case of an alcoholic, the best course of action would be to buy him a loaf of bread or get him into a treatment program. As Jesus said, we must be wise as serpents and gentle as doves. Burden bearers must combine good judgment with a sympathetic attitude.

Still, the Bible charges that "all must carry their own loads." It does not give a time limit; it may take months, even years. But eventually our burdened brothers and sisters in Christ must be challenged to give up the power of always being needy, to wean themselves from dependence on their problems and to become responsible before God. They must stop using past and present suffering as an excuse for bitterness and self-pity and decide what they can do, considering their circumstances, to serve God. To do anything less is to deprive them of God's grace and strip them of human dignity.

At this point burden bearing must give way to admonition, gentle restoration to firm confrontation, for the principal problem has shifted from adversity to resistance, irresponsibility and disobedience. Sooner or later we may be forced to ask of our friends the question that Jesus asked of a cripple, "Do you *want* to be healed?" If the answer is in fact no, then the disease itself has become a secondary issue and their attitude the primary issue. We will need to address that attitude.

The final word in the Bible is always good news, however burdened or free we are. There is one burden all of us have that no human being, save one, can bear. That is the burden of our sin. Jesus came to bear that burden for us. "Come to me, all you that are weary and are carrying heavy burdens, and I will give you rest" (Mt 11:28). Jesus was incarnated, suffered and died on the cross to free us from a burden that is beyond our power or anyone else's power to overcome. To rid ourselves of that burden, we must go to him.

PART 4
CONFRONTATIONAL COMMANDS

11

STIR UP
ONE ANOTHER

We have two commands left to explore. These two are what I call the confrontational commands. The very term *confrontational* implies a resistance to Christ that must be overcome, a resistance that requires the difficult and risky work of confrontation. I have two kinds of resistance in mind, and these correspond to the two commands we will study. The first kind of resistance is willful and rebellious; it manifests an intentional decision to disobey God's word. We will address that problem in the final chapter on admonition. The second kind of resistance is not so much willful as it is unintentional, an expression of inertia rather than of change, a matter of natural inclination more than of defiance. It is the human condition at its unselfconscious worst. It may be the more deadly of the two simply because we are unaware of it, like death by gradual poisoning. It may take more time, but in the end it is as effective as death by a nuclear blast.

It is obvious by now in our study of these commands that the Christian life is not an easy journey for casual weekend strollers. It is more like a strenuous climb on a footpath through the Rockies than a sidewalk stroll at the beach. Jesus called it "the narrow way" and warned us of its cost.

He said that in the Christian life death precedes life, losing comes before gaining, renouncing the world is an initial step that we must take to inherit eternal life.

Many of these commands assume this kind of tough journey. For example, we are charged to comfort one another because discipleship often leads to loss and grief. We are commanded to bear one another's burdens because circumstances often knock us off our feet. We are called to serve one another because the way of Christ exposes how desperately needy we are. We are told to encourage one another because it is sometimes hard for us to keep following Christ. These commands imply that the Christian life is difficult. It seems at times to demand more of us than we are capable of giving.

Capable, perhaps, but not unwilling. The distinction is important. Jesus looks for intent and desire in us more than capability and success. What matters is that we *want* to measure up to the full stature of Christ, however far we fall short. Though desire may not eliminate all of our problems and get us to the goal, it nevertheless points us in the right direction and reveals what is the deepest longing of our hearts. It establishes a trajectory in our lives. The mutuality commands we have studied so far assume at least some openness to and desire for spiritual growth. They imply that, in spite of the difficulty of the Christian life, most Christians really do want to make progress. They want to grow and change and become like Christ.

Most Christians, but not all. These final two commands deal with the "not all" group of people, which most of us probably fall into at least some of the time and maybe more of the time than we would like to admit. Sometimes Christians don't want to grow and change and become like Christ. Sometimes Christians don't want to journey down the path of the Christian life. Sometimes Christians don't want to pursue the highest and best that Christ promises, to which he calls us. In these circumstances the Bible commands us to "stir up" (RSV) and "admonish." We are called to "stir up" believers who suffer from inertia and need to get going again. We are commanded to "admonish" believers who are moving in the wrong direction and need to be turned around.

Uncomfortable Claims

The Gospels make one point very clear about the ministry of Jesus. Jesus upset people. It didn't matter whether they were his followers or his opponents. His words and deeds surprised, shocked and baffled his contemporaries. The Gospel of Mark uses words like *marvel* and *astonish* and *fear* to describe the kind of reaction that met Jesus. People could not figure him out. He broke their stereotypes of a human being, a teacher, a rabbi, a Messiah and whatever else they thought Jesus was. He seemed to think in larger categories. He had an expansive vision of life. He made everything in religion more extreme. He made bigger promises; he made bigger demands. Both followed logically from the claims he made about himself, which were even bigger than were his promises and demands. This "I am," this "Son of Man," this healer and teacher, this audacious human who claimed the prerogative to forgive sins—this man promised eternal life and then demanded that people deny themselves, take up a cross and follow him.

In no book of the Bible are God's promises and demands more radical than in the book of Hebrews. It contains big promises that correspond to the final revelation from God that was Jesus.

Therefore he had to become like his brothers and sisters in every respect, so that he might be a merciful and faithful high priest in the service of God, to make a sacrifice of atonement for the sins of the people. Because he himself was tested by what he suffered, he is able to help those who are being tested. (Heb 2:17-18; see also 4:15-16)

Yet the book of Hebrews also contains big demands. These, too, correspond to the final revelation that God gave in Jesus. The author warns believers because he believed that Jesus was the last word we would receive from God. Jesus made ultimate claims; the final word has been spoken; the last and best hope has come. So we must take Jesus Christ very seriously. He is God become human; he is Lord. He deserves our complete submission and total obedience. Hence no demand is too great and no effort should be spared to strive to do what God commands. "Take care, brothers and sisters," the author warns, "that none of you may have an evil, unbelieving heart that turns away from the living God" (3:12; see also 10:26).

The command to "stir up one another" is given in the context of these big promises and big demands. Much is given to us; much is demanded from us. We cannot have one without the other. Observe the big promises and demands in the passage that immediately precedes this command.

> Therefore, my friends, since we have confidence to enter the sanctuary by the blood of Jesus, by the new and living way that he opened for us through the curtain (that is, through his flesh), and since we have a great priest over the house of God, let us approach with a true heart in full assurance of faith, with our hearts sprinkled clean from an evil conscience and our bodies washed with pure water. Let us hold fast to the confession of our hope without wavering, for he who has promised is faithful. (Heb 10:19-23)

The author begins the passage by giving two big promises: we can be confident of our status as children of God, and we can be secure in our relationship with God. In the former case, our confidence comes because Jesus has made the holy of holies accessible to us through his death. He has opened up a new and living way. Our status as heirs of God's full blessing is pure gift; it is given through the work of Christ on the cross. In the latter case, our security comes because Jesus is now serving as our great high priest in heaven. He sits at the right hand of the Father, where he functions as our mediator and advocate. He is our representative before the Father; he is also the Father's representative before us. He is a merciful and attentive go-between, a divine ambassador who is making former enemies into friends.

But the author does not stop there. He makes two big demands as well. He tells us that we must "approach" God. We must nurture our relationship with him and never presume upon his kindness by thinking that his promises release us from the responsibility to seek God with heart, soul, mind and strength. God must be our goal, our passion. We must be single-mindedly devoted to him and pursue him as if he were life itself, because he *is* life itself. We must also "hold fast to the confession of our hope without wavering." We must persist in faith, endure when times are tough, hold on when everything in our immediate circumstances screams that God is distant, that faith is futile, that prayer is empty, that worship is a sham.

It is not easy to believe God's big promises, nor is it easy to meet God's big demands. That is why the author of Hebrews tells us "to stir up one another." "Let us consider how to stir up one another to love and good works, not neglecting to meet together, as is the habit of some, but encouraging one another, and all the more as you see the Day drawing near" (10:24-25, RSV). God's promises seem almost too grandiose to believe, his demands too difficult to fulfill. We can't believe alone, and we can't obey alone. We need each other's help and support. In the Christian faith, no one dare journey alone, for no one can make it alone.

The Comfort Zone

Faith and obedience often come hard because of doubt, struggle, temptation, exhaustion, busyness. Yet in my mind the greatest obstacle we face in the Christian life is not these difficulties, however serious and prevalent they are. The greatest obstacle is more subtle. It is deadly because it is hard to detect. Sometimes it seems to be the opposite of a problem. That is why the Bible is so clear in warning us and condemning it. The Bible calls this problem "lukewarmness." I shall call it the problem of inertia.

Inertia in the Christian life is dangerous because it seems so natural and justifiable. It is like water that flows naturally to the lowest elevation possible, where it can rest peacefully after cascading down mountainsides and meandering through broad valleys. People have a natural inclination to seek that same state of rest, comfort, ease. We like things to be convenient and controllable, stable and predictable. We want "givens" in our lives because they provide us with security. Consequently, we often fall into predictable patterns of behavior—in private life, in relationships with family and friends, and in the larger society. It thus happens inevitably that free choices soon become necessities, spontaneous activities become habits, innovations become traditions. What constituted bold action at one time sooner or later turns into "the same old thing." We like to settle down into a routine. We tend toward inertia. Rushing rivers, in other words, always end up emptying into placid lakes.

Examples are not hard to come by. Take personal habits. Most people follow a daily schedule. They get up at the same time, dress in the same kind of clothes, eat the same kind of breakfast, work at the same jobs (at home, factory, school, store, office or wherever), pursue the same interests outside of work. We are creatures of habit. It is true of all of us, however disciplined or lazy, whether morning person or night owl, regardless of our age, occupation, background and interests.

Marital roles follow the same rule. Husbands and wives naturally fulfill different roles. They practice division of labor. One takes out the garbage, the other does the dishes. One dusts, the other vacuums. One cares for the children, the other puts bread on the table. One takes the kids to daycare, the other picks them up. One coaches soccer, the other handles music lessons. Perhaps they divide home responsibilities evenly. Perhaps one does most of the work, the other very little. The point is not how but that they divide the labor. Each fulfills a different role.

Social interaction within larger groups follows the same pattern. How groups function demonstrates that same tendency toward predictability and stability. I work as a professor on a small college campus. I frequently observe student behavior outside my office window. I watch the same herds of students move toward the dining hall at about 5:15 every afternoon. I see those same groups frolic on the lawn in the fall and act out rites of courtship every spring. Students could turn the tables—as I'm sure many do—by noting the predictable social patterns that faculty follow.

There is a good reason why we fall into habits, fulfill roles, follow patterns, obey rules. Imagine what life would be like if we didn't! We need predictability to make life stable, comfortable and efficient. It would take an enormous amount of energy and security to adjust to a life that was never the same from day to day. Review how you lived yesterday and you will understand what I mean. What if you didn't have a set time to get out of bed because you didn't know what you were going to do all day? What if there was no food in the cupboards because you hadn't thought about what you were going to eat for breakfast? Or what if you went to your job, where you had worked for ten years, only to discover that you had been replaced without warning and for no good reason? Life is built on habit, order, routine, role, responsibility. Without such predictable patterns we would live in chaos and constant anxiety. We assume—rightly so—that life tomorrow will be roughly similar to life as it was yesterday. We depend on routine as much as we depend on the sun coming up.

Yet stability and predictability cost us something. The cost is sameness, blandness, boredom and sometimes injustice. Again, consider personal habits. There is nothing wrong with following a set schedule from day to day. But what happens when that schedule keeps us from enlarging our world by having new experiences or taking on new challenges? Or take marital roles. There is nothing wrong with fulfilling different roles. Yet the roles that husband and wife decided to follow early in marriage may be unfair when children come, or the husband goes back to school, or the wife gets a different job. Feminists have argued that the massive exodus of women out of the home and into the work force over the past two decades has not been accompanied by a massive change of roles at home. Many wives, in effect, work shifts—one at the job, the other at home. Or take institutional rules. There is nothing wrong with developing policies that make institutions run more efficiently. Yet sometimes rules that were made for the sake of efficiency and productivity under one set of circumstances may under other circumstances stifle creativity; rules that were made to put the most experienced people in positions of authority may eventually give way to an "old-boy network" that keeps new blood from rising to the top.

What is true in ordinary life and secular society is also true in the Christian life and the church. We need and desire stability. We like things predictable. Routine helps define who we are. For example, a personal habit like daily devotions helps to nurture faith. I have a friend who has read through the whole Bible once a year for twenty years now. That habit has enabled him to build personal discipline, expand his knowledge of Scripture, deepen his love for God. Likewise, traditions in the community of faith give us a sense of identity and continuity. I for one like familiar liturgy, older hymns, a printed prayer book. A set church schedule helps us to order our week around spiritual activities. We can look forward to Sunday worship, a midweek educational program, a morning Bible study, an important committee meeting.

Still, a routine poses the risk that personal devotions will grow stale, worship dull and lifeless, a small group ingrown and exclusive, the church schedule inflexibly tied to forms that cannot adjust to changes in culture. I know of people who gave sacrificially to the church during their early years of marriage but have not increased their tithe since then, although their income has at least tripled. Their giving may be predictable; I'm not sure that it is right. I know of churches that have worshiped the same way for twenty-five years; they minister meaningfully to the people who are familiar with the liturgy but ignore the needs of secular outsiders who are unfamiliar and probably uncomfortable with such formality. I know of denominations that have defended their institutions and traditions at the expense of outreach and evangelism.

This is the problem of living in the "comfort zone." The comfort zone in Christianity refers to that place in our Christian experience where we feel comfortable and secure, perhaps too comfortable and secure. Comfort zone Christianity appeals powerfully to certain impulses within us. It is inevitable that Christians eventually settle down to a routine—we build our institutions, develop our liturgies, establish our traditions, form our groups, perform our services. There is nothing wrong with this. If anything, routine protects us from unnecessary change, from a restlessness that dissipates spiritual energy, from the kind of spiritual mobility that makes us unstable, too easily driven and tossed by the winds and waves of contemporary culture. The impulse to change too quickly can entice us to embrace every fad that happens to come along without considering whether or not it reflects a genuine movement of the Spirit. Routine and tradition protect us from becoming prisoners to the spirit of the modern age. They keep us from reacting against the past and rejecting what has gone before simply because it represents tradition.

But comfort zone Christianity is still dangerous. It leads to laziness of spirit, deadness of faith, a routine that gives the appearance of religion without cultivating a heart for God. It allows us to assume a posture of ease and to take the path of least spiritual resistance. It makes us nice, decent and respectable. It leads to spiritual inertia—dead worship, exclusive churches, lifeless devotions, token service, easy giving, superficial knowledge of the Bible. It is, as the Bible calls it, lukewarmness, which is more perilous than open rebellion (Rev 3).

Jesus said that the new wine of his message and ministry—the new wine of the gospel—must be poured into new wineskins. The old wineskins cannot contain the radical power, energy and vitality—the big promises and big demands—of the gospel, which will burst them. We cannot therefore maintain traditions, theologies, institutions, groups, programs and habits if they keep us from drinking the new wine of Jesus! We must be flexible, adaptive, creative, eager to change.

Beyond the Comfort Zone

The mutuality command "Consider how to stir up one another to love and good works" is intended to push Christians *beyond* the comfort zone. Outlined in the biblical command are five steps that must be taken to obey this command.

The first step is concentration. We must *consider* how to stir up. The Greek word used here means "to take notice of," "observe carefully," "contemplate," "fix the eyes of the spirit on." It is the kind of word that describes how an artist gazes at a subject, how a surgeon studies an x-ray, how a scholar combs through data, how two lovers look longingly at each other.

Concentration implies that we think carefully and creatively about the needs of the people in our churches whom we are called to stir up. It requires us to tailor general principles of Christian living to fit individuals whose background, experience, problems, needs and desires differ from each other as much as the appearance of their faces. People are not all the same; consequently, we should not treat them all the same way. We must discern how to apply this command uniquely to each individual in our circle of friends at church. One may need to change careers, another to remain in a job that she would love to leave. One may need to evangelize a neighbor, another to help a neighbor to find a job. One may need to join a small group, another to quit one. One may need to memorize the book of Colossians, another to pray the "Jesus Prayer" one thousand times a day. One may need to go back to school, another to give time to an organization like Bread for the World or Habitat for Humanity.

I know of someone who keeps a section in his journal on the needs of his family and friends. As he prays for them he jots down ideas and insights. He may think of an appropriate gift for his daughter's birthday, which is still months away; he writes the idea down so that he will be able to surprise her with a special gift when her birthday arrives. He may gain an insight about a defect in his son's personality; he takes time to reflect on that insight in his journal so that, at the proper time, he will be prepared to talk thoughtfully about it with his son. He may spot signs of an unusual talent in a friend; he records those observations in his journal so that somewhere down the line he will be able to affirm that gift in his friend. He is mastering the first step of this command. He is learning to concentrate on the needs of others.

The second step involves strategy. We must consider *how* to stir up. It is not enough to think about the needs of our Christian friends. We must think about how our friends can change and grow. We must be deliberate. We must come up with specific plans and outline possible steps of action. It is one thing to think about a friend's need to master the basics of Christianity; it is another thing altogether to give him two good books on Christian discipleship and then propose that you read them together. It is one thing to believe that your church needs to experience deeper fellowship; it is another to go away for half a Saturday with twenty key members to design a program to start or revitalize small groups in the church. Christian faith flounders when we talk endlessly in generalities and neglect to turn our ideas into a specific course of action. We obey this command when we develop a concrete strategy—start a soup kitchen, write letters for Bread for the World, initiate an evangelistic Bible study in our neighborhood, start a second worship service, plan a weekend retreat on the spiritual disciplines, memorize the book of Colossians, attend a marriage renewal seminar.

The third step calls for action. We must consider how to *stir up*. In the Greek language the word was used originally to describe the effects of a high fever on a person. It leads to a paroxysm, frenzy, delirium. The New Testament applies the term to how people influence each other, whether for good or for evil. It is possible to "stir up" one another through irritation, disagreement, manipulation or injustice; this type of influence is usually bad. But it is also possible to "stir up" one another through inspiration, challenge and example; the result in this case is usually good. In either case, the word conveys the idea of a feverish activity. It is not like stirring a thick pot of soup; it is more like stirring a bowl of cream until it becomes butter. *Whip up* is a good synonym. This command demands immediate, energetic, creative action.

The fourth step sends us in a specific direction. We must consider how to stir up *to love and good works*. In other words, we must care about people, and we must commit ourselves to important causes. People are important to God. God wants us to treat people as ends rather than as means. Years ago I memorized 1 Corinthians 13. Every so often I review that chapter and evaluate my life in its light. I always come to the same conclusion: I am ashamed at how loveless I am. I can point to many accomplishments; I have many competencies that I have developed over the years. I have pursued many interests and hobbies. But I question how well I have learned to love.

Love, of course, is what people are crying for in our culture. This command requires that we challenge each other to love people—church people, neighbors, family members, colleagues. They must be our supreme concern in life, not (taking my own interests as an example) reading good books, building furniture, following the Dodgers, tending my garden, playing tennis, camping and backpacking, writing and teaching new courses. It is a sin to reverse the divine order, turning the penultimate into our ultimate concern. Jesus commands us to love God and neighbor even above ourselves.

One way we love people is by investing in causes that meet their needs. Christians are not wanting for good causes these days. I receive probably five hundred letters a year from Christian organizations that represent some great cause. I can't embrace them all; but I can embrace one or two. Recently I met a man who, on his retirement, sold his home and now pulls a trailer around the country to communities where he can help build churches. I know a physician who travels to Latin America one month a year to provide free medical care to villages. Never before has the church had so many opportunities to serve human need. What is lacking is not the causes but the willingness to give our time and energy to them.

The final step centers on the need for support—*not neglecting to meet together*. Christians can't stir up one another if they never see each other. There must be consistent participation, regular attendance. That standard presents a difficulty for people who live in a highly mobile, fragmented, leisure-oriented society. Many churches virtually shut down during the summer months because so many of their members leave for extended vacations or spend the summer at their cabins and cottages. Not that attendance improves that much during the other nine months. The school year (the calendar that many churches seem to follow) doesn't necessarily mean that church programs will attract maximum participation, since many church members go away for weekends or choose to give their time and energy elsewhere. It all adds up, killing momentum and undermining continuity. Spotty attendance hurts the church's ministry. Sunday-school teachers have difficulty building on what they taught the week before. Choir directors can't introduce new and challenging music. Small groups flounder. Ministries to needy people die. How can a church grow in numbers and depth if well over half of its membership is hit-or-miss?

How One Small Group Obeyed This Command

The Bible contains many examples of stirring up. Mordecai stirred up Esther to courageous action when he said, "Perhaps you were brought into the kingdom for such a time as this." The apostle Paul stirred up Philemon to care for his runaway slave. The author of Revelation stirred up the seven churches to faithfulness and service during a period of intense persecution. These biblical illustrations are useful examples of how to obey this command.

The church provides many settings in which we can obey this command. One of the most obvious settings is a small group. I have been in many small groups over the years. But the most memorable and significant was the group I started during the first year of my plunge into pastoral ministry. The six of us intended to meet for six months. We met instead for over four years, every Thursday morning at 6:00. It is the closest I have come to experiencing the full impact of this command over a long period of time.

At first we studied a book of the Bible. We were all very pious, and the group was safe. But soon we began to talk about what the message of the Bible meant for the way we lived—in our homes, at church and work, in the neighborhood. First we discussed our marriages, then friendships, then work. We expressed our deepest feelings, we revealed our weaknesses, we talked about our nagging questions. We challenged each other to become true disciples, and we discussed the obvious struggles of trying to be true disciples. We tried to strike a balance between service in the community and commitment to family, between

211

business at church and ministry to people, between time on the job and volunteer activities.

We became fast friends. We came to know each other well. One member of the group confessed his addiction to pornography. Another member sought our advice about buying a rundown house (the only kind he could afford) and then asked us to help him fix it up. We comforted each other during times of pain and grief. We encouraged each other when we were fatigued and lacked zeal. We had loads of fun together.

In short, we learned to obey the mutuality commands together. This group, in fact, was my first foray into studying these commands in depth. We took about two months to explore six or eight of the commands that this book covers. That was over fifteen years ago.

Intimacy in this group did not just happen. At some point each member of the group took the risk to challenge, confront and push the others. Sometimes we climbed all over each other. We did not settle for anything less than the best of what each of us could be. We told Bill that he had better attend to the needs of his wife before he found himself without one. We told Aaron that his anxiety at work would not increase his income, so why continue it? They told me to cool my intensity and mitigate my drive or everyone in the church would be exhausted. The group flourished because we dared to stir up one another to love and good works. I shall never forget those Thursday mornings—and all the other times we had together. I miss those friends very much.

How One Pastor Obeyed This Command

Small groups provide one setting to stir up one another. Eventually, however, a church must consider what this command implies for its total program and mission. I know one pastor who learned to stir up a declining congregation to love and good works. I believe his example and the church's story are useful because the church is quite ordinary, similar to most congregations in America. It is not located in a middle- to upper-middle-class community that is experiencing significant growth in population. It does not have lavish facilities or a perfect location. It is not a new congregation without a past to determine what its future will be, or will not be. It is not loaded with money. And its members are not highly professional or sophisticated. Yet it is an unusual church because it has carved out for itself a fruitful ministry in a depressed neighborhood after having endured a precipitous decline throughout the 1960s.

At that time the present pastor, Case Boersma, accepted a call to the church. I know Case well, and I consider him to be exceptionally good at knowing how to stir up. He has led the church to renewal and growth. It has become over the past twenty years one of the flagship churches of a midsize mainline denomination and a model for congregational renewal in a changing neighborhood. The church has tripled in size and offers a wide variety of programs in the community.

Case is energetic and visionary. He has a simple and clear theology of renewal, and he has applied this theology to the church for twenty years now. "Stirring up," he wrote to me, "demands an ethos and atmosphere of GRACE. Grace keeps a church from falling into the traps of reductionism and works righteousness." The first business of the church is to "create a womb of grace where healing and hope can abound. Without this 'womb,' in an age filled with fragmentation and quiet despair, the process of 'stirring up' only leads to further despair and greater levels of complacency. The key to creating this 'womb' is love, *unconditional love,*" embodied, as he put it, in the work of Christ on the cross, which creates level land on which everyone can stand.

Pastor Boersma is aware that stirring up the congregation to love and good works leads to a kind of death—the death of the familiar, of attachment to the past, of control and power. He realized soon after arriving at the church that, for the church to change, it would have to go through grief.

Life is obviously about change. Change invariably leads to loss; loss to grief; grief to anxiety; and finally, anxiety to hostility. We need, therefore, to acknowledge grief. We need to understand and choose to walk with the grieving. We need to lift up the truth that our God

213

is a God who calls us to change. We are "pilgrims on the move" and not settlers in the parlor. As I reflect back, I can recall sharing new ideas and watching, feeling and sensing the "pillars" of the church react with fear. It was my goal to listen to them, encourage and affirm them.

Yet he did not shrink from challenging the church to move forward. He kept holding up a vision of what the church could become. "People become 'stirred up' when they see a vision which is Holy Spirit birthed and inspired. This vision needs to be something which is larger than they are." He advocated the practice of "writing new chapters" every three years so that the church would develop a sense of history and see that progress has been made. "The congregation must be educated to understand that approximately every three years or so some new chapter needs to be written in obedience to the Holy Spirit. The Spirit causes new needs to be recognized; new programs to be developed; new approaches to meet the needs of the hurting."

His church has witnessed several major changes over the past twenty years. It transformed the image it had of itself. It expanded the staff. It intensified ministry to youth and family. It initiated a ministry to the Hispanic population. It deepened its ministry of prayer and enlarged its music ministry. It renovated the sanctuary. It developed a number of programs to meet needs in the community.

Pastor Boersma has called the people to prayer and praise. He confesses that without these spiritual disciplines the life of his congregation would wither, however busy it would appear to be in running its many programs. In his mind it is not enough for the people to do the work of God; they must also be the people of God, and they must practice the presence of God.

When God's glory is revealed to his people, they are "stirred up" by his majesty, love, power and presence. Our Saturday evening prayer services (at 7:00 and 9:00 p.m.), our Sunday evening praise service, and the emphasis on prayer in all musical endeavors have been pivotal in the "success" that our church has known recently. We find that

God's Spirit is released through contemplative prayer. The inner person is recreated. This enables us to love and serve again, joyfully. Pastor Boersma is a master at affirming members of the congregation for their obedience to Christ, and he draws attention to them so that others have examples to follow. "People who are on the frontier of faith, people who have borne their crosses with great dignity, people who have understood the price tag of Christian life and leadership, people who have passed on the baton of faith to the next generation, need to be recognized as models worth emulating." At the same time he is sensitive to the people who feel left behind and left out. He therefore spends a great deal of time listening to angry, disappointed, frustrated and critical people. But he does not allow such negativity to keep him from nudging the congregation forward.

This simple theology established the foundation for his ministry from the very beginning. During his first five years at the church, he emphasized hope and vision—hope that the church had a bright future ahead of it, vision that it could reach outsiders. He began to outline a strategy for renewal. He was persistent and repetitious—preaching on it frequently, reviewing it monthly at the elders' meeting, mentioning it at Bible studies, church potlucks and informal coffees. He dealt with the grief and absorbed the criticism; but he would not let up on the pressure. When the church began to grow he added staff, printed a weekly newsletter and started new programs. Above all, he and his family gave of themselves; they were very visible, amazingly energetic, extremely encouraging, consistently joyful. The church reversed the decline, added new members and reached out to the community. It also developed a new image of itself; members were proud of the church, eager to support new programs and willing to invite their friends. The church eventually became a dominant institution in the community.

This success did not mean that the church was spared from problems. Success itself posed a problem, because the church grew beyond what its facilities could handle. Loss of control and the absence of the familiar taxed the tolerance of the old-timers, who felt supplanted by new blood.

Pastoral leadership became more important in the minds of some members than the involvement of ordinary church members. Finally, "Americanized Christianity" has tempted many church members to seek a convenient faith that embraces happiness, prosperity and success but avoids commitment and sacrifice.

Continuity and Change

How radically should the church change? That question forces us to consider the outside limits of this command. How far should we go to "stir up" one another? How far is too far? Is it possible for us to change everything about ourselves? Is it possible for a church to change everything about itself? Is it right and healthy to change so radically? The church that Pastor Boersma serves is different now, yet people who have been gone for many years and have returned to visit mention the continuities as well as the changes. They say that the old church is still somehow there, however noticeable the changes. The leadership is largely the same as it was ten or fifteen years ago. The morning order of worship is the same, as are the church's location and facilities. The church has the same faces in it and the same feel to it. The changes are significant, but not so radical that the church of the present is a stranger to the church of the past. It has undergone several radical surgeries; yet the body is still the same.

This sense of continuity with the past should put our minds at ease. It implies that stirring up is best done by appealing to the best self that we already are in Christ, to the best church or institution that lies latent under the surface of the one that presently exists. Lutheran churches don't have to become Baptist churches to be renewed; they just have to figure out how to become better Lutheran churches. Small churches don't have to become superchurches to minister fruitfully in the name of Christ; they just have to discern how they can serve Christ as small churches. Liturgical churches don't have to throw tradition out their stained-glass windows to make worship lively; they just have to effect renewal by reinvigorating their liturgy.

What is true for churches is also true for individuals. Quiet and sensitive people don't have to become noisy and aggressive; activists don't have to become contemplatives; scholars don't have to become popularizers. Stirring up means that we become all that God meant us to be. It is not helpful or possible to stir up people to something that they are not or never could hope to be. It is not right to stir up a church to change so much that it becomes unfamiliar with the church it once was. Stirring up preserves the best of what we already are, the best of the tradition our church embodies. Continuity and change are partners, not enemies.

Both are important. Change pushes us beyond the comfort zone; continuity keeps us from forsaking the usable past. We need discernment to shape our vision of what stirring up requires, both for our friends and for our churches. The fact that daily devotions become routine does not mean that, in the name of renewal, we should reject that discipline. The fact that liturgy can degenerate into dead formality does not mean that liturgy itself is bad. Volunteer service that has become methodical and wearisome does not give us an excuse to give all of our time to contemplative prayer and meditation.

Sadly, much of the history of the church can be summed up in its reaction to what went before. When a religious tradition goes bad, a new movement may reject it entirely; soon that new movement becomes a tradition and, over time, it too goes bad. Another movement emerges and reacts against it, and so the cycle repeats itself endlessly. The secret of stirring up is balance—to push people, churches and Christian institutions beyond the comfort zone without breaking continuity with the past. Balance requires us to expand our vision of discipleship, not to change it entirely; to enlarge our capacity to know and obey God, not to swing periodically from one extreme to the other.

12

ADMONISH
ONE ANOTHER

A dmonition is the mutuality command that we obey the least often, and even when we attempt to obey it, we usually do the worst job of it. Unlike gossip, slander, criticism and rejection—other behaviors that, like admonition, concentrate on the negative aspects of people and come all too naturally to us—admonition seems awkward and contrary to our basic nature, like throwing a baseball with the opposite hand. We tend to avoid admonishing others as assiduously as we avoid being admonished by others. Still, it is a command in the New Testament. In fact, it is mentioned more often than nearly all of the other mutuality commands. Perhaps, as we shall see, for good reason.

We hesitate to admonish, for both good and bad reasons. On the good side of the ledger, we recoil from admonishing our brothers and sisters in Christ because we feel unqualified and unworthy. "Who am I to tell him to change? I've got enough problems of my own!" Such hesitation reveals our fear of being judgmental and intolerant, of picking the splinter out of someone else's eye before we remove the log out of our own. Ironically, a sober awareness of our own shortcomings may actually keep us from obeying this command at just the point where we are most able to do it well. Hesitation can be healthy because it builds humility. It becomes unhealthy only when it excuses us from doing the unpleasant but necessary business of admonition.

There is another good reason why we fail to obey this command. We feel a strange kind of relief and camaraderie with people who have weaknesses and problems similar to ours. We think to ourselves, "Well, at least I'm not the only one who has that problem!" We find comfort when we meet people who struggle with obesity, like we do, or who fall easily into depression, or who lose their temper at the least provocation.

I have three delightful children who happen to be very testy. Sometimes their spiritedness wears me out. I wonder if something is wrong with me, especially when everyone else's children seem to behave so perfectly. Their kids never run around after church like mine do! Their kids never whine and cry like mine do! Their kids never fight like mine do! Then suddenly I observe problems in other people's children—a brother pops a sister on the head, a six-year-old screams uncontrollably because she doesn't get her way, a ten-year-old mouths off to her father after being scolded. I realize that I'm not alone anymore, that my friends, who seem to be normal and healthy Christians, still struggle with how to be good parents, that there are good people out there whose children are imperfect. That knowledge comforts me.

Perhaps the most common cause of our failure to admonish, however, originates from our familiarity with those closest to us. We have an amazing capacity to adapt to the people we know well, to tolerate idiosyncrasies and to accept them for who they are, even when they are at their worst. Perhaps love is the reason for this. Or it could be our own need for survival, since we realize—perhaps unconsciously—that the cost of admonition is too high. We would rather keep the peace than have to deal with a strained relationship, hurt feelings, misunderstanding, anger—typical responses that often greet admonition. This familiarity may explain why some wives seem to tolerate intolerable irresponsibility, rudeness and selfishness in their husbands, why some churches maintain loyalty to a pastor who is not doing the job or why friends overlook, even chuckle affectionately at, obnoxious behavior in a neighbor.

But we also hesitate to admonish for at least one bad reason—a reason that reveals the wickedness of the human heart. We derive a strange pleasure in spotting weaknesses in other people, especially our Christian "enemies," and we like to tell our friends about those weaknesses. In other words, we prefer gossip to admonition. If it were simply a matter of cowardice and humility, then our hesitation to admonish people in the light of the knowledge we have about them would be understandable. Unfortunately, our real motivation is not cowardice and humility but power. We gain power over people when we know their weaknesses and reveal them to our friends.

Christians are no strangers to this habit. Perhaps it is even worse among Christians, because we can masquerade our gossip in such pious language. "Please pray for her," we say after having already said too much.

The ethos of our culture does not make admonition easy. Our culture has exalted toleration to the level of a creed. People are therefore quick to accuse their critics of being "judgmental" and "intolerant" and "insensitive" when they try, however graciously, to confront problems. They often hide behind the uniqueness and difficulty of their circumstances to excuse their behavior. "You just don't understand, you don't know what I have had to endure these past three years," someone says to a friend who thinks that she does understand and doesn't like what she sees. The statement is true, of course. No one knows exactly what another person feels and experiences. But does that mean we can say nothing at all after listening to someone's tale of woe except "Oh, how sad"? Are we always the victims of our circumstances? Does our environment excuse us from having to take responsibility for the choices we make?

Still, no excuses are good enough to excuse us from the obligation to obey this command. We are responsible for one another. That is the simple and frightening truth. We might not believe it; we might not accept it. But we cannot change it. What I become depends on how my Christian friends respond to me when I'm at my worst as well as at my best. The same holds true for them. And God will judge us for it. The prophecies of Ezekiel (for example, Ezek 33) contain sober warnings aimed at those who disclaim responsibility for others. These passages say that we are like watchmen who have been appointed to look out for a city. If an enemy comes and we warn the city, but our warnings go unheeded, then the destruction of the city will be the people's own fault and they will have no one to blame but themselves. If, on the other hand, we fail to warn the city, then the fault will be our own and we will have to take the blame for it. The enemy refers to the sins of the people of God. We are responsible to warn them about their sin. If we fail, then we will also be held responsible for their disobedience. The prophetic tradition—to my knowledge unique to Hebrew faith—reminds us that God holds his people accountable for their behavior and chooses to use people like us to remind them of that fact. We are called to be "watchmen" for one another. We are commanded to admonish.

We are not left, then, with much choice. And it makes good sense, once we consider the nature of discipleship. As I said in the last chapter, the path of discipleship is more like a footpath in the Rockies than like a boardwalk along the shore of a placid lake. It is not meant for weekend strollers but for serious hikers. It is a steep, rugged, narrow path. A tough path requires a tough faith. Tough faith requires tough love. Tough love requires that we show loyalty and concern for people in a variety of ways—encouragement, comfort, service, forgiveness. And admonition.

The question, therefore, is no longer whether we *should* admonish but *when* and *how*. We must learn to do it well. Scripture commands us to admonish one another, and it also tells us how. The apostle Paul will be our example; Jesus' instructions will give us the guidelines.

The Meaning
The Greek word for admonish means to "set right, correct, warn, lay on the heart of someone." It denotes confrontation, challenge, correction

of someone. Behind it lies the assumption that something is very wrong with that person's life. That wrongness requires admonition.

Admonition fits in well with and completes the metaphor of the journey that I have already used to explain the meaning of other mutuality commands. Comforting, for example, requires that we stop at the side of the road for a while to be with Christian friends who are waylaid by some grief. Bearing burdens requires that we get broken Christians back on their feet so that they can resume the journey of faith. Stirring up requires that we get lukewarm Christians, who have been living too comfortably, going again. Encouragement requires that we keep faithful people going when they face challenges and difficulties.

Admonition demands that we turn disobedient Christians around. It raises questions about the direction of their lives. It has a predictive dimension: we see what will happen if their present direction does not change. We warn them of the consequences of their present course of action. Appealing to their conscience, we challenge them to make a choice. "Here are the alternatives: your way or God's way. Which shall it be?"

On more than one occasion the New Testament writers put teaching and admonishing together (see Acts 20; Col 3). The two are necessary companions; one is incomplete without the other. Teaching appeals largely to the intellect, admonition to the will. Teaching deals with content, admonition with implications and application. Teaching sets a general course of direction, while admonition corrects a course that has gone awry. Teaching assumes openness and interest; admonition must confront opposition. Teaching sets the standard; admonition holds people up to it when they have chosen to compromise.

Admonition will have a harsh edge to it sometimes. The Bible contains many examples of brutal confrontation. The prophet Nathan says to King David, "You are the man!" (2 Sam 12:7). Jesus addresses Simon Peter, "Get behind me, Satan!" (Mt 16:23). Paul instructs the Corinthians, who had someone in the church who was practicing sexual immorality, "to hand this man over to Satan for the destruction of the flesh, so that his spirit may be saved" (1 Cor 5:5). As these references indicate, admonition is not something that Christians will readily welcome. It is therefore important that we be forbearing first. We must learn to love our Christian brothers and sisters as they are, to accept and affirm them before we challenge them to change.

Admonition can never be used as an excuse to clobber a friend because she does not measure up to what we think she ought to be. It does not give us license to lord it over others. First we give slack, listen, sympathize and affirm. Then we ask, "Is anything hindering my friends from growing in Christ? Are they wandering off course?"

Those questions are critical. While we should forbear always, we should admonish seldom. In many cases problems in our friends and in ourselves are not the result of defiance and rebellion but of weakness, vulnerability, human finitude. Time and experience will correct most of them. We must use a discerning eye. We don't take an eight-year-old to the doctor because he isn't five feet tall yet. We realize that it takes time to grow up into the full stature of manhood. We take him to the doctor only if something is hindering his growth, if he is not growing naturally, as an eight-year-old ought to. Likewise, we don't take a four-year-old to a reading specialist if she doesn't know how to read. We know that time and experience will probably make her a reader. People need room to grow into Christlikeness. Admonition is reserved for those few cases when something is keeping a Christian friend from maturing naturally in the faith. It corrects a course, turns someone around, challenges a problem, confronts resistance to God's Word. It addresses attitudes and behaviors that impede growth.

Before we admonish, therefore, it is important that we try to understand the basic nature of people. There is a subtle difference between the unique personality of a person and the perversion of a personality that results from disobedience to God's commands. The former requires the development of character, which enriches personality as morning sunlight draws out color in what appears to be a gray, lifeless world; the latter requires admonition so that defects can be corrected and Christian growth resumed.

Take a busy, active, productive person. She is always the one to volunteer for responsibilities, and she always gets the job done well and on time. Of course there is nothing wrong with being active and busy. Yet lately we have noticed that she has become frantic, nervous. She arrives late and unprepared to meetings; she is doing her work poorly. She seems to be neglecting her inner life and therefore lacks serenity when she is busy. It is time for admonition. "I have always admired your energy and commitment, but recently . . ."

Or take a naturally affectionate person. He loves to embrace his friends, male and female alike. He is passionate, emotional, demonstrative. We appreciate his outgoing personality, his expressiveness, his affectionate nature. But lately we have observed that he seems to be sending a slightly skewed set of signals to several women at the church. Others have noticed the change too. The time has come for admonition. "I have always enjoyed your warmth and affection, but I've observed lately that . . ."

The point is, we should not admonish Christians for their idiosyncrasies and imperfections. If we did, we would be admonishing people all day long. Admonition would become a wearisome, oppressive business. Rather, it should be reserved for problems that prevent Christian growth, not problems that normal Christian growth will solve. Thus we should not admonish serious people for being serious, unless they have become excessively self-serious. We should not admonish spontaneous people for their free-spiritedness, unless their spontaneity makes them consistently irresponsible. We should not admonish disciplined people because they live in a routine, unless their discipline makes them inflexible. We should not admonish conservative people for their conservatism, unless that conservatism has made them negative, critical and self-righteous.

Again, admonition requires discernment. "Who is this person?" we should ask. "Is she heading in the right direction or is she wandering off course?"

Admonition tries to correct the wrong direction that a friend's life has taken. It should not then be reserved—as it often is—for those big, juicy, scandalous sins that titillate us and make for delicious tidbits of gossip. Admonition is best practiced before the damage is done. We should admonish at the beginning stages, when a wrong course has been set but the consequences of it have yet to be experienced. I have heard horror stories from more conservative churches about young unmarried couples who were dragged before the entire congregation to confess the sin of fornication. They were found out because the woman became pregnant. I do not deny that they sinned. But how much good is accomplished by their humiliation? The proper time for admonition is not after the woman is pregnant but before, when couples are experimenting with sex but are unaware of the consequences, both physical (pregnancy, sexually transmitted diseases) and spiritual (lack of trust and intimacy, moral compromise, shame). If admonition was appropriate once the pregnancy had happened, it should have been leveled at the larger church family, who sat there gawking, snickering and shaking their heads. The real sin that needed exposure was not fornication, however bad that is, but hypocrisy and judgment.

Admonition, in short, does not wait for the consequences of sin to become apparent to all before it goes to work. It challenges lust before it turns to adultery, greed before it eases into materialism, anger before it becomes violent and abusive, little lies before they grow into big ones, factionalism before it causes a church to split.

The Purpose

The apostle Paul gives a positive and a negative purpose for admonition. To the Christians living in Colossae he wrote: "It is he [Jesus Christ] whom we proclaim, warning [admonishing] everyone and teaching everyone in all wisdom, so that we may present everyone mature in Christ" (1:28). Paul is referring to the goal of having the full expression of Christ's perfection formed in us. There is a tension in Paul's theology at this point. We are new persons because of what Jesus has done for us. The newness is already ours—it has already happened *to* us by the imputation of Christ's righteousness into our lives. But it must also happen *in* us through the work of the Holy Spirit. In Christ we have been adopted as children of God; through the power of the Holy Spirit we must begin to act like it. We belong in the family of God; now we must live that way. Our responsibility as children of God is to close the gap between our status as saints and our daily behavior as sinners.

Admonition corresponds to this positive purpose. We see what our friends already are through the work of Christ on the cross and what they can become through the work of the Holy Spirit. We tremble when we consider their potential glory. Consequently, we won't let our friends settle for anything less than the best. That vision of glory excites us; that same vision leads us to admonish them. "That won't do," we say to them about some sinful habit. "Not when you consider what God has in store for you." Admonition in this positive sense functions like a good coach who is convinced that her team of average players can become the best in the league. She pushes them, pleads with them, demands a great deal from them because she believes that they have a great season ahead of them. She lifts up their level of performance because she knows that it can be higher, much higher.

Paul mentions a negative purpose for admonition too. In his farewell sermon to the elders of the church at Ephesus he warned them of perils that would shortly come upon the church. He said that "fierce wolves" would soon attack the flock. Those wolves were pagans who wanted to keep unsavory company with weak Christians in order to destroy their faith. Their religious ideas were speculative rather than revelational, and their behavior was immoral rather than upright. Paul was concerned about their deleterious influence on vulnerable Christians. He understood human nature. He knew that something about new ideas and base conduct entices Christians, drawing them away from true faith.

Still, that was not Paul's only concern. He believed that perils would also arise from within the church, "even from among you," he said in his farewell message. In this case Paul was referring to church leaders who would lead ordinary believers astray. Paul realized that this inside threat was worse than the outside one because the leaders used a religious disguise to hide their true intent. As it turns out, Paul's fear was well founded. Later on he wrote two letters to Timothy, who was serving as the pastor of the church at Ephesus. In those letters he intimated that the elders had not heeded his warning. Consequently, the church had to contend with false teachers who were distorting apostolic teaching. They were telling people what they wanted to hear, "tickling their ears," as he put it.

Paul was alarmed by still one more peril. This one originates from within each individual. In his first letter to the Corinthians Paul admonished the believers there because they had become arrogant and self-seeking (1 Cor 4). They were so hungry for power and influence that they recoiled from people like Paul who were too weak and ordinary, too humble and good, to merit respect and obedience. They boasted about their wealth and status; the apostles boasted only about the grace of God at work in their lives. So Paul warned them about what was happening to their own souls. The quest for power was corrupting them, and they didn't even know it. They had become self-deceived.

Over the years I have met many people who violated biblical absolutes and did not feel any pangs of conscience until the reproofs of life knocked them off their feet. They were completely self-deluded. As one woman said to me about a church split in which she participated, "I justified myself at every stage of the conflict. I was completely convinced that I had a good reason to join the splinter group. I had a foolproof case." Then she added, "It is frightening to consider how easily we can deceive ourselves."

The juxtaposition of this negative and positive purpose motivated Paul to admonish his brothers and sisters in Christ. He understood the high stakes—the promises and the perils—of discipleship. So he did not hesitate to plead, warn, threaten, confront and appeal to the conscience of his fellow Christians when they were drifting off course. Their maturity was more important to him than was his popularity; being loving was a higher value to Paul than being liked. He wanted them to become mature in Christ; he wanted them to be spared from compromise. He resorted to every conceivable method of motivation—including admonition—to get them and keep them on course.

The Act of Admonition

Jesus outlined how we should address the kinds of offenses in the church that call for admonition.

> If another member of the church sins against you, go and point out the fault when the two of you are alone. If the member listens to you, you have regained that one. But if you are not listened to, take one or two others along with you, so that every word may be confirmed by the evidence of two or three witnesses. If the member refuses to listen to them, tell it to the church; and if the offender refuses to listen even to the church, let such a one be to you as a Gentile and a tax collector. Truly I tell you, whatever you bind on earth will be bound in heaven, and whatever you loose on earth will be loosed in heaven. Again, truly I tell you, if two of you agree on earth about anything you ask, it will be done for you by my Father in heaven. For where two or three are gathered in my name, I am there among them. (Mt 18:15-20)

What can we learn from this passage about admonition? First of all, admonition is best done privately. Admonition that includes no one but the offender and confronter builds trust and eliminates the nasty complications that arise when people who are not part of the problem or the solution get involved. Too much talk spoken by too many people who have too many opinions undermines the work of admonition. It makes it difficult for a person, already cautious and resistant, to change when he discovers that uncommitted, uninformed and unloving people know what should have been kept private.

In my mind we have too many unnecessary conversations in the church about other people's problems. We like to be insiders and know something about everyone, especially when the information we have doesn't actually require us to do something about it. But information that does not lead to obedience is dangerous. Admonition demands that we do something about what we know. It requires that we deal directly with people. We must "speak the truth in love" to the only person who needs to hear the truth, the only person who can do something about the truth. Admonition keeps things private. It goes public only when, as Jesus intimated, there is a hostile response. And by public I mean to people of experience, wisdom and authority—the elders of the church—who are in a position to deal firmly and redemptively with the problem. Then, only after every option has been exhausted, should the offender be asked to leave the church.

Private admonition will protect us from using others' faults as leverage to gain power over them. The danger of admonition is that fallen human nature can turn a legitimate occasion for admonition into a power struggle between two proud people. The quest for power, in turn, tempts the admonisher to go public before it is the proper time, because public exposure of an errant brother gives one power over another. The admonisher demonstrates by word and spirit that she is not so much interested in restoring her brother as she is in gaining power over him. The admonished senses that taking to heart the admonition is tantamount to giving up and giving in. He feels exploited, humiliated, defeated. Privacy, however, transforms the whole dynamic of admonition. The confronted does not feel that he must defend himself before the entire community. Repentance does not spell defeat. There is no sense of "You lost, I won" or "I told you so." Privacy keeps power from becoming the central issue; it therefore draws attention to what matters most—the need to repent and make one's life right with God.

Second, admonition is best done positively. The purpose is, as Jesus taught, to "regain" a brother or sister. Admonition does not just put down; it builds up. It does not simply point out a weakness but tries to replace it with a strength. It corrects a wrong course by helping to set a right one. It aims at restoring, making right, solving the problem. It gets people going in the right direction again. No one likes to be told about failures if that person does not sense that the critic is interested in making him a success. As I pointed out before, criticism of weaknesses, like the demolition of a condemned house, is the easy part. It is usually a simple task to tear something down. The building of strengths is the difficult work. Telling a friend that she must break off an affair is one thing; helping her to rebuild a marriage is another. Harping on someone's need to lose weight is one thing; helping him to change eating habits is another. Admonition demands the kind of long-term commitment that enables us to see our friends all the way through to repentance, recovery, restoration. As Jesus said, we want to "regain," not simply to reprove.

I asked the academic dean at a Christian liberal arts college to reflect on his years of experience as a Christian leader in both church and college and to distill insights about the use of admonition in his position. In a long letter to me he addressed two issues: the spirit of admonition and the method of admonition.

Doug used the examples of two critics from his past to make the point that one must "earn the privilege" to admonish. The privilege is earned, he said, by the spirit that is communicated to the one who needs admonition. "My first critic," he wrote, "accurately assessed my short-comings, my need for growth."

I couldn't argue with his evaluation, but I bristled when I heard it. What was all wrong was the spirit in which he offered his criticism. It was a judgmental spirit. From his perch of superiority, he verbally beat me with a catalogue of how I failed to measure up to accepted standards of performance. And, of course, he was right. I had failed to measure up. But his insistence on putting me down instead of building me up only made me defensive. He hadn't earned the privilege of being my critic.

The second critic, Doug continued, communicated a different spirit.

I never perceived my second critic as a critic. I perceived him as a caring friend. His was a spirit of helpfulness and kindness. I knew that he cared enough about me to want me to grow. And so I didn't bristle at his suggestions for growth, his criticisms. I even sought them out. He helped me immensely, not with a spirit of superiority, but with the humility of a fellow Christian pilgrim who acknowledged his own need to grow. He had earned the privilege of being my critic by first being my friend.

This second critic had learned to exemplify the "rare combination of being both critical and kind at the same time."

This kind of positive admonition appeals directly to the conscience, the deepest part of a person's life. When we admonish we must address not simply the unacceptable behavior but the worldview that supports it. Sin is bad as an action because it leads to self-destruction. Sin is bad as a thought because it leads to self-delusion. The mind is frighteningly capable of justifying sinful actions. It can embrace a worldview that seems perfectly reasonable. That is why, as Paul said, we must do more than "put off" bad habits and "put on" new habits. We must also "be renewed in the spirit of our minds" if we want real victory. Paul understood that the transformation of the mind is as important as is a change in behavior (Eph 4:22-24).

But the mind is stubborn and quick. It does not like being told it is wrong. It can maneuver adeptly to counter any logic we may use to prove it wrong. Consider this example. A missionary on the field works with ten colleagues, and none of them can stand to work with her. She is bossy, selfish and critical. She spoils the unity of the group. All are agreed that she has a serious character problem. But no one dares to confront her. She is a master at playing the victim. She complains that no one understands her and that everyone is out to get her. Her logic makes her unapproachable.

Or consider this example. An associate pastor at a large church builds a successful youth program, but it comes with a price. He criticizes his staff, dominates their time and energy and insists that they think his way or quit his ministry. He leaves little room for diversity. Yet he deflects criticism by claiming to be a prophet. "Prophets are never popular," he says. "No one likes people who speak the Word of the Lord." His close identification with God makes it impossible to correct him.

Or consider this example. A woman who has struggled with lesbian tendencies for years finally joins the lesbian community and becomes a militant advocate. She is also a Christian and claims biblical justification for her chosen way of life. Using a "justice hermeneutic," she criticizes the "heterosexism" of the Bible, and she justifies lesbianism by claiming that God's grace gives her freedom to be unashamedly who she is. She turns the tables on biblical morality by claiming that traditional sexual ethics is a product of heterosexual dominance and oppression. Her logic has made what the Bible would call a sin a normal and healthy pattern of behavior.

Admonition cuts through distorted logic by transcending it, refusing to argue, avoiding intellectual power struggles. It appeals to the conscience. It does more than prove and argue; it convicts instead. It appeals to the highest and truest self in a Christian, the self that is being shaped into the image of Christ. It asks, "Is this what God wants for you? Is this how God intended life to be lived? Is being so right really worth it when you consider the price that you are paying?" Admonition summons people to Jesus Christ, to repentance and forgiveness, to death and resurrection. It calls people to spiritual transformation. That is the most positive message that we can possibly give.

Third, admonition is best done prayerfully. Admonition is risky business. There is no guarantee that our friends will welcome our admonitions, repent of their sin and decide to live differently. They may take offense, reject our pleas, cool to our friendship. They may even rally a group of sympathetic friends around their cause. Paul understood the risks. On more than one occasion his admonitions were not received enthusiastically. His first letter to the Corinthians, for example, was dismissed by some members of the church. They challenged his authority and continued to tolerate ungodly behavior and to believe false doctrine. So Paul had to write what some scholars call "the severe letter" to expose their sin. So anxious was he over their response to this letter, now lost to us, that he could not even preach. He wanted to know the outcome to this painful dispute.

Prayer greases a tense situation, prepares the heart (both theirs and ours), softens the will. Prayer sends the Holy Spirit ahead of us so that the most important work—making someone open to God—is already done before the actual admonition is given. Prayer protects us from the presumption of thinking that our words are enough. It keeps us from overestimating our own human powers to effect real change. The deepest parts of people are beyond our reach, however sincere and loving we are. Only God can touch those deep parts. Prayer invites him to.

Offenses Needing Admonition

The church is deeply divided, perhaps worse now than ever, over what problems, if any, deserve admonition. Admonition implies standards. Standards imply rights and wrongs. What constitutes right and wrong is presently up for grabs. Such confusion makes admonition difficult. How can we obey this command if it is impossible to agree on basic doctrinal and moral standards? It appears that today one can believe and do almost anything and still be a Christian.

Christianity is a religion of the book. So what does the Bible teach? What beliefs and behaviors did the biblical authors single out for admonition? I believe that these can be broken down into three categories. The first involves theological problems. The most important by far concerns our view of Jesus Christ, or what theologians call Christology. The New Testament boldly proclaims that God has come himself in the person of Jesus Christ, who was perfectly divine and perfectly human. This Jesus was born of a virgin, lived a sinless life, suffered and died, and was raised from the dead. On the cross he dealt once for all with the sins of the world. Anyone, therefore, who believes in Jesus will become the beneficiary of his atoning work. That person will receive forgiveness of sins and the gift of eternal life.

The apostle Paul argued that Christ's nature and Christ's work are the dividing line that determines whether or not one is a believer. Everything else, however important, is secondary. In his letter to the Galatians he called a curse on anyone who altered the basic message of the gospel. When ministering in Antioch he admonished Peter because Peter had required Gentiles in Antioch to become Jews before becoming

Christians. That meant that the gospel was less than sufficient to make one right with God. "Christ or nothing!" was Paul's battle cry.

Admonition must begin at this point. If one's basic theology is wrong, then everything else we could potentially confront is beside the point, like trying to treat symptoms of a disease when the disease itself is completely overlooked.

The second category comprises moral problems. In this case I am referring to the kinds of moral problems that manifest defiance against God, not struggle before God. As I argued in the chapter on burden bearing, there is a subtle difference between a person who slips into sin and a person who plunges into sin. Some believers are made vulnerable to sin because of their circumstances. Other believers choose to sin simply because it will give them pleasure and power. It is this latter group that needs admonition.

Moral problems require admonition at the earliest stages of development. Paul listed the "big sins" in several of his letters (Rom 1; 1 Cor 6; 1 Tim 1). He said that fornicators, idolaters, adulterers, male prostitutes, sodomites, thieves, the greedy, drunkards, revilers and robbers will not inherit the kingdom of God—unless of course they repent of their sin and trust in Jesus alone for forgiveness and salvation. Once becoming Christian, people need to be kept from falling into sin that may remain attractive. They need to be admonished when old and familiar sins start to regain a foothold, before "little" sins, so innocent and pleasurable, become big ones, as they usually do. As the old proverb goes, an ounce of prevention is worth a pound of cure. Admonition concentrates on lust, materialism, covetousness, appetite—habits of the mind that eventually surface in ungodly behavior. Admonition addresses attitude as well as action, corrects character flaws before they become moral tragedies, goes to the mat over small compromises before they erupt into big crises.

The third category involves church disputes and divisions. By far the greatest cause of church disunity is self-righteousness, which is easy to spot in others but not so easy to spot in ourselves. Self-righteousness surfaces when we isolate some distinctive about ourselves or our group—

ethnic, cultural, political, doctrinal—that gives us the right to think ourselves superior to another person or group. The most prevalent distinctive that divides Christians today is based on the ideological distinction between the right and the left. Christians on both sides have decided that views on abortion, homosexuality, South Africa, censorship, pornography and ecology are more important than the gospel itself. Both sides have aligned themselves with a political party at the expense of unity in the one issue that matters the most—who Jesus Christ is and what he did. Such an ideological division is a violation of the unity of the church in Jesus Christ. It puts power and influence higher than loyalty to the church.

Jesus was absolutely intolerant of the self-righteousness of the Pharisees, who believed that one had to become a strict Jew in order to be acceptable before God. Paul wrote that Jesus' death broke down the "dividing wall of hostility" (NIV) by abolishing in his flesh any kind of distinctive that makes one group feel superior to another (Eph 2:11-22). The only thing that ultimately matters is that we know and trust in Jesus Christ (Phil 3:7-9). In fact, Paul considered that his pharisaical social status and accomplishments—the distinctives that made him feel superior to others, especially Christians—were like garbage because they had kept him from knowing Christ.

Self-righteousness divides the church, the very church that the New Testament declares is one. There is "one" Lord, "one" faith, "one" God (Eph 4:5-6; see 1 Cor 12). The church is united in Christ, not in one particular theology, political ideology or ecclesiastical polity. People who divide the church for any other reason than the preservation of the gospel itself need to be admonished.

Levels of Responsibility

Who should be admonished is one question, who should do the admonishing is another altogether. Our level of responsibility depends on the intimacy of the relationship and the nature of our own authority. I have found two general rules useful. The first is that intimacy of relationship and authority of office give us the right to admonish. The second is that complexity of situation, ambiguity of offense and lack of accurate information should make our admonitions tentative.

The first rule addresses the right we have to admonish. We have the responsibility to admonish our closest friends, not strangers in the church. The reason is simple enough: we know our closest friends better, and we are in a better position to perceive their strengths and weaknesses. Similarly, as church leaders we have the right to admonish believers who are under our authority. Again, the reason is simple: church leaders have been entrusted with the authority to be teachers and shepherds of the flock. Our responsibility to admonish will taper off as relationships become more superficial or authority is lacking. In other words, we should be most attentive to the needs and problems of those closest to us, those under our authority and not those whom we know only through chance encounters, hearsay, rumor or gossip. What have I to say intelligently and redemptively about the Methodists down the street? a newcomer in my church? the Catholic hierarchy? My responsibility in such cases is to pray for them, not judge and admonish them, unless my stature, knowledge and position allow.

The second rule addresses the manner in which we should admonish. Not all admonition demands a "Thus says the Lord." Forthrightness is appropriate some of the time, but not all the time. Admonition does not always have to be harsh and direct. Sometimes it is best to ask a question and negotiate a tentative solution. "I am confused by your behavior," we may say to a friend. "First you're rude to me; then you treat me like your best friend. Is something bothering you about our relationship?" That kind of mild admonition reflects an open attitude. It invites conversation and mitigates defensiveness. It is appropriate when we are concerned but feel uncertain, when the problem is serious but not critical.

Rarely does a problem demand a prophetic word. Such an occasion occurs only after questions or negotiations have failed, and may even put a person at greater spiritual risk. Sometimes I talk to my children about dangers that I want them to avoid. For example, I tell my three-year-old that he may not cross the street by himself. I take great pains to explain the reasons why. During these discussions my children ask questions to clarify the rules and to reach understanding. Occasionally they complain about the rules and suggest alternatives. Sometimes I don't discuss but command. If my son is racing full speed toward the street on his Big Wheel, I don't take the time to explain the rule. I shout at him to stop dead in his tracks.

The same principle applies to admonition. It is one thing when we feel concern about a teenager's friendship with a disreputable group of people. That kind of concern calls for long conversations. It is another thing when that teenager is planning to go away with the group for an unchaperoned weekend at a cottage. Likewise, it is one thing to observe that trouble is brewing between rival groups in our church. That kind of trouble requires constructive conversation in small groups and a sermon series on the unity of the church. It is another thing when one of those groups is organizing its own Sunday-evening worship service in anticipation of a church split. Whether we should discuss or confront, negotiate or rebuke depends on the severity of the problem, the risk posed by the problem and the attempts we have made in the past to deal with the problem.

Difficult Cases

If admonition is hard enough to do under normal circumstances, it becomes even harder in complex cases. I want to explore several of these situations. The first concerns parties in the larger church of whom we are suspicious and with whom we have sharp disagreements. I disagree, for example, with prochoice groups in my own denomination. Am I responsible to admonish them because I think that they are wrong? Should I organize a group to counter their influence? Should I lead a crusade against them? Or should I remain silent and let the disagreement stand?

If we follow the guidelines for the levels of responsibility that I just outlined, it follows that I lack both authority and intimate knowledge to assume the right to admonish advocates of a prochoice policy (unless of course they happen to be close friends of mine or members of the church in which I have authority as a leader). It seems that the best strategy is not to admonish but to become acquainted with both the people and their ideas. I could, for example, have a face-to-face conversation with a person of a prochoice persuasion. I could read the literature of the movement thoughtfully and carefully to become better informed. I could frequently remind myself that prochoice is not a monolithic ideology, nor are prochoicers evil and calloused human beings. Before I ever get to the point of considering admonition, in other words, I could befriend, listen, probe and understand. That is far more constructive than what we usually do, which is label, caricature, distort and dismiss.

The second complex case involves Christian authors and speakers who communicate their ideas to a wide audience and exercise an influence far beyond the reach of their personal friendships or local church. What should we do, for example, if we read an article in a Christian magazine, study a Christian book, listen to a Christian tape, watch a Christian television program or hear a Christian speaker and disagree strongly with the message? Do we have the right to admonish? Again, we must remember that in such circumstances our level of responsibility is not very high. But does that mean we have no responsibility at all to warn the church of a theology or ethic that departs dangerously from what we consider the biblical truth? Should we not warn Christian friends about a particular program, book, seminar, church, movement or preacher that poses a serious threat to the Christian faith?

Again, it seems to me that we should attempt to listen and to understand before we act. Watching one television program does not make us experts. Nor does listening to one sermon. Nor does reading one article. We should become informed first. Once informed, we should also try to communicate directly with the party about whom we are concerned to get more information, clear up confusion, raise questions. Only then, it seems to me, do we have the right to go public and expose the errant message. And then under one condition—that we deal with the issue itself, not the person. A book is not a person; it only contains a person's ideas. A sermon is not a person; it only communicates a little of what the preacher believes. If we write a book review to challenge an author's point of view, we should stick to the issue itself and be as fair as we can, avoiding any hint of condemning the author. We should report to our friends that we believe a televangelist's preaching is errant, not that the televangelist himself is demonic. We should discipline ourselves to say no more than is warranted by the evidence that we have.

The point is, we should not pretend to be experts on people we do not know, and we should avoid saying something about authors or speakers outside of what is contained in their books or messages. We should claim expertise only when it is earned, after we have done our homework well. Then we should stick to the issue at hand—the content of a book, the message of a sermon—and not wander off into territory that is forbidden by our ignorance or their privacy. The command to admonish does not give us the right to destroy anyone with whom we happen to disagree, however wrong they may be. Robert E. Lee's motto is a good one to follow: "I have fought against the people of the north because I believed they were seeking to wrest from the south its dearest rights. But I have never cherished toward them bitter or vindictive feelings, and I have never seen the day when I did not pray for them."

The third case concerns evaluations in Christian institutions, which of course includes the church. Do institutions have the right and responsibility to admonish employees who are not doing their job? Missionary organizations, parachurch movements, Christian colleges, Christian businesses, denominational bureaucracies and individual congregations all face this complex issue. How do we evaluate poor performance in a redemptive way?

I asked Doug, the academic dean whom I quoted earlier in this chapter, to outline how he approaches evaluations, both official and informal, of faculty members at the college he serves. I believe his insights are applicable to many settings, especially to churches and church bureaucracies. These are the guidelines he tries to follow:

1. Be quick to speak publicly of a person's abilities and accomplishments.

2. Never speak publicly of a person's weaknesses and shortcomings.

3. If you have a criticism of a person's performance, go directly to that person.

4. Take the time needed to develop caring relationships with the people who report to you, creating a spirit of helpfulness, not judgment, earning the privilege of being critical.

5. Don't wait to spend time with a person until you have a criticism of his or her performance.

6. Cultivate the habit of looking for the good in people and events.

7. In a comprehensive performance evaluation of anyone, start with and highlight the person's strengths and accomplishments (the good news); then present honestly and kindly your perceptions of need for further growth—he or she will thank you if it is done in the spirit of helpfulness, not judgment.

He concluded:

Many of us are associated with institutions claiming to be guided by Christian principles. What is the telltale sign of fidelity to that claim? Not the growth of our institution; not the size of its budget; not the profundity of the publications and speeches of its members. It is "that we love one another." That is no easy task. It requires kindness. It also requires being critical. That's a rare combination.

Admonition as a Two-Edged Sword

I talked with a good friend of mine, Elizabeth, about the subject of admonition, because I knew that her recent experience had exposed her to the two-edged sword of admonition. Her experience led her to admonish; it also invited others to admonish her. Elizabeth was appointed to serve on a church committee that was charged with the responsibility of selecting a new hymnal for worship. Elizabeth has conservative theological convictions. She is thoughtful, hardworking, serious about her faith and committed to developing Christian character. She is one of the sharper people I know. Her experience on that committee is useful because it reveals how important it is for people who admonish to be open to admonition.

The pastor asked each member of the committee to review three hymnals. Elizabeth did her review very thoroughly. She read the lyrics of every hymn, took notes on changes in language, observed additions of new hymns and eliminations of old hymns, and analyzed the usefulness of the hymnal to a typical middle-class congregation. She became immediately aware of three issues. First, she was by far the most conservative member of the committee. That made her feel isolated and forced her, as she said, "to do [her] homework well." Second, she discovered that she had done her homework so well that she was far more prepared than the other members of the committee to discuss the strengths and weaknesses of each hymnal. The knowledge she had acquired intimidated some of her colleagues on the committee. Third, she responded most negatively to the one hymnal that the committee was already receiving pressure to adopt—the most theologically liberal of the three hymnals.

She decided soon after the committee was organized to express her concerns in writing. What started out as a short letter turned into a long paper that provided insightful analysis of the one hymnbook around which most of the dispute revolved. She managed in those twenty-some pages to challenge everything that many educated people in American culture—and therefore many Christians—consider "politically correct," including commonly held assumptions about feminism and inclusive language. I read her paper. Whether one agreed with it or not, it was an impressive document.

That paper had a huge impact on the proceedings. It polarized the committee, incensed the chair, who favored the hymnbook that Elizabeth was attacking, and eventually sent ripples of controversy through the whole congregation. The committee had hearings—even brought in experts in theology, church music and feminism—just to deal with

Elizabeth and her paper. It was obvious that every member of the committee disagreed sharply with Elizabeth. Some even intimated that she should wise up and enter the twentieth century. One man called her a Pharisee who was "dropping a nuclear bomb on a mosquito."

However stiff the opposition from the committee, Elizabeth managed to hold her own without getting defensive. Soon word leaked out to the congregation about her paper. Members of the congregation began to request copies. Others started to study the proposed new hymnal with greater seriousness, as if the decision whether or not to adopt it was an important one, which of course it was, since the hymnbook would function every week for many years to shape theological convictions in the church. In other words, people began to think theologically about what they were going to be using in worship, and they began to evaluate the new hymnbook according to their understanding of Scripture. Elizabeth had in effect admonished the congregation to repent of its slothfulness, theological ignorance and naiveté. She had charged fellow members to become mature in their thinking.

Over the next months the church became as polarized as the committee, except that the church sided overwhelmingly with Elizabeth. The elders called a congregational meeting just to deal with some of the tension and to head off a possible church split, which the church seemed to be moving toward all too speedily. Finally a new committee was formed, this one with three more members. There was greater variety of convictions among members of the new committee—more conservative voices, in other words—and greater commitment to move carefully and thoughtfully toward selection of a hymnal. The committee has yet to make a final recommendation.

I believe that Elizabeth demonstrated courage and humility throughout the process. Her convictions infuriated some members of the committee. Some were nasty to her. The chair and her family have since left the church. Yet Elizabeth remained peaceful, kept discussion confidential and did not recruit a party to support her. Perhaps the reason she acted as blamelessly as she did is that she, the one who did so much admonishing, was herself open to admonition.

Elizabeth told me that when the dispute reached its tensest moments, she lost perspective and became completely absorbed by it. She might have lost patience, attacked the opposition, become self-righteous and recruited an army of defenders if she had not been admonished on four separate occasions.

The first occasion occurred when her own teenage daughter asked Elizabeth one day, "You mean to tell me that the feminist movement is more important than the gospel? Mom, you are behaving as if I should warn my friends about the evils of feminism, not tell them the good news about Jesus." That word brought her up short.

A few days later her husband began to raise questions too. He cautioned her: "Be careful. Cultivate a gentle spirit. Don't get defensive." He also suggested that, regardless of the outcome, they not leave the church. "The selection of the hymnbook is important," he said, "but not that important. It is not an issue that merits leaving the church." And then, speaking for the whole family, he pleaded, "Elizabeth, let it go. We want our mother and wife back. You have let this thing go too far."

About a month later she read this paragraph from Osward Chambers. It provided still another word of admonition.

Am I set on my own way for God? . . . Every time we stand on our rights and insist that this is what we intend to do, we are persecuting Jesus. . . . I may teach sanctification and yet exhibit the spirit of Satan, the spirit that persecutes Jesus Christ. . . . God has to destroy our determined confidence in our own convictions. . . . When we serve Jesus in a spirit that is not His, we hurt Him by our advocacy for Him, we push His claims in the spirit of the devil.

Finally, she called a friend after having sent her paper to him to get his evaluation of it. He, too, spoke a word of warning.

You are developing a siege mentality, Elizabeth. You have an Elijah complex. You seem to think that you are the only person left alive who has not compromised biblical convictions. That is simply not true. Other people have decided to express the same convictions differently. Give them the same respect you want to receive.

So it was that the admonisher received admonition. She learned that the great peril of confronting others was that she herself could all too easily become inaccessible to criticism. She also learned that theological controversy carries with it the risk of distorting perspective, leading to defensiveness and self-righteousness. Admonition of someone else's weakness does not mean that one is spared from the need to receive admonition for one's own. Errant theology in someone else, in other words, does not justify ungodly character in oneself. In fact, it is openness to admonition that makes one a good admonisher. If we are willing to have someone spread mustard on our own sandwich, we will learn better how to put just the right amount on someone else's.

Admonition is the last resort, the final weapon, the riskiest move we make in our relationships with fellow Christians. It rightfully comes at the end of this book. Our success at admonition will depend not simply on the openness of other people but also on our own commitment to obey all of these commands. Greeting our brothers and sisters in Christ will show that we embrace them; forbearance will demonstrate that we are willing to give them room. Confession will communicate our humanity, service our lowliness and humility, comfort our sympathy for their losses and pain, encouragement our appreciation for what they do well. Admonition must be the follower, not the leader of the list. I think that we will discover then how seldom we will have to practice it.

Epilogue

I am reminded almost daily of the enormous challenge Christians face to make the church what Jesus intended it to be. What I read in religious periodicals, what I hear from friends and colleagues, what I observe and experience in my contact with fellow believers yanks me back to reality when I become excessively idealistic and naive. The church—local, denominational, global—seems to work overtime at making its witness in the world ineffective, if not altogether scandalous. It faces serious difficulty in settling disputes about biblical authority, missionary strategy, homosexuality, abortion and public policy, to say nothing about more local disputes like church architecture, preaching styles, anthem selections, elections of leaders, church programs and personality conflicts. It makes one dizzy to think about how much trouble the church faces, how often the church is divided, how quickly the church wanders off course.

None of these problems will be solved easily. Many will not be solved at all. I'm not sure that it matters all that much. I for one am not convinced that unity in the church depends on uniformity of belief and style, except of course in the essentials.

Jesus' new commandment demands special attention during the many moments we don't get along with fellow Christians but still want to be the church. It is pluralism that makes love hard; it is also pluralism that makes love necessary. That is why I prefer the strategy of learning to love one another when there is every reason not to. That is love's greatest

test. As Paul wrote, love does not insist on its own way. It is not self-righteous, though it must still be grounded in the truth.

This book was never intended to settle differences in the church by eliminating those differences altogether. I am too much the realist for that. I have concerns, as most Christians do, about errant doctrine, ethics, behavior and attitude. I am not a relativist. Prochoice Christians bother me as much now as they did before I set out to write this book. So do theological liberals. And I will continue to try my hardest to persuade them to change their position. The same is true for any number of other issues.

But can the church be the church in its pluralism? Yes and no. Some teachings, like the divinity of Christ, are so central that their compromise threatens the very life of the church. As I argued in the chapter on admonition, some issues are too important to ignore and compromise. The basic gospel is one of those nonnegotiable standards, as the church has affirmed now for almost two thousand years.

Still, pluralism is inevitable and in many cases probably healthy. The new commandment was given at least in part to keep the church united even in its pluralism, to make the church one in its diversity. I believe that the mutuality commands of the New Testament offer specific guidelines for how Christians can remain loyal to each other even when they dislike each other and disagree with each other.

I envision the church being something like a big Italian family where there is no shortage of difference of opinion and heated conflict. Sometimes big fights break out and neighbors shudder, wondering whether the family will stay together. But when an outsider attacks one of its members, the family pulls together, stands as one and defends its own. Loyalty undergirds it. They might not always get along, but they still know to what family they belong.

This book has presented a modest plan to help the church function as a family. It has not whitewashed difficult problems, advocated tolerance as an absolute good or dismissed disagreements and divisions in the church as irrelevant. As I have said before, I am not a relativist. I believe that there is an absolute truth, revealed in Scripture, that we must know, believe and live by. But neither has this book answered every question, solved every dispute, revealed the right and wrong position on every issue. Instead, it has attempted to show what Christians must do and how the church must function when every question cannot be answered, every dispute cannot be resolved, every issue cannot be answered with a clear right and wrong, however zealous we are to discover the truth revealed to us in Scripture. It has pointed to the way of love. That does not make questions, disputes and issues less troublesome, only less significant in light of Jesus' ultimate standard.

There is something as important as being right, however important that is. That something is being loving.

In his book *In the Name of Jesus*, Henri Nouwen suggests that we often fail to love because we are too set on gaining power. Love gets lost in our fight for what we believe is right or what we assume is due to us.

What makes the temptation of power so seemingly irresistible? Maybe it is that power offers an easy substitute for the hard task of love. It seems easier to be God than to love God, easier to control people than to love people, easier to own life than to love life.[1]

Nouwen argues that the quest for power may actually reveal a fear of the intimacy that comes with love. It is a way of putting off relationships. "One thing is clear to me: the temptation of power is greatest when intimacy is a threat. Much Christian leadership is exercised by people who do not know how to develop healthy, intimate relationships and have opted for power and control instead."[2]

Jesus Christ, the Lord of the church, calls us to obey one supreme command—to love one another as Jesus has loved us. No disagreement is so important, no division so final, no clash so intense that we are relieved of the responsibility to live like Jesus. As he loved even his enemies who sent him to the cross, so must we love others. As Jesus said, "Love one another as I have loved you."

Notes

Chapter 4: Forbear One Another
[1]Dietrich Bonhoeffer, *Life Together* (New York: Harper & Row, 1954), p. 98.

Chapter 5: Forgive One Another
[1]Lewis Smedes, *Forgive and Forget* (San Francisco: Harper & Row, 1984), pp. 130-31.
[2]Ibid., p. 133.

Chapter 6: Confess Sin to and Pray for One Another
[1]Bonhoeffer, *Life Together*, p. 112.
[2]Ibid.
[3]Ibid., pp. 112-13.
[4]Henri J. Nouwen, *In the Name of Jesus* (New York: Crossroad, 1989), p. 46.
[5]Ibid., pp. 47-48.
[6]Ibid., p. 49.

Chapter 8: Encourage One Another
[1]"In 'The Church of the Locked Door,' " *Newsweek*, August 19, 1991.

Epilogue
[1]Nouwen, *In the Name of Jesus*, p. 59.
[2]Ibid., p. 60.

Questions for Study and Discussion

Chapter 1: The New Commandment
1. There are two reasons this book was written, as the chapter indicates. The first has to do with the pluralism we find in the church today. Can you think of examples of pluralism from your own experience? What were the consequences of this pluralism in the life of the church?
2. The chapter suggests three possible responses to such pluralism. What are they? What are the strengths and weaknesses of each?
3. What does this chapter mean by "diversity of belief"? "Diversity of style"? Can you cite examples of each from your own experience?
4. The author mentioned his own experience of catastrophic need to show that the church is capable of functioning as the community God intends it to be. Have you ever seen the church at work in a similar way?
5. Read John 13:34-34; John 15:12-13; John 17:20-23; 1 John 4:11-12, 20-21. What do these passages say about love and unity in the church?
6. What does the apostle Paul say about the unity of the church in Ephesians 2:11-22 and 4:3-6, 13-16?
7. How do you think your church needs to grow in love and unity? Are there specific areas in which such growth is especially important right now?

Chapter 2: Greet One Another
1. What does it mean, according to Jesus' words in Luke 11:42-44 and Matthew 5:43-48, to take initiative and to be generous in our greetings? Jesus used Gentiles and Pharisees as negative examples. Have you ever

met people like the Pharisees who expected greetings before they gave them? Or like the Gentiles who only gave greetings to those who returned the favor? Have you behaved similarly?

2. The apostle Paul was a master at greeting people, as his letters demonstrate. Read Romans 16:1-16. How does Paul acknowledge people in these verses?

3. As you reflect on your past, can you remember times you were acknowledged in a way that made you feel important? Can you remember ever being overlooked or snubbed? Identify some concrete ways in which you can acknowledge people. How can your church acknowledge people?

4. The apostle Paul showed that another good way to give greetings is to commend accomplishments. How did he do that for Phoebe? Reflect on times you received a commendation that you did not expect. How can you do that for others?

5. Paul often exhorted believers to greet one another "with a holy kiss." Can you think of appropriate ways in our culture to demonstrate affection in your friendships and in your church?

6. Many of the letters contained in the New Testament close with a blessing. What does the Bible teach about the divine blessing? Have you received a divine blessing from others? How can you bestow the blessing of God on others?

Chapter 3: Be Subject to One Another

1. How is the dance a fitting metaphor for God's intentions for Christian relationships?

2. Why is the idea of subjection so offensive to people who live in the modern world?

3. As the chapter indicates, subjection is the mutuality command that directs how Christians should live in the social order. In your mind, why is social order necessary? How is it fallen? How have you experienced the social order at its best and at its worst?

4. There are two popular solutions to the problem of living in the necessary but fallen social order. The first is radicalism; the second is conservatism. Explore these two solutions. What are their strengths and weaknesses? How does subjection differ from both?

5. What does subjection mean? Do you believe that there should be limits to it?

6. How does subjection have the potential to transform the church (as a social order) without destroying the church?

7. What do you think subjection requires from your church, considering the practical problems that it presently faces?

Chapter 4: Forbear One Another

1. What does *forbearance* mean? Why is the word preferable to *politeness* and *tolerance?* Why should forbearance be considered a foundational command for the church?

2. What makes forbearance such a difficult mutuality command to obey?

3. How has God demonstrated forbearance? How has God done that in your life?

4. What in your mind does it mean "to give people room" to be who they are? How will the virtue of meekness help?

5. Read Romans 14:1-4; 15:1-2; and 1 Corinthians 9:19-23. What does Paul say about "strong" believers' responsibility to serve "weak" believers? How will this Pauline principle provide room for people to be themselves? How much room should believers be given? How much is too much? Can you think of times when people gave you room to be yourself? Were you ever given too much room?

6. What does it mean, in your opinion, to give fellow believers "room to become" what God wills? How will patience help? Can you think of examples of people who simply outgrew problems and weaknesses? Do you think people are always capable of changing when they need to? What should the church do if people are not willing to change or capable of changing?

7. Forbearance requires the church to give people room to contribute their gifts, though they are imperfect people. Think of a time you learned a valuable lesson or received a valuable gift from an imperfect person. What kind of guidance does Paul give about such a situation in Philippians 1:12-18? How will the virtue of "lowliness" help? What does it mean for you right now to have a teachable spirit?

8. What, in your mind, are the limits of forbearance?

Chapter 5: Forgive One Another

1. What offenses in the church require forgiveness as opposed to forbearance?

2. Why is it so hard to forgive, especially fellow believers? What factors make forgiveness especially difficult, if not impossible?

3. What makes it possible to forgive? What in your mind keeps Christians from forgiving?

4. What is the cost of forgiveness? Of unforgiveness?

5. Forgiveness has its limits. It cannot accomplish everything that is necessary for redemption and restoration. What, for example, will forgiveness *not* do? What does forgiveness have the potential of accomplishing?

6. Are you in circumstances right now that require forgiveness? What would it mean for you to forgive? What steps should you take?

Chapter 6: Confess Sin to and Pray for One Another

1. How has the self-help movement contributed to American culture? What in your opinion are its weaknesses? Do you believe that the problem of sin can be solved by human effort and goodness alone?

2. What potential does the mutuality command of confession have for uniting and building the church? Dietrich Bonhoeffer called it the "break-through" to community. What did he mean by that?

3. James associates sin and sickness, confession and health. What do you believe is the relationship between sin and sickness? What biblical support can you cite? What is the relationship between confession and health?

4. Jesus commanded his followers in Matthew 5:23-24 to be reconciled to each other before they offered a gift to God. Why is this so important?

How do the pressure to be perfect and the fear of vulnerability keep leaders and the entire church from being the community God wants the church to be?

5. Should there be limits to confession? Guidelines for how it is to be done? How can your church begin to create the kind of community that allows for vulnerability, weakness and confession of sin?

6. Why is the ministry of mutual prayer in the church so often neglected? How can this ministry be cultivated in the whole life of the church? How can you begin to develop this ministry?

Chapter 7: Serve One Another

1. What does service mean for the church? Why is it necessary? Who in particular needs to be served?

2. Can you think of a time you were served by fellow Christians in your church? How did that experience affect you?

3. Why does service require sacrifice? What does it mean to have "equality" as the goal? What does Paul say about this in 2 Corinthians 8:12-14?

4. Why is it especially important for leaders to become servants? Why is it so difficult for them? Do you think it is right that powerful and gifted people give up some of their power and neglect some of their gifts in order to serve others? Why?

5. How does service require time? What principles will help Christians to use their time wisely?

6. How can money be used to serve others? What is the potential of wealth? The danger of wealth? Again, what principles of stewardship will enable Christians to use their money to serve others rather than to indulge themselves?

7. How can people's expertise be used to serve the church's mission?

8. How can you—and how can your church—begin to use time, money and expertise to serve? What needs are you aware of right now? What opportunities do you have to serve specific people? How can you and your church function as advocates for the needy?

9. How can you link yourselves to others so that you are serving as a team instead of as isolated individuals?

10. How can you and your church begin to build an organization that makes service possible and helpful? Should strings be attached to the service you render? What kind?

Chapter 8: Encourage One Another

1. How does encouragement function as the "maintenance" ministry of the church? What kinds of people are most in need of encouragement? What does it mean to encourage?

2. When is encouragement especially needed? Reflect on occasions in your life when you desperately needed encouragement. What did it feel like to receive such encouragement—or not to receive it?

3. What role does personal example play in the ministry of encouragement? Have you ever been encouraged by the example of another Christian? What did it do for you?

4. How is encouragement an art? Explore this art, especially in the case of writing letters, entertaining guests and using humor. Have you ever seen encouragement become an art?

5. How can your church cultivate the art of encouragement? Are there individuals and groups who need encouragement?

6. How can you begin to encourage your friends?

Chapter 9: Comfort One Another

1. Explore the kinds of losses that people often suffer. The apostle Paul uses the word *affliction* to describe such losses. What kinds of affliction are mentioned in the Bible?

2. What does it require to offer good comfort? Have you ever needed comfort? What helped and what hindered?

3. Are you in a situation right now that requires you to give comfort? What should you do?

4. Grief is work. Losses can be so overwhelming at times that the easiest way out is to ignore or deny them. What, in your mind, does it mean to face the darkness of loss directly? What does that require?

5. What kind of understanding can comforters offer? What kind of practical help? How can comforters challenge grieving friends to embrace life, even as they face some kind of death? What does it mean to write a new story for one's life?

6. How can your church become a community of comfort? What did the apostle Paul say about this in 2 Corinthians 1:3-9?

7. What hope is provided by a Christian worldview, as Paul outlined in 2 Corinthians 4:7-16? How can you nurture that hope in yourself and your friends?

Chapter 10: Bear One Another's Burdens

1. What does it mean to bear one another's burdens? Why is the story of the good Samaritan a good example of burden bearing?

2. What is the "occasion" for burden bearing? Do you know people whose circumstances have made them vulnerable to sin and whose bad decisions only complicated the problem? How has life in the modern world made burden bearing even more difficult?

3. What is the prerequisite to burden bearing? How does that prepare the way for the act of burden bearing? What do you think it means to get people back on their feet spiritually? Emotionally? Socially? Physically?

4. How can your church develop a balanced strategy in bearing burdens? For example, how can you strike a balance between individual initiative and corporate responsibility? Between engagement and distance? Between short-term and long-term solutions?

5. What are the perils of burden bearing? Have you ever experienced any of these perils? How?

6. What does it mean to "test your own work" and "look to yourself, lest you too be tempted"?

7. The goal of burden bearing is to get people back on their feet. What does that mean in practical terms? If you once had burdens that have since been relieved, what did it mean for you to get back on your feet?

What does it mean if you have burdens now? What does it mean for burdened members of your church?

8. What should the church do for chronic burdens, or for people who don't want to get back on their feet?

Chapter 11: Stir Up One Another

1. What are some of the big promises and big demands that the Bible mentions? What big promises and big demands appear in Hebrews 10?

2. What is the problem of the "comfort zone" in Christianity? Why is it easy to fall into this comfort zone? Can you identify the comfort zones of your life? Of your church?

3. What does it mean to "stir up one another"? What are the five steps that the passage in Hebrews outlines for us?

4. What did you learn about stirring up from the two case studies in the chapter?

5. How can you begin to apply this command? How can your small group? How can your church?

Chapter 12: Admonish One Another

1. Why do we hesitate to admonish?

2. What does Ezekiel 33 imply about our responsibilities for one another? What does it mean to take personal responsibility for each other?

3. Admonition requires that we confront people when they are headed in the wrong direction and turn them around. How is that best done? What is the relationship between teaching and admonition?

4. What does it mean to be aware of forces and habits that are hindering our friends from growing in Christ? What would you consider to be reasonable expectations of brothers and sisters in Christ? Can your expectations be too high? How do you determine what those expectations should be?

5. What is the purpose of admonition, both negative and positive?

6. What is the best way of doing admonition, as Jesus outlined in Matthew 18:15-20? Consider the three basic principles of privacy, positiveness and prayerfulness. What do you think it means to appeal to someone's conscience? How can logic function negatively to make people inaccessible to admonition?

7. What offenses require admonition? Which situations are obvious? Which are ambiguous? How should the church handle these?

8. What does the chapter say about levels of responsibility? What are the difficult cases mentioned in the chapter? Can you think of any others? How should these be handled?

9. Are you in any circumstances right now that call for admonition? What should you do? How should you do it?